ONE NATION UNDER SIEGE

ONE NATION UNDER SIEGE

Congress, Terrorism, and the
Fate of American Democracy

Jocelyn Jones Evans

THE UNIVERSITY PRESS OF KENTUCKY

Scholarly publisher for the Commonwealth,
serving Bellarmine University, Berea College, Centre
College of Kentucky, Eastern Kentucky University,
The Filson Historical Society, Georgetown College,
Kentucky Historical Society, Kentucky State University,
Morehead State University, Murray State University,
Northern Kentucky University, Transylvania University,
University of Kentucky, University of Louisville,
and Western Kentucky University.
All rights reserved.

Editorial and Sales Offices: The University Press of Kentucky
663 South Limestone Street, Lexington, Kentucky 40508-4008
www.kentuckypress.com

14 13 12 11 10   5 4 3 2 1

Library of Congress Cataloging-in-Publication Data

Jones Evans, Jocelyn.
  One nation under siege : Congress, terrorism, and the fate of American
democracy / Jocelyn Jones Evans.
     p.   cm.
  Includes bibliographical references and index.
  ISBN 978-0-8131-2588-6 (hardcover : alk. paper)
  1. United States. Congress. 2. United States. Congress—Security
measures. 3. United States. Congress—Constituent communication.
4. United States Capitol (Washington, D.C.—Security measures. 5. United
States Capitol Visitor Center (Washington, D.C.) 6. Civil right—United
States. 7. National security—United States. I. Title.
  JK1021.J63 2010
  328.73—dc22
                          2010006312

Member of the Association of
American University Presses

CONTENTS

FIGURES AND TABLES

FIGURES

TABLES

PREFACE

Rare are those moments when political scientists find themselves in the midst of political crisis as both observer and participant. As a political scientist specializing in the study of Congress, I was working on Capitol Hill in Washington, D.C., as a 2001 American Political Science Association Congressional Fellow. While on the Hill, I sought to gain a better understanding of the basics of congressional life, including how Congress works, how bills become law, and how members of Congress make decisions. That year involved a steep learning curve as I juggled the responsibilities of both a full-time Hill staffer and an advanced graduate student conducting interviews and gathering data for my dissertation on women and politics. I had the privilege of working in a leadership office and consequently had great access to members, personal staff, committee staff, party staff, lobbyists, bureaucrats, and a host of other political elite. This made elite interviews much easier to secure and research much easier to conduct. It was within this milieu that I experienced both the terrorist attacks of 9/11 and the subsequent anthrax attacks in October 2001.

On 9/11, I remember being interrupted from my dissertation work to go with some friends in the office down to the cafeteria in the basement of the Longworth House Office Building for our ritualistic morning dose of caffeine. They asked me if I had seen the breaking news of a plane flying into one of the World Trade Towers. I had not even had enough time to turn on the television in my cubicle, so I just listened as they bounced ideas back and forth about possible culprits. There was no question in their minds about whether it was an intentional attack. Given the number of easily identifiable foreign threats to American security, they did not need to ask why it had happened. Rather, the question was who was responsible.

When we returned with our coffee and sodas, we entered an office scene I will never forget. In most offices of members of Congress, televisions are mounted in the corners almost to the ceiling. This makes them viewable to anyone in the office or in the waiting area. They are also sprinkled throughout staff cubicles and members' chambers. Every room has a television, and every station is tuned to either C-SPAN or the news.

One of the key points made by Senate Majority Leader Tom Daschle in his account of this event concerns the centrality of the media as a source of government information. The events on 9/11 made this reality painfully clear.

> It's hard to fathom—or maybe we simply don't want to believe—that our leaders in the upper levels of government in Washington, the people we turn to for confidence and security in times of crises, might, at just such a time, be as utterly clueless as everyone else. But the fact is that while we often are privy to sources of communication and information that the average citizen does not have, we just as often get the only information we have from the same place everyone else gets it—in many instances, from television. Walk through the Capitol on any given day, and you'll see a TV in every House and Senate office tuned in to CNN or C-SPAN. Those sets are turned on from the moment the office is unlocked in the morning until the last person leaves late at night. In the chaos and confusion of September 11, I was as dependent on the network television reports—at least early on—as everybody else.[1]

When we entered the office, we were looking at a sea of throats. All eyes were on the televisions mounted high in the corners, and all mouths were dropped wide open at the sight of a second tower on fire. My friend (who is now my husband) took his soda to his corner cubicle and began to surf television stations to find additional information. He then went around the corner to the chief of staff's office to be the first to notify her of the attack on the Pentagon. Our world, Washington, D.C., was under attack. Everyone in the office scrambled for a phone to call loved ones. I called my mother. She begged me to leave the building.

Office personnel frantically began calling the "authorities" around the Hill to identify the plan of action. Capitol Police were at a loss. They were waiting for directions from the Speaker's Office. The Speaker's Office was at a loss. To our knowledge, nothing like this had ever happened

Smoke from the Pentagon is visible from the parking lot outside of the Cannon House Office Building. (Photograph taken by the author.)

before. Individual offices began to evacuate the Capitol grounds. "Keep your cell phone on!" The words rang out from every office up and down every hall.

I was parked in Lot 7, just below the Cannon House Office Building on C Street. I offered to take those staffers without a car with me, away from the Capitol. As we hurried to the parking lot, we smelled smoke. To the southwest of the Capitol, you could see it billowing over the trees. The Pentagon was on fire.

We drove southbound on I-395 before authorities closed it to through traffic. The radio stations issued unsubstantiated reports of bombs at the White House, at the State Department, and on the Mall. For the first and only time in my life, I remember rolling down the windows to see and to hear the news for myself.

Our destination was an apartment in Arlington at the Courthouse metro stop. We turned on Washington Boulevard and stopped at a gas station to refuel before working our way through the heaving traffic. The attendant pumped our gas and shared his experience with us. He had watched a plane pass over his station before plowing into the side of the Pentagon. It was an American flight, and the crash was intentional. On

Smoke from the Pentagon is visible from I-395. (Photograph taken by the author.)

the roads, emergency vehicles slowly screamed through the rows of cars. Ambulances passed with doors gaping open to provide room for more wounded as they made countless trips back and forth to the Pentagon.

At the apartment, I tried to distract myself. The Pentagon was in plain view from the thirteenth floor. It was ablaze. (It would smolder for several more days.) I cooked and cleaned and focused on providing creature comforts for all those staffers who had gathered to be together in this apartment on such a strange day. A video message from Osama bin Laden was followed by breaking news of harrowing tales from New York City and our very own backyard. The constant tickers across the television screen eventually became too much to process. It was all just too much to bear.

The next day we returned to work, but there was nothing normal about it. The phones did not ring. Constituents did not visit. Planes did not fly. Life did not return to normal.

Within hours that Wednesday morning, staff began to don swatches of red, white, and blue ribbon purchased at the House Gift Shop in the basement of the Longworth House Office Building. We were all wearing safety-pinned ribbons by day's end. These symbols of patriotic unity soon

View of American flags draped outside the House office buildings after 9/11.
(Photograph taken by the author.)

appeared on all the news stations and eventually became the icon for
remembering the 9/11 event.

Over the course of the next few days, offices across Capitol Hill
draped huge American flags vertically from their windows to signify that
the country was in mourning. Stores nationwide had difficulty keeping
enough flags in stock to satisfy the demand caused by the events of 9/11.
Yet there was something particularly striking about this outpouring of
patriotism by those working in and around our nation's Capitol. These
flags served as a symbol to the world of the courage and resilience of
democratic government in the brutal face of terrorism.

Just a month later, as life began to return to normal, a letter laced
with anthrax was discovered in Senator Tom Daschle's (D-SD) office.
I remember this experience as being quite different from the events of
9/11, but just as significant and disturbing. On Capitol Hill, mail typically
is opened by the interns or the legislative correspondents. These positions usually are filled by the youngest adults on the Hill. Interns are in
their early twenties, and legislative correspondents are not much older.
Given that no one knew how widespread the anthrax attack would be,
the incident in Daschle's office struck fear in the hearts of administrative

personnel across the Capitol campus. How would offices protect their youngest staff from the faceless yet deadly weapon of anthrax?

Immediately the House and the Senate leadership debated over the appropriate course of action. To end the session and close the Capitol Complex would communicate that the attack had succeeded in disrupting legislative life. On the other hand, the leadership did have to consider the health and safety of the thousands of congressional staff under their supervision. This event provided me with a rare opportunity to appreciate the power of the Speaker of the House and the Majority Leader of the Senate to serve as chief administrators of Congress. Speaker Dennis Hastert (R-IL) opted to end the House's session and evacuate the Capitol grounds, while Majority Leader Daschle initially chose to keep the Senate in session. It was also interesting to witness the discretion exercised by individual offices over evacuation. Several members of Congress chose to defy Capitol Police orders. By staying on Capitol Hill, they placed their staff in the precarious dilemma of either doing their jobs or listening to their parents and loved ones.

All offices ultimately were evacuated for an indefinite period of time. For staff, that was probably the most difficult feature of the whole event. For those used to the fast-paced, relentless hours of Hill life, an indefinite evacuation rattled the nerves. Only the most critical members of congressional staff reported to duty during that period, the chiefs of staff and legislative directors. The entire Capitol Complex was screened for anthrax, and several buildings tested positive for contamination. In a piecemeal fashion, staff slowly began to return to their offices once the space was officially decontaminated. Some staff returned within two weeks. Others were sent to work at off-site locations while their offices were systematically cleaned by the CDC (Centers for Disease Control and Prevention). It would be months before things fully would return to normal around the Capitol.

I left Washington, D.C., in November 2001 to finish my dissertation, but I would never leave the experiences emblazoned in my memory by that fall. After a few years of teaching and the successful publication of my dissertation, I returned my attention to the impact that the events of 9/11 and anthrax had made on the offices, the staff, and the life on the Hill that I had come to know and appreciate. What I discovered over the course of my investigation provides the substance for this book.

I find myself faced with the same question that concerned Richard

Fenno in the aftermath of the 1988 Republican National Convention. After following Senator Dan Quayle for six years as part of a book project on the U.S. Senate, Fenno had both gathered rich historical, personal, and political detail about Quayle's life and career, and in the process become his friend. Fenno knew that he had important information about Quayle that could inform the media and voters, but he also knew that his friendship might taint his ability to offer objective treatment of Quayle's candidacy for vice presidential office. Placed in this unique situation, Fenno realized the fundamental difficulty associated with being both a participant in and an observer of politics.[2] As a participant observer, how does one achieve a suitable balance between access and objectivity? Throughout this text, I have tried to be sensitive to the potential bias caused by my unique position as a congressional aide during these attacks. Consequently, the conclusions are based not solely on my own recollections, but also on the reflections of more than seventy-five political elites, each with differing backgrounds and perspectives on the impact of terrorism on Capitol Hill.

It is my hope that this book sheds light on a congressional culture that is not easily measured but that is nevertheless real and has changed over the last several years. For the academic, this work draws from multiple theoretical frameworks, multiple methods, and multiple data sources to capture the full extent of the change on Capitol Hill and the meaning implicit in it. For the student, this book is about real congressional life. It is about the fascinating people, the awe-inspiring place, and the unique culture that pervades the Capitol. Most of all, however, it is about the changes that crisis events can bring to such an important place.

ACKNOWLEDGMENTS

I cannot believe this journey has come to an end. Every moment I spent working on this project was captivating and enlightening. I am so blessed to study something I enjoy and to write on subjects that continue to excite my intellectual curiosity. My life has been so full, and I owe so many for making it so.

First, I offer my sincere gratitude to the practitioners who contributed to my understanding of legislative life on Capitol Hill. The American Political Science Association's Congressional Fellowship Program offered the invaluable opportunity to watch and record congressional politics firsthand. Without this once-in-a-lifetime experience, I never would have "been at the right place at the right time" and this book never would have been written. I also am hugely indebted to the staff of the particular office that hosted me during my fellowship year on the Hill. This affiliation provided me with access to members, personal staff, committee staff, lobbyists, administrative personnel, and others. Through these connections, I established a network of contacts that served me well upon my return to conduct elite interviews in the summers of 2005 and 2006. All of those who welcomed me into their offices and spent precious time entertaining my naive questions also deserve my thanks and the thanks of our profession. Political science depends on the willingness and openness of public servants to share their experiences so that we can truly understand what it is that we study. The comments shared with me by these individuals brought life on the Hill alive and enriched the text beyond any analysis I could provide.

They say "A picture is worth a thousand words." In the study of Congress, it may be said that "An interview is worth a thousand data sets."

Thank you all for sharing your memories with me. I only hope that I have recounted your reflections in a way that captures their essence and maintains their integrity.

Beyond the congressional support for this project, I must also recognize the institutional support I received to complete this study. I owe a debt of gratitude to the faculty and staff in the Department of Government at the University of West Florida for providing the funding and research support, the intellectual sounding boards, and the great dose of patience necessary to complete this project. My special thanks go to Alfred Cuzán, Michelle Hale Williams, David Alvis, and Jongseok Woo for listening to me go on and on about terrorism and the Hill. I hope that this product was worth all of the talk. The University of West Florida also provided me with two Creative and Scholarly Activities Grants that subsidized travel to the field site in 2005 and 2006 and funded two teams of research assistants to accompany me in collecting interview data. The experience enjoyed by these students was priceless, and UWF deserves much credit for prioritizing education even when it takes students outside of the classroom. I would be remiss if I did not directly thank each and every student who assisted me in this project. This book has been a work in progress for several years. Generations of students have contributed to its culmination. In chronological order, they include: Olivia Lagergren, Stephen and Teresa Stanquist, Patrick Cabeza, Ryan Smallen, Alexis Trout, Danielle Manjikian, Ryan Cunningham, Maureen Yann, Sarah Sanders, Bryan Waters, and Zachary Hensley. Thank you all. I finally finished it!

I would also like to take a few lines to recognize the mentorship that I received at Berry College and the University of Oklahoma. Peter Lawler at Berry College continues to guide me in my professional development. He has encouraged me for more than a decade, and I would not be where I am today without his influence. In terms of this project, I would like to thank him for the insightful comments he has provided in reviewing successive drafts. He first introduced me to the big questions of politics and philosophy, and I will spend the rest of my life trying to find answers. I thank him tremendously for that. Several faculty members at the University of Oklahoma have also shaped my career in remarkable ways. My deepest gratitude belongs to the faculty and staff of the Carl Albert Center and Department of Political Science for shepherding me through graduate school, conference activity, classroom instruction, the job market, and professional development. I would like to specifically thank Ron Peters for challenging me to think about Congress in a qualitative and historical way. I would like to thank Gary Copeland for "holding my feet to the fire" throughout the process of writing my dissertation. The publication process is difficult, and all work needs revision. Finally, I would like to thank Keith Gaddie. More than any other influence in my professional life, he has consistently encouraged me to write and to send my work out for review. It takes guts to do what we do, and Keith challenges and expects me to draw upon my inner strength. Thanks for believing in me.

Without the close and insightful comments of the reviewers and editors associated with the University Press of Kentucky, I would be producing a much weaker text. Their firsthand experience in Congress and extended years of service in academia provided remarkably constructive criticism. I am so fortunate to have received such helpful advice. Stephen Wrinn, director of UPK, saw something in this project and has patiently and gently steered me through the process of revision and publication. It has been a joy to work with all of the editorial and production staff. I hope that the book lives up to your expectations.

In addition, several individuals offered critical feedback on panels at various political science conferences, and a few deserve particular mention. Jacob Straus reviewed the chapter on office administration and helped to shape my vision for this text back in 2006 at the Midwest Political Science Association meeting. Joe Stewart and Brian Harward provided clear and constructive advice on the historical chapter at the 2007 meeting of the Southern Political Science Association in New Orleans. Similarly, David Parker and Christian Grose reviewed the chapter on anthrax and the mail and provided an incredibly engaging discussion about representation and constituent correspondence at the 2007 Midwest Political Science Association meeting in Chicago. These encounters were tremendously helpful, and I thank you all.

Finally, I would like to thank those who put up with me through this entire process. Mentors, colleagues, and students assist from afar. Family lives with you. My mother, Glenda, and my father, Mike, are amazing and wonderful people. They sacrificed so much for my education, and they continue to sacrifice so much for my professional success. Always a phone call away, they loved me through this project, and I love them for who they are. After receiving a contract for this book from UPK, my husband, Jeremy, bragged about me over dinner to some friends. "She is going to publish her *second* book!" I love you, Jeremy. I love that you are proud of me. And I love that you are in my life now and till the end of time. You are my sunshine.

INTRODUCTION

Congress as an Adaptive Institution

> I have to say that I often sit in my office and reflect on all that happened between the election of 2000 and the election of 2002, and I realize that it is unlikely the events of those two years will ever be repeated. In many ways, that's a good thing. . . . I think historians who have the luxury of time and perspective will look back and see these as revolutionary times. As a nation, we are making monumental decisions about our very identity as a society and role on this planet—decisions that will affect our citizens and the entire world for many years to come.
> —Senate Majority Leader Tom Daschle

In the fall of 2001, two devastating but separate terrorist attacks threatened the U.S. Capitol. The first threat occurred on September 11, 2001, when a coordinated terrorist plot included a hijacked plane possibly directed at the Capitol Building. Fortunately for the institution, the passengers of Flight 93 thwarted the attack and diverted the plane from D.C. airspace. Nevertheless, this massive scheme caught the Capitol Police sorely unprepared to handle a security threat of this magnitude. The second threat occurred in the months following September 11, 2001. In October, mail containing anthrax spores was discovered in several buildings, ultimately leading to the evacuation of the Capitol Complex. Some buildings remained closed for three months to undergo thorough decontamination. Yet again, the Capitol lacked appropriate security mechanisms, this time to prevent biological threats from infiltrating the mail system or to detect them once they had entered the buildings.

In the aftermath of these two distinct attacks, Capitol Hill experienced a deluge of administrative, structural, and environmental changes in the name of security. After the dust settled, what was left was a different climate that has persisted to the present day. This shift in mentality and in operations highlights a fundamental tension in democratic political systems between security and openness, between public accessibility and fortification against attack. As Charles Goodsell elaborates:

> The issue of access to government buildings in a democracy is complex because they serve, at the same time, as symbols of democratic governance, on the one hand, and symbols of hated authority (at least to some) on the other. Citizens can rightfully demand ready access to them in fulfillment of the democratic ideal. Yet, increasingly, government buildings are the targets of shootings, bombings, and other forms of violent disruption. This makes it difficult to determine an appropriate balance between security and openness. The resolution of this dilemma is the most fundamental way in which the statehouse influences human behavior.[1]

The image of the American statehouse portrayed by Goodsell is one of extreme accessibility. He examined state legislatures before the turn of the twenty-first century, when open campuses, lacking fences, barriers, security checkpoints, metal detectors, or uniformed guards, created the appearance of public accessibility. These key features of the statehouse served to overshadow the subtle means of securing these public spaces, such as security cameras, bulletproof glass in key officials' office windows, silent alarms, and officers in civilian attire. For Goodsell, the statehouse was "not a fortress, but a carefully, if unobtrusively, monitored building."[2] The architectural features of American statehouses that simultaneously provided openness but incorporated subtle monitoring achieved "an effective balance between the needs to celebrate and protect democracy."[3]

Goodsell's depiction almost serves as a memoir of the statehouse of the past. In the same year his book was released, the accessibility of statehouses was severely curtailed nationwide. His reflection that "the statehouse is the most unfortress-like public building type in America" is now a subject of debate in the post-9/11 environment.[4]

Tracing the steps taken by the U.S. legislative branch in the time since the attacks of 2001 provides an awareness of the reconstituted balance between openness and security on Capitol Hill. The indelible imprint of this brief period on the nation's Capitol is captured through an examination of the changes to office administration, constituent correspondence, the committee structure, and visitor management. This adaptation serves as a testament to the fragility of our democratic culture and governance. At the same time, it highlights the resilience of our legislative institution.

While there is some scholarship on institutional change and the triggers that lead to it, there is very little examination of the impact of these changes on political actors themselves. This work explores the attitudes and histories of those political actors involved in implementing the institutional changes demanded by September 11 and anthrax. It seeks to answer how these events changed the way members of Congress and their staff view their jobs, manage their offices, maintain constituent representation, adapt to Hill safety, legislate in an era of "Homeland Security," and evaluate the restructured committee system and oversight processes of the institution. Consequently, this book serves as an important addition to the field of congressional studies in two ways. First, it treats Congress not just as an institution, but as a people who constitute a community and express a distinctive "culture." Second, this book explores the impact of the terrorist attacks of 2001 on not only the structure and function of Congress but also the climate and culture of Congress. In this way, it provides a more holistic understanding of both the congressional environment and the factors leading to institutional change. The following section explores some of the traditional approaches to studying Congress and situates my work within this theoretical and methodological dialogue.

Theoretical Approaches to Studying Congress

The congressional literature suggests several appropriate theoretical perspectives for understanding the impact of security threats on the daily workings of the U.S. Congress. Useful approaches for this analysis include a historical approach, an institutional approach, a new institutional approach, a systems approach, and an organizational theory approach. Each of these five perspectives provides a unique lens for examining Congress. When taken together, they come closer to capturing the institutional culture of Congress and the way in which it responds to its external environment.

The Historical Approach

From a historical perspective, Congress can be viewed as an assembly of representatives, a set of public buildings, and a bureaucratic organism. As such, it has expanded and evolved for more than two centuries. Congressional historians suggest that the Capitol Building itself has gone through several phases of construction to address legislative growth and meet the demands of a changing political context. From the initial 65 members of the House and 26 members of the Senate, the Capitol Building grew to hold 535 members of Congress and 4 delegates from U.S. territories and Washington, D.C. Suffering multiple fires, quartering troops during the Civil War, and weathering architectural, technological, and political transformations, the Capitol Complex evolved to address the needs introduced by historical change.

Studying Congress apart from its historical past is detrimental. Without a historical orientation, one cannot fully understand the institutional heritage of Congress and the impact of the broader political and social context in shaping its legislative activity. As Elaine Swift and David Brady argue:

> Our ahistorical focus on the contemporary Congress leads congressional theory to overestimate the impact of endogenous factors, particularly institutional actors. Absent an historical perspective, institutional actors appear to be behaving relatively free of external constraints and pressures. Unsurprisingly, we therefore tend to see them as the primary institutional dynamic and assign them undue causal weight. Congress's past suggests otherwise. From an historical perspective, we can appreciate the impact of exogenous patterns and forces that are often too subtle or inchoate for contemporary scholars and participants to adequately discern.[5]

The Institutional Approach

Congress also is an assembly that can be viewed as an institution for several reasons. First, it is well-bounded. In other words, membership in Congress is exclusive. To be a member of the House of Representatives, one must be elected by the majority of voters in a congressional district. To be a member of the Senate, one must be elected by the majority of voters in a state. Second, Congress is complex in its internal organization in that the committee and subcommittee systems provide a sophisticated division of labor. Similarly, the party system further organizes members and distributes power throughout Congress. Third, the rules of procedure in Congress are universalistic in that they apply to everyone equally. For example, parliamentary procedure governs debate on the floor of the House of Representatives. Finally, Congress is automatic in its decision making in that there are norms that guide the behavior of its members. The "seniority rule" in Congress, for example, dictates that the most senior member on a committee is named as the chair or ranking member.[6]

While the level of institutionalization of the contemporary U.S. Congress compared to previous periods is a matter of debate, it nonetheless remains quite bounded (or distinctive) and complex.[7] Part of its boundedness includes a distinct organizational culture in which its inhabitants are thoroughly immersed. A good example of this dynamic is the publication and distribution of a daily congressional newspaper, *The Hill*. This newspaper covers everything about Congress, from current legislation under consideration, to the personalities and politics behind legislative work, to the battlefields of congressional elections, to relations with the executive branch, to the more casual buzz of staff life. The paper states, "Capitol Hill is also a local community like a small city, and in our pages are its culture, social life, employment, security, shopping, dining and recreation."[8] This description conveys the sense that Congress is a unique entity with definite boundaries and complex networks. According to the institutional perspective, the focus on why and how bounded and complex institutions develop and the impact of external conditions on this development is fundamental to understanding Congress.[9]

The New Institutional Approach

In recent decades, social scientists have returned attention to the role of institutions in shaping political and social behavior. New theories of institutionalism have developed from economics, sociology, anthropology, history, and political science.[10] Advocates of new institutional approaches treat institutions as political actors with identifiable collective interests and motivations.

Those who utilize a new institutional approach attempt to find answers to three important questions: "how do actors behave, what do institutions do, and why do institutions persist over time?"[11] Generally speaking, there are two separate responses to these questions, the "calculus approach" and the "cultural approach."[12] For those who espouse the calculus approach, institutions shape the distribution of resources and power relations between actors by managing uncertainty, controlling relevant information, and setting parameters on negotiation. Institutions structure the strategic interactions of political actors who hold competing interests in a system of separated powers. For those espousing the cultural approach, institutions shape the behavior of actors not by structuring the terms of negotiation but by imbuing social meaning, encouraging routine patterns of behavior, and providing cognitive filters for interpreting political life. In this view, "not only do institutions provide strategically-useful information, they also affect the very identities, self-images, and preferences of the actors."[13] When these two approaches are taken together, they suggest that the behavior of political actors "may be influenced both by strategic calculation about the likely strategies of others and by reference to a familiar set of moral or cognitive templates, each of which may depend on the configuration of existing institutions."[14]

Perspectives of new institutionalism cast Congress as an institutional actor in a separated system of institutional actors (the executive, the legislative, and the judicial branches) making rational decisions out of self-preservation and self-interest. Often, however, these decisions are based on limited information and limited resources (bounded rationality) and structured by preexisting policies and patterns of behavior.[15] In the case of security, the decisions made by Congress to protect the Capitol Complex from external threats can be viewed as a product of both strategic calculation and bounded rationality. Over the two centuries of congressional history, the institution has systematically increased security in response to external threat, but it has done so by implementing feasible changes in a piecemeal fashion, given resource constraints and limited information. Similarly, the development of the committee system in Congress illustrates the principles of new institutionalism. As the executive branch has developed new departments and agencies, Congress has responded by adding new committees to facilitate oversight and protect its policy interests. The development of the new Homeland Security Committee in the House and the restructured Homeland Security and Governmental Affairs Committee in the Senate are just the most recent examples of this institutional phenomenon.

The Systems Approach

From a systems approach, Congress is a bounded entity or "black box" pressured by outside forces to respond to changes in the environment

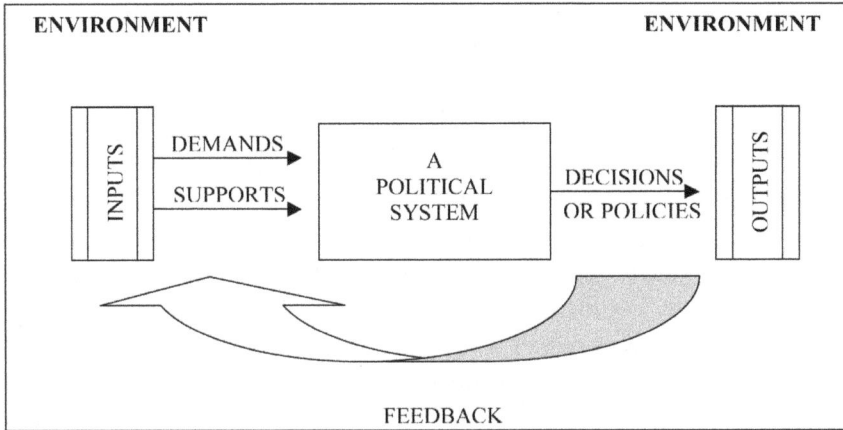

Figure I.1. Political Systems Model. *Source:* David Easton, *A Framework for Political Analysis* (Chicago: Univ. of Chicago Press, 1979), 112.

and judged by the changes it introduces. Arguably the first political scientist to suggest placing political institutions within their social environment was David Easton. In his classic "black box" or "systems" model of government, he highlighted the role of public pressure in influencing the activity of government and leading to policy change. Easton's political systems model of policymaking suggests that government institutions are clearly responsive to their external environment.[16]

As figure I.1 suggests, pressures are placed on government in the form of demands and supports that are then transmitted into policy outputs. These policy changes then lead to a new set of demands and supports in the form of public feedback.[17] Pressures introduced by the environment set the institutional agenda by creating opportunities or opening "policy windows" for change.[18] John Kingdon calls those with the desire to advance change "policy entrepreneurs," and they, whether out of perceived pressure, ideological orientation, political calculation, or institutional position, make change possible.[19]

Congress acts like a system in a number of ways. When considering the impact of crisis on Congress, it is clear that the congressional system reacts and responds to external threat. From the very first attack on a visitor to the nation's Capitol, the attack on President John Quincy Adams's son in the Capitol Rotunda in 1828, Congress has responded by adjusting security around the premises. Events such as 9/11 and the anthrax attacks of October 2001 are just the most recent environmental impacts creating new demands for the institution and ultimately leading to changes in policy concerning security and access.

The Organizational Approach

Congress also can be viewed as an organization. The organizational features of legislatures "define the situation in which legislative activity takes place, structure legislative behavior and activity, and establish the ways in which legislatures operate."[20] The organizational features of Congress include not only the formal legislative process, but also informal norms of behavior and patterns of socialization. It regularly has been noted that members of Congress conform more or less to distinct norms of behavior, including the norm of apprenticeship, the norm of institutional courtesy, the norm of legislative specialization, the norms of reciprocity and deference, and the norm of institutional patriotism.[21] These rules governing behavior promote group cohesion, promote predictability, control conflict, expedite business, advantage certain individuals, and facilitate interaction among members of Congress.[22]

Congress is not only characterized by certain norms of behavior, but also by socialization processes. Scholars have used theories of socialization to understand how members of Congress "learn the ropes" and adapt to congressional life. Legislative studies tend to treat legislative chambers as unique institutions with their own folkways and cultures. New members learn the "nuts and bolts" of House and Senate legislative culture through a process of socialization that includes formal orientation and informal communication networks.[23] Through this process, the "social milieu" of legislative life is passed on from one generation of members to the next.

At the start of each new Congress, *The Hill* publishes a new members guide. This resource serves two separate purposes. On the one hand, it serves to orient new members to the culture and activity of the Hill. On the other hand, it serves to orient old members to newcomers by providing brief biographical information on each individual joining the organization of Congress. *The Hill* is a tangible representation of the political socialization that is central to congressional life.

Understanding Congress as a Culture

While culture is a concept that eludes precise definition and scientific measurement, recognition of the common experience of life on Capitol Hill is critical to a rich understanding of the institution and the behavior of those who inhabit it. If culture is understood from an anthropological perspective to mean a group's shared set of attitudes, values, goals, and practices that are transmitted across generations, then congressional scholarship suggests that Congress has a certain political culture. There are distinct norms of behavior and processes of socialization that persist in Congress across generations of lawmakers. Members of Congress share similar experiences with schedules, travel, budgets, staff, media, housing, interest groups, campaigns, and constituents. Members also share similar values and goals involving representation, public service, reelection concerns, public policy development, and political ambition.

Not only does the U.S. Congress have a distinctive political culture, the House and Senate each has a uniquely identifiable culture. The House and Senate have been coined the "Tuesday-Thursday Group" and "The Senate Club." Ross Baker traces the "distinctive roles and styles" of these two legislative chambers.[24] There are critical differences between the House and Senate, including chamber size, member term-length, constituency character (district versus state), and legislative responsibility. These differences have led to unique rules of procedure, patterns of partisanship, and electoral arenas and horizons.[25] In turn, they have yielded unique cultures recognized by members of Congress, journalists, lobbyists, and staff. Christopher Matthews, a former staffer for Speaker Tip O'Neill, reflected on these differences, stating: "There's kind of an invisible shield across the rotunda. Senators can be on Capitol Hill for years and never cross the Capitol except to hear a State of the Union Message. There's no reason why somebody over there would disgrace himself by going over to the House side, and the House member, for fear of humiliation, would never risk going over there."[26] Differences between the two chambers have also led to distinctive norms and institutional mores. Members of the Senate face strong norms of collegiality, deference, and reciprocity. According to one senator, "There is a great pressure to conform in the Senate. It's like living in a small town."[27] Even given recent scholarly accounts of the erosion of legislative norms, these norms continue to strongly influence behavior in the Senate. Marvin Overby and Lauren Bell challenge students of Congress to pay closer attention to these norms, arguing that in the Senate they "matter a great deal and serve as significant constraints on individual incentives that could be quite detrimental to the welfare of the institution."[28]

According to Alan Rosenthal, legislatures also *reflect* broader political culture. They are "interwoven in the fabric of their states; and the legislative process cannot be considered in isolation from the prevailing ethos, the political ethics, and the capital community in the state in which it operates."[29] Legislative organizations adjust to change in the external environment, whether they are changes in technology, resources, or public attitudes. They further change to meet the political demands required by the executive and judicial branches of government.[30]

In sum, organizations such as the U.S. Congress do not spontaneously develop. They are influenced by several factors. Congress as an organization adapts as a result of planning on the part of its leadership and change in the political environment, in personnel, and in the situational context.[31] Congress both has a culture and reflects the broader culture of American politics.

At its core, this book sits at an intersection of these different theoretical approaches. Congress is an assembly embedded in a rich historical context. It is an evolving institution set apart from other institutions in American government. As such, Congress is a rational institutional actor in a political environment making decisions out of self-preservation and self-interest. It is a part of a political system, responsive to outside pressures and influences. Finally, Congress is an organization with a unique culture and history. As Julian Zelizer suggests, Congress has a life of its own.[32]

In very clear ways, the evolution of Capitol security can be viewed through each of these theoretical lenses to develop a rich picture of institutional culture and responsiveness. Yet none of these approaches taken in isolation captures the complex dynamic of congressional change in its entirety, particularly in terms of securing the Capitol Complex from outside threats. Perhaps this is because previous accounts often explain cultural norms during times of stability. If congressional culture does exist, it is a constant that serves to make congressional life predictable. In a context of change, however, what happens to congressional culture? Do norms of legislative behavior and patterns of office administration remain constant? Or do they evolve and adapt to meet the demands brought about by changes in the political environment? If a new culture develops, then what are the implications of these changes for congressional life and representative politics? This book attempts to both theoretically and practically address these questions by examining the impact of terrorism on the workings of Congress and the culture of Capitol Hill.

The Character of Congressional Change

The previous discussion develops a picture of the U.S. Congress as an adaptive institution, embedded in a social context, with a distinct organizational culture. Organizations such as the U.S. Congress do not spontaneously develop; they also do not remain the same over time. Change is critical to legislative life. "No organization, the House included, can retain its autonomy and vitality if it fails to respond to its changing external environment."[33] The events of 2001 changed the external environment of Congress. To more fully appreciate the significance of this event, this section examines the causes and ramifications of congressional change. The choices legislatures make to respond to environmental pressures (such as those caused by terrorism) hold both practical and symbolic implications for democratic life.

Congressional change can result from both gradual changes in the broader social environment and critical triggering events, such as war or economic depression. In *How Congress Evolves,* Nelson Polsby examines the social bases of institutional change at work in the U.S. Congress from the end of the New Deal in the late 1930s to the Republican Revolution in the 1990s. For an example of a social basis of change, he argues that a change in the environment, namely the invention of air conditioning, resulted in population shifts that in turn affected the partisan cleavages and thereby the membership and behavior of the U.S. Congress.[34] This new technology made it more tolerable to live in a hot climate and led to population shifts from the North to the South, and ultimately impacted the membership of and power distribution in Congress. Aside from his conclusions, Polsby's historical approach is invaluable in that he uniquely embeds the national legislature in its political and social environment and thereby suggests the responsiveness of the legislature to macro-level changes occurring in its environment. He concludes that "understanding how institutions function requires understanding the social contexts in which they are embedded."[35]

Not only does Congress slowly evolve in response to social change, it also evolves in response to crisis. There are certain critical events that are extremely important for triggering change, such as war or economic depression.[36] War often creates a large degree of widespread demand for institutional change and a large degree of widespread autonomy for politicians to implement required institutional changes without suffering electoral repercussions. The terrorist attacks of September 11, 2001, might have provided just this type of critical juncture in that they constituted an international crisis that led to a number of public demands on the institution of Congress. Many policies and structural changes have ensued in response to these pressures. These terrorist attacks "produced unprecedented fear among American citizens about the threats that loomed from international forces, revealing the desperate need for extensive changes in government surveillance and military strategy."[37] In this context of wartime emergency and unified government, Congress was able to pass "sweeping 'homeland security' changes."[38] As this scenario illustrates, it is clear that institutional change can result from trigger events.

It is important to realize, however, that institutional configurations at the time of a crisis serve to limit or advance change within the institution. The size of the opportunity for change depends upon two things: "(1) the degree and scope of demanded institutional changes; and (2) the degree and scope of autonomy the trigger affords state officials from short-term political constraints."[39] In other words, public institutions can only do what they are given the political flexibility to do and what they have the organizational capacity to do.

Congressional change, whether gradual or immediate, holds practical ramifications for democratic politics and symbolic ramifications for democratic life. Charles T. Goodsell, in his book *The American Statehouse: Interpreting Democracy's Temples,* captures the practical and symbolic meaning of political change as illustrated in the architecture of state legislatures. The physical space and shape of capitol buildings, according to Goodsell, convey meaning about the values of the legislatures they house. He explores the "way in which statehouses reflect and affect aspects of authority, influence, hierarchy, and culture as they relate to public governing."[40] Changes to these spaces carry meaning about shifts in public values. Given the centrality of Goodsell's ideas to the changes introduced to the U.S. Congress in the aftermath of the terrorist attacks of 2001, it is important at this juncture to survey his argument in greater detail.

Goodsell grounds his analysis of the social meaning of architectural design of state capitols in a framework consisting of three distinct but complementary lenses. He characterizes these lenses as the expressive lens, the behavioral lens, and the societal lens. "Together, they reveal the ideas and values that were implicitly embedded in statehouse designs by their builders, the ways in which the capitols affect their users, and the impact of these buildings on the broader society."[41]

The Expressive Lens

The architecture of capitol buildings expresses meaning. These structures embody "broad conceptions of what was considered right and proper within a system of state governmental authority during their era of construction."[42] From the architectural imprint of capitol buildings, citizens can glean insight into the dominant cultural "ideals, values, and concepts" of government at the time of their construction.[43] To demonstrate this point, one need only look to the original design for the Capitol Building in Washington, D.C. The location of the building was chosen based on the principle of "superiority of height." The Capitol was constructed on the highest point in the Washington, D.C., region to indicate the primacy of the legislative branch of government in the American political order.

It is interesting to ponder the social architectural meaning of the Capitol Building taken as a whole structure, given the relevance of height to the cultural meaning of the past but the lack of relevance of height in the cultural meaning of architectural design in the present period. If the Capitol undergoes renovation or expansion without recognition of this concept, then can the building still be interpreted? Do architectural layers of meaning still exist? Are these layers cumulative in the expression they give to citizens? Utilizing the expressive lens throughout the following pages, attention is paid to ideas and values embedded in changes to the physical organization and setting of Capitol Hill in reference to the terrorist attacks of 2001 (see table I.1).

The Behavioral Lens

The architecture of capitol buildings also impacts political behavior. While architectural alterations to Capitol Hill may tell us something about the values of the contemporaneous culture, these alterations also shape the behavior of the political actors who utilize the space as a daily work environment. According to Goodsell, this lens suggests "not what buildings say about their originators or eras of construction, but how they may shape the attitudes and conduct of contemporary users and others affected by them. This frame is used to look for ways in which the built environment affects, not reflects, the social world. Putting the distinction another way, architecture is seen not as an imprint of earlier ideas, but as a pathway that steers or conditions current behavior."[44]

Goodsell illustrates his point by directing attention to the refurbishing of the House of Commons after the attacks of World War II. Winston Churchill argued for a reconstruction of the original design due to certain critical features of the chamber that affected legislative behavior. He suggested that within the House of Commons the benches designed for Government and Opposition minimized the potential for ideological faction; the lack of desks kept member lid-banging at a minimum; and the intimate size of the chamber gave the illusion of members at work.[45] Contrast this setting with the chamber of the U.S. House of Representatives, with ample room for every member. On average workdays the chamber is relatively empty and is covered by C-SPAN for all to see.

Churchill's architectural vision of the House of Commons captures it as a uniquely behavioral setting: "There is no doubt whatever about the influence of architecture and structure upon human character and action. We make our buildings and afterwards they make us. They regulate the course of our lives."[46] Churchill perhaps drew his inspiration of institutional determinism from Charles de Secondat Montesquieu. In a text on Roman history, Montesquieu observes that "at the birth of societies, the rulers of republics establish institutions; and afterwards the institutions mold the rulers."[47]

This summary suggests that the use of the behavioral lens assumes that the architectural design and setting of statehouse buildings hold implications for political behavior. While individuals are autonomous agents and can resist this architectural influence, on the whole there is an impact of design on group behavior. In this way, the behavioral lens offers us a unique perspective from which to evaluate the impact of changes to Capitol Hill since 2001.

The Societal Lens

Finally, the architecture of capitol buildings carries symbolic meaning for the society at large. The final lens through which to examine the Capitol is the societal lens, or the ways in which "buildings present themselves to the external society."[48] There exist distinct building types. Take, for example, a church. Stereotypically characterized by a steeple, the church as building type symbolizes not only a social or religious subculture of people, but also a certain orientation to the physical world—the proper relationship of citizen to community. Similarly, certain stereotypical features characterize the American statehouse. The dome of many state capitols, for example, has become the symbol of legislative government. As a symbolic representation of the cap or crown of government, it suggests the sovereign authority of the people's house in a separated system of government. Very often this dome is centered on a bifurcated structure balancing the two chambers of the legislative branch.

While the expressive lens begs us to take heed of the ideas, values, and concepts at play in the original design of the structure, the societal lens begs us to examine the impact of the design on the society. These are not one and the same. As Goodsell argues, "The societal lens draws attention to the effects of the statehouse on the public at large. Citizens do not notice the capitol's detailed embedded expressions or subtle behavioral effects, but they do experience the structure as a whole, in important ways."[49] It is possible that the values embedded in the design might fail to have the desired impact on citizens. Nonetheless, it is just as important to question the symbolism perceived by the public as it is to question the expression embedded in the structural design.

This discussion leads to a theoretical framework for examining the contemporary Congress. The Congress is assumed to be an evolving institution, shaping and shaped by its environment. The social context is recognized as important for understanding the operations of Congress. Finally, three unique lenses (the expressive, behavioral, and societal) hold value for observing the changes to the U.S. Congress following the terrorist attacks of 2001. The following pages outline the methodological approach utilized throughout this book to examine the impact of terrorism on Capitol Hill.

Gathering the Evidence

Much of the research on Congress has focused on the individual motivations of legislators. This scholarship provides rich insight into the goal-oriented behavior, the cues for decision making, the representational styles, and the career patterns of members of Congress. It, however, does not speak to the institution as a whole (the institution as a collective entity with collective motivations). As Julian Zelizer suggests, "In order to

Table I.1: Three Lenses and the Theoretical Framework

	Expressive	Behavioral	Societal
Types of social meaning sought	Ideals and values embedded in features of design	Design elements that shape user conduct	Symbolic impact of design on the public
Issues faced in interpretation	Unstated, subjective, and culturally bound nature of meaning	Degree of causality, individualized and interactive effects	Ambiguity and subjectivity of symbolic meaning
Evidentiary basis of analysis	Observation, comparative analysis, elite interviews, secondary data	Observation, elite interviews, historical record, secondary data	Conceptual reasoning, elite interviews, secondary data
Topic of analysis (by chapter)			
History of attacks on Capitol Complex (chapter 2)	Ideals and values embedded in Capitol design and related to security breaches	Changes in security related to interaction of technological advancement and specific attacks	Symbolic impact of security measures to protect Capitol Complex
Member office administration (chapter 3)	Ideals and values fostered by changes brought about to office administration	Specific policies and operational reforms that change office functionality	Symbolic impact of office protocols on public
Representation and the mail (chapter 4)	Ideals and values present in changes to handling the mail	Policies changing mail delivery and member response	Symbolic impact of reforms to mail delivery on public
Homeland Security committees (chapter 5)	Ideals and values at play in restructuring of committee system	Jurisdictional changes and reorganization to facilitate legislative oversight	Symbolic meaning of committee creation
Visitors Center (chapter 6)	Ideals and values projected by design and construction	Functionality of the space and effects on access	Symbolic meanings of site design

Note: The theoretical framework is adapted from Charles T. Goodsell's analysis in *The American Statehouse: Interpreting Democracy's Temples* (Lawrence: Univ. Press of Kansas, 2001). This table is adapted rather directly from page 9.

understand the institutional changes that [shape] Congress, it is essential to look beyond the motivations of legislators."[50] In large part, the research question asked in this book requires just this sort of broad, institutional perspective. It also requires a meshing of historical, anthropological, architectural, and political analysis.

I am indebted to those political scientists who bravely utilize quasi-anthropological methods to answer their research questions. The foundation they have laid provides this work with its necessary methodological justification. Tracking down the evidence to address the impact of terrorist attacks on the culture of the U.S. Congress ultimately led me to a very similar method and similar data sources as those utilized by Nelson Polsby (see summary on page 19). Consequently, I have arranged my discussion of sources in a similar fashion. From the fall of 2001 to the fall of 2009, I gathered thoughts, references, insights, and reports along the following major lines.

Personal Observation

In 2001 I served as an American Political Science Association Congressional Fellow in a leadership office on the House side of Capitol Hill. I was technically the deputy policy director for one of the party caucuses. Given that I was working on my dissertation on party culture at the time, this opportunity provided me with countless interviews, invaluable meetings, and firsthand observations that continue to bring exponential benefits to my teaching and research. Toward the end of the legislative session, as my fellowship time was quickly expiring, I found myself in a remarkable position of experiencing firsthand perhaps the most dramatic security events to befall Congress in (at least) the last several decades.

On September 11, 2001, terrorists launched an attack with hijacked commercial airliners on major symbols of the U.S. government. The plot targeted symbols including the World Trade Center, the Pentagon, the White House, and the Capitol. Though the historic buildings of the White House and the Capitol were spared, the psychological impact of the day's events was nevertheless immediate and severe across the nation and its capital city. As a firsthand observer of this event and the anthrax attacks that followed in October 2001, I cataloged the newspapers, the stories, the sentiment, and the events that unfolded in Washington, D.C. It was not until after my dissertation was finished and published in early

2005, however, that I returned my attention to the implications of terror to life on Capitol Hill.

When conducting interviews in 2005 and 2006, the climate I encountered was noticeably different from the environment before the terrorist attacks of 2001, and particularly different from the environment Polsby and Fenno described in the 1960s and 1970s. Polsby recounts that in the early days of his academic research on Congress "there were tourists in the Capitol building but security was informal, and the hallways—especially in the office buildings—were not crowded. Not many scholars could be spotted doing what I was doing, which was just watching and listening."[51] While some things have changed since those days, others largely remain the same. Security is much tighter. Those lingering or meandering down hallways, curious as to the purpose of oddly positioned furniture or fixtures, may find themselves apprehended by Capitol Police. Those without official business may not be welcomed by offices to just "soak and poke" as Fenno did in the 1970s.[52] Nonetheless, the House office buildings are not usually crowded, except for perhaps the Longworth Cafeteria, and tourists are limited to a few constituents and special interests seeking out particular members of Congress.

Increased attention to security on Capitol Hill has further limited the congressional access available to political scientists. Consequently, it has further reinforced the distinction Polsby references between conventional anthropological and quasi-anthropological investigation. While total immersion at the field site is relatively impossible for congressional scholars in today's security environment, sporadic immersion provides the next best option. Repeated trips to the field site allow congressional scholars to piece together a rather rich understanding of legislative life. In addition, there are other sources of data from which congressional scholars may check their firsthand observations (see summary on page 19). Pulling these accounts together, one may create a narrative of congressional adaptation and change that reasonably reflects reality and allows for corroboration by others. Firsthand observation through a quasi-anthropological investigation of Congress constitutes one data source for this analysis.

Elite Interviews

Given that I utilize both a historical and a quasi-anthropological methodological approach to tackle the cultural impact of security breaches

Central Characteristics of a Quasi-Anthropological Approach

- Rather than total immersion in a social setting for long periods of time, use of periodic firsthand observation—sometimes by permission—with interaction kept to an unobtrusive minimum.
- Use of multiple sources and types of data, including eyewitness testimony, newspaper accounts, and official records and statistics.
- Use of "thick description," involving the development of a coherent narrative from the disparate data sources that captures the worldviews of the subjects in native language.
- Use of copious personal notes from the research site as well as those of others.
- Availability of the research site for observation by others.

Source: Adapted from Nelson W. Polsby, *How Congress Evolves: Social Bases of Institutional Change* (Oxford: Oxford Univ. Press, 2004), 168–170.

on Congress, the second data source I include in this analysis is a set of firsthand interviews. The interview data are taken from over seventy-five elite interviews conducted between the summers of 2005 and 2006. The interview set draws from a variety of perspectives, including those of members of Congress (both House and Senate), personal staff, committee staff, Capitol Police, Capitol historians, policy analysts, lobbyists, and D.C. tourism representatives. The interviews include reflections of members who serve on the Homeland Security and Intelligence committees in the House and the Senate as well as staff who work for members on these committees. They further include both personnel who worked on the Hill before 9/11 and those who began working there after 9/11. The interviews are supplemented with primary and secondary sources as well.[53]

These conversations over the summers of 2005 and 2006 must be classified as in-depth, open-ended elite interviews. It was never my intention to quantify the responses taken from my subjects. Rather, it was my intention to listen to and learn from these political and administrative elite, to draw from their insights the appropriate avenues of inquiry given my general research question. In the end, I draw great parallels between Goodsell's treatment of interviews and my own. In conducting research, he treated his interview subjects as "informants instead of respondents, asked not to generate objective data about causal variables, but to open a window into a subjectively experienced, complex, and unique world."[54]

The Written Record

I further draw on primary and secondary data sources to provide an assessment of the major congressional changes brought about by terrorism, including the major security breaches on the U.S. Capitol grounds, the impact of these breaches on office administration, the development of the committee system to accommodate homeland security, and the evolution of the Capitol Visitor Center. This category of data includes excerpts from the *Congressional Record;* reports by the Congressional Research Service; estimates from the Government Accountability Office; stories from *The Hill, Roll Call,* and *Congressional Quarterly;* and major newspaper accounts of the subject in question.

Documents and Statistics

The final general resource from which I draw information includes statistics on individual members of Congress taken from references such as *Congressional Quarterly's Politics in America,* official congressional Web sites, and reports of the Congressional Research Service. These sources provide additional evidence to support the evaluations of the interview subjects and my personal observations.

Nearly ten years have passed since the terrorist attacks on 9/11. The data for this project largely span this decade, covering the initial responses to the attacks, the creation of the Homeland Security committees in both the House and the Senate, and the construction of the Capitol Visitor Center, a project envisioned decades ago and finally opened to the public in December 2008. The conclusions reached in this book are the result of reflections I have had over the last decade of observing changes to Capitol Hill. Zelizer's recent study of Congress emphasizes that government reform can and often does move at a snail's pace. It is a "slow, messy, and complex process."[55] Contrary to common depictions of institutional reform in textbooks, "change takes a long time and does not tend to occur in the dramatic bursts of innovation."[56] The changes brought about by recent security threats are no different. A near decade of observation, a rich combination of data sources, and an assortment of both quantitative and qualitative methodological techniques provide a much clearer picture of the lasting implications of terrorism for our nation's Capitol.

Outline of the Book

The introduction has sketched the events spurring this analysis of congressional adaptation and change. It has laid a foundation based on the existing research on Congress as an evolving institution and the various methodological approaches for evaluating congressional change. Finally, it has presented a set of three distinct lenses for examining the institutional changes brought about by the terrorist attacks of 2001. Through these lenses, the expressive lens, the behavioral lens, and the societal lens, the significance of congressional changes introduced since 2001 can more fully be appreciated.[57]

After laying this theoretical groundwork, it is necessary to outline the trajectory of the text. The book is substantively divided into four sections. After examining the historical setting of congressional adaptation to change, I turn to an examination of the changes introduced in member offices in terms of both office management and communications. I then examine the changes introduced to the committee system, and finally I address the massive changes introduced to visitor management on Capitol Hill. These four substantive sections, broken down into five chapters, mount evidence to support the conclusions presented in the final chapter of the text.

In chapter 1, I trace the history of physical attacks on the U.S. Congress, beginning with the burning of the Capitol by the British in 1814 during the War of 1812 and continuing through the twenty-first century to the present. I argue that the Capitol has always been a symbol of liberty and self-government. Consequently, it always has been a target for those who would wish to criticize American political leadership. In addition, each attack on the nation's Capitol has reminded Congress firsthand of the fundamental tension in this country between security and liberty. Congress consistently has chosen the side of security, systematically increasing physical security to the buildings, members, staff, and personnel. Drawing from a variety of theoretical perspectives, I use historical analysis and elite interview data to suggest how the institutional culture of Congress is impacted by its environment and does respond in tangible ways to buttress itself against similar vulnerabilities in the future.

In chapter 2, I examine the changes introduced to office administration. Previous research regarding legislative staff has been limited to a few primary areas: types of staff, staff characteristics, staffing reform, and staff influence on members of Congress.[58] While this research confirms the centrality of legislative staff to the policymaking process, few studies focus on the administrative behavior of staff in personal offices of members of Congress.[59] A far less studied aspect of Congress is the administrative personnel serving outside committee, party, and member offices. Those faces in the basement of the House and Senate office buildings or in the buildings neighboring the Capitol that implement the administrative policies of congressional leadership on a daily basis to keep the legislative branch operational are a significant part of "how Congress works." The terrorist attacks of September 11, 2001, and the subsequent anthrax attacks of the same year brought critical changes to all offices and all personnel on the Hill, involving staff training, preparedness, responsibility, and protocol in case of an attack on Congress.

I further examine staff turnover across time to identify the impact of 2001 on staff tenure at the aggregate level. A major finding of this chapter is that post-9/11 security measures have had a tangible impact on Capitol communications, office coordination, administrative responsibilities, constituent responsiveness, and security of members' personal staff. These changes potentially hold implications for office morale and job satisfaction but appear to be unrelated to staff tenure.

In chapter 3, I look specifically at the administrative changes introduced by Capitol Police for handling congressional mail in the aftermath of the terrorist attacks of 2001. Some of the most significant changes involved congressional office communications and accessibility to constituents. For example, mail is now sent to a processing facility, where it is "cleaned" or irradiated to decontaminate it. The process can delay the mail, sometimes by up to two months, and the chemical treatment alters the appearance and durability of the letters by the time they reach congressional offices. Members have responded by instituting a number of office-level policies to accommodate the new security-driven protocol. For instance, most offices now utilize e-mail as their primary mode of correspondence.

I argue that these changes hold significant implications for constituent responsiveness and representation. To examine these changes in communications and accessibility, I combine both quantitative analysis of member contact information with qualitative analysis of interview data.

The quantitative data includes office-level indicators of correspondence policies obtained from office Web sites, as well as member-level indicators of party affiliation, seniority, and electoral vulnerability. Findings suggest a widespread shift in constituent communications, and qualitative evidence attributes this shift in part to changes in institutional protocol for handling office correspondence since 2001. Members are reluctant to simply comply with new protocols for handling constituent mail (instituted by the Capitol Police for the purposes of security) because the process for screening the mail is too time consuming and destructive and thus inhibits constituent responsiveness. This chapter speaks to the evolutionary nature of congressional operational norms, the role of historical context in shaping the representational relationship between member and constituent, and the tension between security and liberty in a democratic institution threatened by terrorism.

In chapter 4, I follow the changes in the committee structure in the House and the Senate. One theme of this chapter is the bicameral character of the congressional restructuring of the committee system. The two chambers adopted different approaches to adapt the committee system to meet the challenges of oversight and legislative productivity posed by the new broad policy domain of homeland security. This chapter further explores the jurisdictional battles that ensued following the decision to restructure the committee system. These battles over turf have held significant consequences for legislative productivity and effective oversight of the new Department of Homeland Security. Finally, the activities of these committees have been a source of bitterness and resentment across Capitol Hill, due in part to the inequitable formula for allocation of homeland security grant monies.

In chapter 5, I trace the impact of security threats on the project development and management of the Capitol Visitor Center, which was under construction from 2001 to 2008 and was opened to the public on December 2, 2008. Drawing from the theoretical perspective of the advocacy coalition framework as well as the literature on privatization and government contracting, I examine the evolution of the policy debate surrounding the Capitol Visitor Center and the subsequent debate over management of the massive project.[60] It was difficult for Congress to provide necessary oversight for the project in part because of the evolving security demands of the CVC and because of its contracted-out management. The results were major delays and cost overruns.

Examination of the Capitol Visitor Center project highlights the frustrations inherent in collective decision making for a body in which power is fragmented and decentralized, as it is in the U.S. Congress. The Capitol Visitor Center warrants attention. It will be a central feature of the Capitol experience for future generations of visitors to Washington, D.C.

In chapter 6, I present the major conclusions of the text. A return to the three lenses offered by Goodsell reveals that the security threats introduced in 2001 led to substantial changes in the core structures and operations of Congress. The shape these changes took expressed the particular value structure and priorities of the governing majority. They further impacted the way the Hill conducts its day-to-day operations. Finally, these changes symbolize a marked movement from an open and accessible Capitol Hill atmosphere of decades past to a new security-sensitive atmosphere for the future.

Conclusion

This volume is a unique addition to the study of Congress. While others have examined the impact of 9/11 on executive power, bureaucratic organization, public policy, and jurisprudence, no book to date has been written on the impact of the events of 2001 on the U.S. Congress. In part, this is due to the theoretical and methodological difficulty of this task. It requires moving beyond statistical analysis of roll-call voting and electoral returns. Though these techniques are valuable to our understanding of legislative behavior, they cannot identify or explain the changes that have occurred on Capitol Hill as a result of terrorism.

A full understanding of the long-term implications of these events for legislative life requires a combination of disciplinary perspectives, including those stemming from history, anthropology, architecture, public administration, and political science. It requires examination of all aspects of congressional operation, including changes to committee structure, jurisdiction, and behavior; changes to office organization and administrative procedures; changes to security infrastructure and protocol; and changes to the physical setting of the Capitol Complex. It requires examination of a wide array of readily available resources, including primary sources, such as government documents, contemporaneous newspaper articles, and individual accounts by those experiencing firsthand the changes introduced by terrorism.

From this examination, it is the argument of this book that the fall of 2001 and the years that immediately followed constituted a historically significant period of time that led to profound changes in the institution of Congress. My hope is that this work provides an original and valuable contribution to our understanding of Congress through its nontraditional combination of ideas and analytical approaches. I hope that it engages the reader with its rich historical detail and firsthand political anecdotes. Finally, I hope that it challenges all students to think holistically about the political culture in which our legislative body operates and to incorporate this view into their own studies of Congress.

RECONCILING SECURITY AND LIBERTY

Attacks on the Capitol and Corresponding Changes in Security

> Even with outside help, the Capitol's earliest watchmen could not adequately protect members of Congress. In order to meet this primary responsibility, the Capitol Police has steadily added officers, equipment, and expertise to its operation, usually in response to perceived threats to security and expansion to the building and grounds.
> —"The Capitol Police," *U.S. Senate Art and History*

While the terrorist attacks of 2001 alerted Americans to the vulnerability of our economic, political, and military institutions, these events are only the most recent in a long history of attacks on our nation's symbols of freedom. The Capitol Building, perhaps the most recognizable symbol of modern democratic government in the world, has been the target of several of these attacks. As the above quote suggests, the Capitol security force has grown in tandem with each additional threat, from its original size of a single guard in 1801 to the approximately 1,700 officers that serve on the Capitol Police Force today.

The focus of this chapter is the historical evolution of the institution of Congress and the security of its buildings, including the Capitol. While the fall of 2001 brought increased attention to the Capitol as a potential target for terrorist activity, this season was just part of a long history of physical threats to Capitol Hill by those wishing to voice political protest. It is apparent through an examination of this history that the threats of 2001, though perhaps the most familiar and potentially devastating, actually were by no means the most severe. The changes introduced by this series of events also are simply the latest in an evolution of changes in security protocol to accommodate emerging threats to the facilities and personnel comprising the Capitol Complex. Finally, while perhaps not historically unique, these events did introduce major changes to security protocol that have affected the culture of congressional life. The most notable of these changes concern the visibility of Capitol security, the accessibility of Capitol facilities, and the sensitivity of Capitol personnel to potential security threats.

This chapter recounts the history of attacks on the nation's Capitol to understand the evolution of threats as well as the evolution of required security measures to protect the members of Congress, their staffs, and the facilities of the Capitol Complex. This chapter paves the way for an examination of the unique impact of September 11, 2001, and the anthrax attacks of October 2001 on the culture of the Hill.

The Capitol has always been a symbol of liberty and self-government. Consequently, it has always been a target for those who would wish to criticize American political leadership. In addition, each attack on the nation's Capitol has reminded Congress firsthand of the fundamental tension in this country between security and liberty. Consistently choosing the side of security, Congress has gradually increased physical security for the buildings, members, staff, and personnel. In order to place the attacks of 2001 in historical context, this analysis first presents a timeline of physical attacks on the nation's Capitol and then weaves secondary historical analysis as well as firsthand interview accounts of the impact of these events on the culture of Capitol Hill.

A Chronology of Attacks on the Capitol: 1814–1998

With 9/11 as our contemporary frame of reference, it is hard for many Americans to imagine that the Capitol or our other institutions of government, finance, and defense have ever been so vitally threatened. In fact, the history of our democratic institutions is speckled with stories of foreign invasion, militant protest, and personal vendettas. The following few pages survey this history to provide a more accurate perspective of the true institutional impact of 9/11 and anthrax on our nation's Capitol. Perhaps the most serious attack on the nation's Capitol in U.S. history was the British invasion of Washington, D.C., in 1814.

Burning of the U.S. Capitol in the War of 1812

According to Anthony Pitch, author of *The Burning of Washington,* little is known of this war, which actually took place on American soil. "It's so humiliating," stated Pitch. "I don't think people want to know about the destruction of the White House and the Capitol and that the president fled the city."[1]

The United States declared war on Britain on June 18, 1812. For a few years, the British were distracted by war with the French, but with the defeat of Napoleon the British turned their full attention to fighting the young United States. It is curious that the British would attack Washington, given Baltimore's strategic value just to the north. Apparently, in order to inflict a significant psychological blow, the British sought to attack the fledgling nation's capital city.[2]

After destroying many settlements up and down the shores of the Chesapeake Bay, the British turned south with their sights set on Washington, D.C. When word reached the nation's capital of the British intent to invade, "ninety percent of the 8,000 residents . . . fled, abandoning those who couldn't or wouldn't leave."[3] Those few who remained took responsibility for salvaging the young nation's treasures and records from the destructive hands of the British. The enemy troops arrived at the Capitol at 8 P.M. on August 24, 1814, and set it ablaze. Moving from the Capitol to the White House to the Treasury, they burned everything of public significance to the Americans. The next day they burned the State Department and War Department, as well as a few other points of interest.

One of the most famous stories of this event is that of First Lady Dolley Madison saving the portrait of George Washington by Gilbert Stuart. Knowing the British were marching toward the White House, she refused to leave until the portrait was saved. In a letter to her sister Anna, she expressed the fear and loss associated with this significant attack on the capital city.

[My husband] desires I should be ready at a moment's warning to enter my carriage, and leave the city; that the enemy seemed stronger than had at first been reported, and it might happen that they would reach the city with the intention of destroying it. I am accordingly ready; I have pressed as many Cabinet papers into trunks as to fill one carriage; our private property must be sacrificed, as it is impossible to procure wagons for its transportation. I am determined not to go myself until I see Mr. Madison safe, so that he can accompany me, as I hear of much hostility towards him. Disaffection stalks around us. My friends and acquaintances are all gone, even Colonel C. with his hundred, who were stationed as a guard in this inclosure. French John (a faithful servant), with his usual activity and resolution, offers to spike the cannon at the gate, and lay a train of powder, which would blow up the British, should they enter the house. To the last proposition I positively object, without being able to make him understand why all advantages in war may not be taken.[4]

Others watched from safety as the nation's capital was set ablaze. Pitch captures the perspective of Mordecai Booth, who served as an American scout during the attack: "The Capitol was burning. As the flames took hold, the magnitude of the calamity struck home. The landmark, notable as much for its artistic beauty as for its symbol of democratic freedoms, was doomed. Booth watched as the dancing flames spread unchecked. Soon the familiar wings were shrouded in flames and belching smoke. It was a conflagration of unprecedented scope. The majestic building atop its hill burned like an incandescent beacon. Booth felt pain and revulsion. It was a sight 'so repugnant to my feelings, so dishonorable, so degrading to the American character, and at the same time so awful.'"[5]

The Senate reconvened for a new session on September 19, 1814, a month after the British invasion. With the Senate wing of the Capitol lying in ruins, the Congress met in the only available building, Blodgett's Hotel. From this location they discussed possible alternatives for rebuilding the nation's capital. They discussed moving the capital to a more defensible and comfortable location (given that Washington, D.C., constituted little more than a swamp on the Potomac). They eventually settled on rebuilding the American symbols of democratic limited government on their existing sites. While construction was under way, Congress met in a satellite location nearby for another four years.[6]

Dignitaries, Fires, and a Royal Beating (1824–1828)

In response to the visit of the Marquis de Lafayette to the Capitol in 1824 as well as a fire in the Library of Congress in 1825, President John Quincy Adams created a watch force in 1827 of four men to guard the Capitol and all those visiting the area. But when President Adams's son was attacked in the Rotunda while visiting the Capitol the following year, the city of Washington extended its police jurisdiction to include supervision of Capitol Hill. This act in 1828 marks the official founding of the Capitol Police.[7]

Attempted Assassination of President Andrew Jackson (1835)

In 1835, President Jackson was the subject of an attempted assassination in the Rotunda of the Capitol Building. Richard Lawrence fired two pistols at the president during a funeral service in the Rotunda. Fortunately for President Jackson, both guns misfired and Lawrence was captured.[8] Lawrence apparently suffered from mental illness.[9]

Armed Exchange between Senators (1850)

Just two weeks after Vice President Millard Fillmore had addressed the Senate concerning the role of the presiding officer in maintaining order, a remark during Senate debate by Senator Thomas Hart Benton (D-MO) challenging the motives behind Senator John C. Calhoun's recent farewell address incensed Senator Henry S. Foote (D-MS) to the point of drawing his pistol. Ultimately, the two senators were restrained by fellow lawmakers. This exchange had two long-term effects on the institution. First, senators were discouraged from wearing firearms on the Senate floor. Second, the Senate strongly opposed a recommendation from the Rules Committee in 1856 concerning appropriate floor debate procedure, preferring instead to be chastened by the institutional norm of senatorial courtesy.[10]

Brooks and Sumner (1856)

In 1856, Senator Charles Sumner (R-MA) attacked Senator Andrew Butler (D-SC) in his infamous speech on the floor of the Senate, "A Crime Against Kansas." Sumner found Butler comparable to Don Quixote in all but one respect. Unlike the reputable mistress of Don Quixote, Sumner suggested, Butler had chosen "a mistress to whom he has made his vows, and who, though ugly to others, is always lovely to him; though polluted in the sight of the world, is chaste in his sight—I mean the harlot slavery."[11] Taking offense for his uncle, Representative Preston Brooks (D-SC) entered the Senate chamber and beat Sumner unconscious with his cane. Though Sumner survived, he was unable to return to the Senate for three years. Brooks resigned after being censured by the Senate, but he was reelected to defend the honor of his southern district in the years following the Civil War.

Shooting of a Former Member (1890)

In February 1890, William Taulbee, a former Democratic member from

Kentucky, was shot and killed by Charles Kincaid, a *Louisville Times* newspaper reporter, just outside of the House on the stairs leading to the basement. The shooting was in retaliation for threats hurled by Taulbee at Kincaid for exposing a sex scandal involving the former member.[12]

Bombing of the Capitol (1915)

The next attack on the Capitol took place on July 2, 1915, during World War I. In an act of protest against American financial involvement in the war, Erich Muenter, a former professor of German at Harvard University, detonated a bomb inside the Capitol.[13] Muenter entered the Capitol with a bundle including three sticks of dynamite. He intended to spark an explosion in the Senate chamber, but, finding it locked, he settled for the Senate Reception Room. Muenter saw his attack as an act of political protest rather than an act of violence. He intentionally targeted the Capitol during an extended Senate recess and set the bomb to detonate just before midnight to minimize casualties. The very next morning, Muenter attempted an assassination of J. P. Morgan Jr., the principal financier for supplies to the British. According to Muenter's letter to the *Washington Evening Star* explaining the attack, he intended the bomb to "make enough noise to be heard above the voices that clamor for war. This explosion is an exclamation point in my appeal for peace."[14]

Attempted Assassination in a Member's Office (1921)

The day after his retirement from the Senate, Charles B. Henderson from Nevada was attacked by a constituent. There are conflicting stories concerning what exactly transpired. By one account, Henderson was stabbed in the wrist and shoulder when he threw up his arm in self-defense. By a second account, a constituent frustrated over a Nevada land deal entered Senator Henderson's office, shot him in the wrist, and then surrendered.[15]

Gunman in the House Gallery (1932)

A common theme of attacks at the Capitol is that those who seek to terrorize the inhabitants are often driven by a cause or an issue. They wish to make a statement by threatening the building in which national policy is made. In 1932 an average department store clerk held the House gallery hostage, waving a loaded revolver and demanding to address the chamber. Marlin Kemmerer, a twenty-five-year-old from Allentown,

Pennsylvania, demanded twenty minutes to speak to the House about the nation's economic crisis. He was persuaded to put down the gun by Representative Melvin Maas, a veteran of World War I, before any shots were fired.[16]

Assassination Attempt in the Capitol Tunnel (1947)

On July 12, 1947, William L. Kaiser of Columbus, Ohio, followed Senator John W. Bricker of Ohio as he rode a subway car through the Capitol tunnel to a quorum call.[17] Kaiser fired two shots from a .22 caliber target pistol at close range but barely missed the senator's head. Kaiser had targeted Bricker because of a personal financial loss in the liquidation of the Columbian Building and Loan Association in their home state of Ohio fifteen years earlier. Bricker had served as attorney general of Ohio at the time of the liquidation.

Interestingly, Kaiser was a former Capitol police officer. He had been replaced when Bricker took office. At the time, positions on the Capitol police force were doled out as patronage. Though Kaiser suggested no ill will concerning his replacement, this certainly explains his dexterity in navigating the tunnel as well as his familiarity with Capitol employees and easy identification of Senator Bricker.[18]

Capitol Shooting by Puerto Rican Nationalists (1954)

Perhaps the most notorious shooting incident was by Puerto Rican nationalists in the House chamber on March 1, 1954, during a congressional debate on an immigration bill. Lolita Lebrón, Rafael Cancel Miranda, Andres Figueroa Cordero, and Irving Flores Rodriguez unfurled a Puerto Rican flag and unloaded thirty rounds from automatic pistols on 240 members of Congress. Ultimately, they only wounded 5 members. After serving twenty-five years in prison, the three nationalists still in prison had their sentences commuted by President Carter in 1979. A bullet hole in a desk on the House floor remains as a testament to the event.[19]

Capitol Bombing by Vietnam War Protestors (1971)

The Senate switchboard received a bomb threat at 1:00 A.M. on March 1, 1971. Roughly thirty minutes later, a bomb detonated in a restroom near the Senate Foreign Relations Committee offices. A description of the event in *Time Magazine* suggested that part of its significance was the placement of the bomb: "The explosion occurred in the original section of the Capitol, begun during George Washington's term in office and restored after the building was burned by the British in 1814. . . . Architects and engineers will spend weeks searching for damage around the fragile west front of the building, which is already buttressed to support cracks in the sandstone facing."[20] The Weather Underground, a protest movement opposed to U.S. involvement in Laos, claimed credit for the bombing; however, no suspects were ultimately found.

A Bomb Explodes in the Capitol (1983)

On November 7, 1983, a bomb exploded at 10:58 P.M., on the second floor of the Capitol's north wing outside the Senate chamber.[21] Members of a militant organization operating under a number of aliases, including the Armed Resistance Unit, the Resistance Conspiracy, the Revolutionary Fighting Group, and the Red Guerrilla Resistance, targeted the Capitol in protest of U.S. military action in Grenada and Lebanon. The Senate had adjourned at 7:02 P.M., and a reception near the Senate chamber had ended just after 9:00 P.M. Consequently, no one remained in the corridors of the Capitol Building when the bombers notified the Capitol switchboard, claiming credit for the blast that would happen just minutes later.[22] The group also contacted the *Washington Post* warning of an imminent explosion.[23]

While no one was hurt, the bomb hidden under a bench did blow off the door to the Democratic Leader's office, then inhabited by Senator Robert C. Byrd (D-WV), damaged the Republican cloakroom, and destroyed furniture and shattered glass. In the aftermath of this attack, several additional security measures were introduced. This single incident is responsible for the permanent closure of the area outside the Senate chamber, making it off-limits to the public.[24]

Those involved were arrested on May 11, 1988, and charged with bombing not only the Capitol, but also several other locations in Washington, D.C., including the National War College at Fort McNair, the Washington Navy Yard Computer Center, and the Washington Navy Yard Officers Club. The group "describing itself as a 'Communist politico-military organization'" was also charged with bombing several buildings in New York, including the Federal Building on Staten Island, the Israeli Aircraft Industries Building, the South African consulate, and the offices of the Patrolmen's Benevolent Association. All of these attacks occurred between January 1983 and February 1985.[25] The members of the group indicted for involvement with the Capitol bombing among others included Marilyn Buck, Laura Whitehorn, and Linda Evans.[26]

Two Capitol Police Offers Shot and Killed (1998)

On July 24, 1998, Russell Eugene Weston Jr. shot and killed Capitol Police officer Jacob Chestnut and Capitol Police detective John Gibson on the House side of the Capitol. Injured in the incident were both a tourist and the gunman himself. Weston suffered from schizophrenia.

Weston entered the building through an entrance known as the Documents Door.[27] Though this particular entrance is reserved for members, staff, press, and visitors on official business, Weston charged through the metal detectors while armed, and began to run once the alarms sounded.[28] When Officer Jacob Chestnut attempted to stop Weston, the gunman shot and killed him. Weston then entered a door closed to the public that led to the Majority Whip's office (then inhabited by Representative Tom DeLay, a Republican from Texas). John Gibson, dressed in plain clothes and stationed outside the office door, was shot by Weston. Though mortally wounded, Gibson returned fire. A wounded Weston was arrested and later committed to a mental institution. As a member of the Capitol Police's improved dignitary protection unit, Gibson represented one of the many changes in security since the 1971 and 1983 bombings.[29]

Contemporary Institutional Responses to Attacks

As the above chronology suggests, the Capitol has been the target of several attacks, some personal and others symbolic. Responses to these attacks have varied.

Several attacks on the nation's Capitol have been accompanied by commensurate improvements in security (see figure 1.1). At the time of the 1954 shootings by Puerto Rican nationalists, the Capitol Police only checked cameras of those entering the House Gallery. Law enforcement understood the Capitol to be both an office building and a tourist attraction. After demonstrators opened fire on the House floor, Capitol Police encouraged Congress to install bulletproof glass in the House and Senate galleries, but the Congress refused. "Members of Congress said they didn't want to lose contact with the public."[30]

Prior to the 1971 bombing, the public had much greater access to

Events compromising security (above the timeline):

- President Adams's son attacked in Rotunda
- House and Senate extensions
- bombing of Capitol
- assassination attempt in Capitol tunnel
- anthrax attack
- armed exchange between Senators
- shooting of former member outside House
- bombing of Capitol
- 9/11 thwarted attack on Capitol?
- Library of Congress fire
- Rep. Brooks attacks Senator Sumner in Senate chamber
- gunman in House gallery
- bombing of Capitol
- second Library of Congress fire
- attempted assassination of Senator Henderson
- two Capitol Police officers shot
- British burn Capitol in War of 1812
- attempted assassination of Pres. Jackson
- Capitol shooting by Puerto Rican nationalists

Timeline: 1800 1825 1850 1875 1900 1925 1950 1975 2000

Actions taken to enhance security (below the timeline):

- Capitol's first watchman
- responsibility for Capitol Police taken by House and Senate sergeants at arms
- magnetometers introduced and surveillance system installed
- Capitol grounds further secured
- founding year of Capitol Police
- Capitol Police Board established
- mail sent for off-site screening
- expansion of Capitol Police jurisdiction
- Capitol Police available to accompany MCs on trips
- dignitary protection
- oversight leads to new uniforms, raise in salary, more officers
- renewed commitment to Visitors Center
- Capitol Police put in uniform and armed
- Congress authorizes new security system
- Capitol Police provide security during impeachment trial
- four-man Capitol watch force
- access to Capitol further restricted

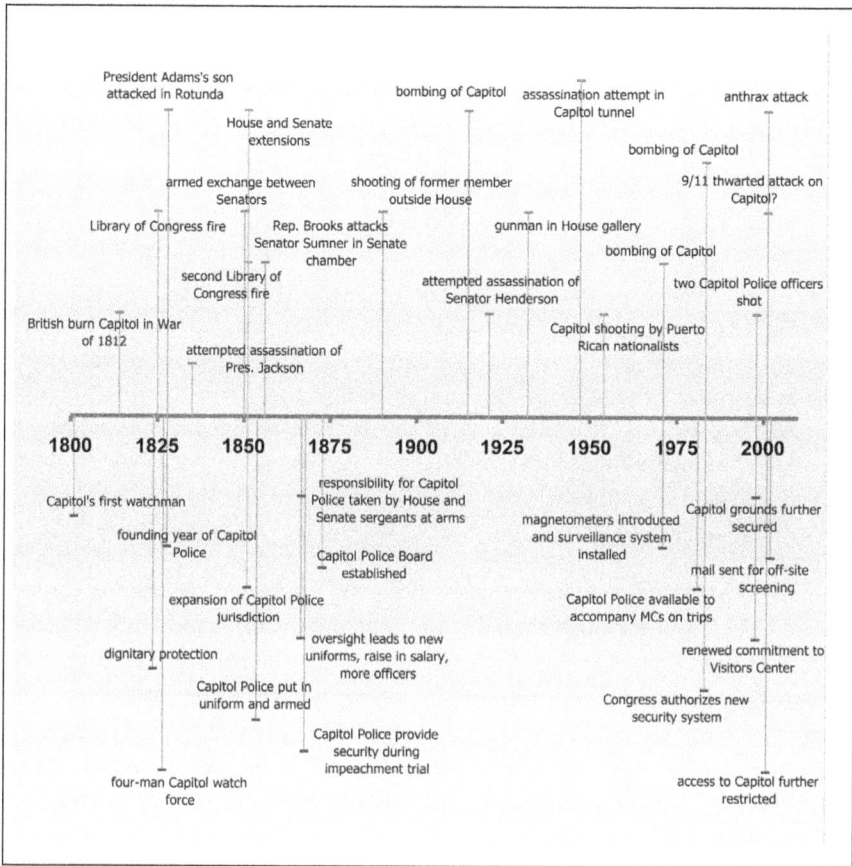

Figure 1.1: Events in Capitol Security. Events compromising security are presented above the timeline, and actions taken to enhance security are presented below the timeline.

the Capitol. According to the House Historian's Office, "The East Front was a parking lot. You could park there when the Congress was not in session." The 1971 bombing came at the end of a year of domestic attacks on thirty-two buildings associated with the federal government. Before the explosion in the Capitol, security had been tightened around federal buildings in response to these bombings and bomb threats. In fact, a few months prior to the March 1971 bombing of the Capitol, a plot to attack the Capitol tunnel system led to the installation of an alarm system and the sealing of most of the manholes.[31]

After the 1971 bombing of the Senate wing of the Capitol, the Capitol Police introduced magnetometers at ten entrances and installed a building surveillance system.[32] Metal detectors were installed outside the visitors' galleries of the House and Senate in 1976.[33] In addition, several other new security measures were instituted. These included:

- Police Force: The Capitol Police force increased from its 1971 size of 622 officers to 1,700 in 2008.
- X-Rays: Packages at ten entrances are inspected by X-ray machines. Guards inspect packages by hand at other entrances.
- TV Cameras: More than one hundred closed-circuit television cameras are stationed throughout the Capitol Complex.
- Alarms: Tunnels from the Capitol power plant to legislative buildings are wired with an alarm system.
- Bomb-Sniffing Dogs: Before the president or foreign dignitaries address Congress, the building is cleared, and dogs sniff for bombs.[34]

A *Time Magazine* article summarized the long-term symbolic impact of the 1971 Capitol bombing, stating: "More troubling than the physical effects of the explosion are the implications for the future. The openness of the Capitol—even to someone carrying 15–20 lbs. of dynamite in a briefcase—has been one of the strengths of the American democracy: the nation's laws have been written within full view of its citizens. Now security measures are likely to be forthcoming, and they will alter the tradition, however slightly."[35]

In the aftermath of the 1983 bombing, the Congress authorized a $725,000 security system, including "hydraulic barriers and unsightly concrete flower pots in various roadways."[36] In addition, metal detectors were installed throughout the building; visitors were restricted to six or fewer entrances; gallery access was limited; and identification badges for all staff and official personnel (other than members) were introduced. Outside the building, Capitol Police introduced further restrictions on parking and traffic flow, and the east plaza of the Capitol was closed to all vehicles.[37]

Responding to Perceived Threats

Actual physical threats to the Capitol Complex have resulted in increased security measures. Capitol security has also increased incrementally in response to *perceived* threats. Over the last thirty years, several events have caused concern for Capitol Police and led to heightened security on the Hill.

During the mid-1980s, Congress suffered no physical attack to its buildings, personnel, or surroundings. Yet the House and Senate considered a proposal from the chief of the Capitol Police to erect a fence around the perimeter of the Capitol grounds. Political scientist Ross Baker recounts this event in his book *House and Senate* to demonstrate the unique cultures of the two chambers of the legislative branch. Through his extended treatment of this incident, we also appreciate the role of *perceived threat* to proposed changes in Capitol security.

From time to time an incident occurs that reminds people, in a dazzling symbolic fashion, just how different the two houses are from each other. One of these epiphanies occurred in the spring of 1986 at a time when Americans had been the targets of repeated acts of terrorism on foreign soil. Concern was expressed that outrages would soon be taking place in this country. Security was beefed up at the White House and at a number of federal facilities around the country. Then, in accordance with what Senator Daniel Patrick Moynihan calls "the iron law of emulation," the legislative branch of the United States government began to demand the same security measures that the executive branch was enjoying.

Significantly, however, the cry for tighter security around the U.S. Capitol was expressed with much greater urgency and passion in the Senate than in the House. While some senators condemned the proposal by a joint committee of House and Senate leaders to install a wrought-iron fence around the Capitol building, the initiative and the loudest defense of the fence came from the Senate.

Senator Alan K. Simpson of Wyoming . . . spearheaded the drive for the fence arguing that if a bomb like the one planted near the empty Senate chamber in November 1983 were to go off while the body was in session a dozen or more members might be killed. Simpson's Democratic counterpart, Minority Whip Alan Cranston of California, tried somewhat unconvincingly to make the project a little less self-serving by asserting that "we have a duty to do all we can" to protect tourists visiting the Capitol.[38]

The reaction of House members was more relaxed. Democratic representative Leon E. Panetta of California explained the opposition of many House members to the fence in terms of differences in the institutional personalities of both houses. "The atmosphere of the House is much different from the Senate," Panetta observed. "We have much more of a free flow here. There's much more mingling here between members and constituents." Former House Speaker Thomas P. O'Neill expressed skepticism about the fence, saying, "I'm not enthusiastic about it, to be perfectly truthful. This is the Capitol of the country, where laws are enacted every day. It ought to be a free institution."[39]

What came out of the episode was a sense that somehow the Senate was more worthy of protection than the House, but also that the House is simply closer to people than is the Senate and that the constitutional design that ordained this closeness has much validity today.[40]

This debate resurfaced periodically throughout the 1990s. The fence has never materialized because members of Congress have consistently disagreed on the purpose for the fence as well as the prudence of building it. One senior Republican member I interviewed reflected on the debate among his colleagues over a fence around the Capitol Complex. The debate over a fence centers on the appropriate balance between security and liberty in shaping the Capitol landscape. This particular member criticized the motivations of those pushing for construction of the fence: "Looking at the old Capitol, it was surrounded by a fence. It would certainly affect the openness of the Capitol. But they [are] not thinking about the need for security, but for historically preserving the Capitol with a decorative fence!"

Others provided a different perspective on the purpose for the fence. According to a representative of the Capitol Police: "It was never really taken too far. Congress frowned upon the idea. It was supposed to be like the fence around the White House. It would still be an open campus. You can't walk up onto the terraces. A fence would increase the freedom people would actually have. It would allow us to screen people further out where we know there is no imminent threat. It's an interesting thought, but it has not been taken too far." Regardless of the motivations behind the proposal, the fence ultimately was rejected in the name of preserving public access to the U.S. Capitol (the openness of democratic government as expressed through landscaping).

During the Persian Gulf War, in the early 1990s, Capitol Police requested a 21 percent budget increase. In part this money would be used for "preventative security functions" taken in response to Operation Desert Storm, according to Senate sergeant at arms Martha Pope.[41] While the U.S. was engaged in the Gulf War, Capitol Police stationed sharpshooters on buildings, placed large cement barriers, and closed surrounding streets around the Capitol. In addition, signs were placed at all entrances requiring screening for visitors lacking proper identification.[42]

After the 1993 bombing of the World Trade Center, members complained about the infrequency of evacuation drills. Capitol Police called in extra manpower and brought in bomb-sniffing dogs to sweep congressional parking lots.[43] The Oklahoma City Bombing of 1995 constitutes the largest act of domestic terrorism in the United States, causing the death of 168 individuals and the injury of more than 680 others. Capitol Police responded to this incident by closing the Rayburn and Longworth horseshoes to through traffic, closing the parking behind the House office buildings, and screening cars entering the congressional parking garages.[44] Bill Livingood, the House sergeant at arms, correlated the security measures to the terrorist attack in Oklahoma, suggesting that the event could permanently impact Hill security. "Everything will be looked at in light of the results of this bombing."[45]

In 2004 a series of bombs detonated on four commuter trains in Spain left 200 people dead and 1,500 injured. Representative Bob Ney (R-OH), then chairman of the House Administration Committee (which oversees the Capitol Police), suggested that the incident served as "a wake-up call." He added, "This is not the time to go backward on our security investment here in the Capitol." Similarly Michael Lauer, the spokesman for the Capitol Police at the time of the Madrid bombings, suggested, "Every time there is an event we obviously re-evaluate our security measures."[46] In response to the London bombings in 2005, the Capitol Police modified more of their security measures and focused attention on vehicular traffic as well as pedestrian baggage. During rush hour, officers were instructed to inspect all large vehicles entering the area. Capitol Police chief Terrance W. Gainer also reported that the force had added manpower, extended officer shifts, and created a constant presence around the Capitol Complex.[47]

Looking from the Vantage Point of the 1998 Shootings

Following the 1998 shootings, the Capitol grounds were further secured inside and out. Inside, the windows were reinforced with bulletproof glass; outside, truck-bomb obstacles were placed around the buildings. In addition, Congress revived discussions of a subterranean visitors' center, originally introduced during the Persian Gulf War, that would

Aerial view of the U.S. Capitol Complex. (Courtesy of the Office of the Architect of the Capitol.)

incorporate security checkpoints.[48] One of the main benefits of the facility would be the funneling of visitors through security checkpoints outside the Capitol Building. Congress further reinforced Capitol security personnel with "more powerful weapons and better bullet-stopping vests."[49] "Guard posts were erected with bulletproof glass, cast-iron posts were installed around the perimeter to stop explosive-laden trucks, and police were given night-vision equipment and devices to detect chemical and biological weapons."[50]

While millions have been spent on sophisticated security, the Capitol Complex is still vulnerable to physical, biological, chemical, and explosive attacks. The Capitol Police face two major problems in trying to secure the Capitol Complex. First, the grounds are expansive and the facilities are intricate. "The U.S. Capitol police force . . . must cover a five-level space that totals 16.5 acres. There are many elevators and stairwells as well as subterranean tunnels and the Capitol Hill subway system."[51] A detailed sweep of just the Capitol Building itself would involve "approximately 540 rooms devoted to offices, committee rooms, restaurants, and storage. The building has 658 windows and 850 doorways."[52] The Capitol grounds cover approximately 274 acres and include more than a dozen buildings.

Second, the grounds hold symbolic meaning that limits the options available for securing this public space. According to John Daniels, former deputy chief of the Capitol Police, "The problem is [that] members of Congress want the Capitol to be a symbol of freedom and an open, democratic society. . . . Trying to balance that and the security issue is difficult."[53] A Congressional Research Service report issued just before the 1998 shooting suggests this inherent tension has been exacerbated by changes in the Hill environment: "The challenge of achieving a secure environment for the Capitol complex, while still maintaining an atmosphere of openness, has become increasingly difficult in this century. . . . Both the potential threats to the Capitol and the number of people using the area every day have grown dramatically."[54] Responses to security threats have largely centered on increasing the size and sophistication of the Capitol Police force and strengthening the security surrounding the Capitol Complex. The changes introduced in the aftermath of the security threats of 2001 involve both of these elements.

A Year of Terror for Capitol Hill: 2001

In the fall of 2001, two devastating but separate terrorist attacks threatened the U.S. Capitol. The first threat occurred on September 11, 2001, when a coordinated terrorist plot included a hijacked plane possibly directed at the Capitol Building. Fortunately for the institution, the passengers of Flight 93 thwarted the attack and diverted the plane from D.C. airspace. Nevertheless, this massive scheme caught the Capitol Police sorely unprepared to handle a security threat of this magnitude.

The second threat occurred in the months following September 11, 2001. In October, mail containing anthrax spores was discovered in several buildings, ultimately leading to the evacuation of the Capitol Complex. Some buildings remained closed for three months to undergo thorough decontamination. The Capitol lacked appropriate security mechanisms to prevent biological threats from infiltrating the mail system or to detect them once they had entered the buildings. Summarizing the state and focus of Capitol security prior to 9/11 and the anthrax attacks, a representative of the Capitol Police asserted, "Before 9/11, all the major issues were robbery, theft, and assault. These still exist, but our focus has changed to terrorism and those types of threats."

The Current Climate

One would be hard pressed to find a member, staffer, or administrator around the steps of Capitol Hill arguing that life after 2001 returned to normal. For those who live on the Hill the current climate is one of frequent security breaches, evacuation drills, changes in protocol, increasingly limited access, and heightened screening. For a summary of changes introduced since 2001, see table 1.1.

For some, these changes provide psychological relief. As one senior staffer in a Republican member's office stated: "Communications from top down is better. The top really is the Capitol Police." Another senior staff person commented: "We all feel generally as staff very secure. We have the best people in law enforcement working here. People may have a lackadaisical attitude about security, but that's because they know they're going to be taken care of."

For others, however, these changes provide psychological angst. As one senior staffer for a Republican member on the House Homeland Security Committee noted: "They're [Capitol Police] overly vigilant. You try to go to the restroom, and you're almost tackled going down the hall. It has really changed the culture around here. Everything now is about security. You can't help but think about it, especially if it is a beautiful clear day."

Another Democratic member of Congress simply summarized, "There's hyper-insecurity about security." A senior legislative aide for a Republican senator on the Intelligence Committee quipped: "It makes me feel more safe to have security officers in full gear. If [security] goes up one more level, they will close off the streets and have military in machine gun nests in the streets." A senior Democratic member on the House Appropriations Committee suggested that it "creates a siege mentality. It's good that we're prepared, but it's also an overreaction."

Part of the increased stress is due to the sheer frequency of security breaches. One Republican member of Congress on the House Homeland Security Committee suggested, "Culturally, it changed everyone. About every day around here we have a security-related incident. Maybe it has gotten to a point where they [Capitol Police] are crying wolf. People might not respond. Last week, a construction guy made a noise in the parking garage that sounded like gunfire. The Capitol Police locked down our office for six hours. It was in a mark-up, wasn't it? We had to shut it down. All the security people are so anal."

Besides increased frequency of security breaches, those around the Hill also note a critical change in the nature of response to security breaches by emergency personnel. One of the most noted observations by members and staff alike concerned the restrictions on access imposed in the months following 9/11 and the anthrax attacks of 2001. A senior

Table 1.1. Changes in Capitol Security since 2001

Access	<ul><li>Public entrances to Capitol severely restricted.</li><li>Several roads surrounding Capitol closed to through traffic.</li><li>Parked police cars strategically pointing outward from Capitol to intercept unauthorized vehicles. Large vehicles regularly redirected.</li><li>Capitol restricted to members, staff, and official business.</li><li>Public tours of Capitol issed by tickets with name and member sponsor—provides access only to rotunda, statuary hall, and the crypt.</li><li>Historic rooms off limits even to leadership staff.</li><li>House and Senate floor off limits unless accompanied by member of Congress.</li></ul>
Searches	<ul><li>Cars entering parking garages must show ID and be searched.</li><li>Bomb-sniffing dogs.</li><li>Mirrors for checking under cars.</li></ul>
Preparation	<ul><li>Member offices equipped with GO-packs, gas masks, and emergency kits.</li><li>Hallways equipped with gas masks for visitors in case of a threat.</li><li>Hallways equipped with air-filtration system to test for harmful agents.</li><li>Mail slots in hallways covered with steel plates to prevent mail from bypassing off-site screening system.</li><li>Green cement bollards installed circling buildings to protect buildings from truck bombs.</li><li>Windows coated with protective layer to limit impact of explosions.</li><li>Routine evacuation drills.</li><li>Office of Emergency Preparedness and Operations established under the Speaker.</li><li>Staff training through respective emergency preparedness offices.</li></ul>
Identification	<ul><li>Members required to wear pins at all times.</li><li>Staff required to wear identification badges at all times—including on weekends and in the tunnels.</li></ul>

Table 1.1. Changes in Capitol Security since 2001 (cont'd)

Communication	• Member offices equipped with enunciators connected to central Capitol Police communication system.
	• BlackBerrys for every staff member that receive e-mails concerning security alerts.
	• Off-site locations established for meeting in case of an emergency.
	• Emergency coordinator in each member office.
Screening	• Incoming mail sent to off-site location for irradiation.
	• No flower deliveries.
	• No packages without congressional ID.
	• No liquids in the Capitol galleries.

Democratic member of Congress said, "I used to walk down with constituents to the Capitol. Now I only do that if I have an appointment in the members' dining room." Similarly, a senior legislative aide for a Democratic member on Homeland Security shared: "It used to be that most staff could take you into the Capitol, but now you have to have a laminated card. It is not as easy to do. It used to be a big thrill to be able to take constituents because only members of Congress are allowed on the floor."

Not only has access to the Capitol been severely limited, but the facilities have also been modified to lend increased protection to members and other Hill personnel. As one Republican member on the House Homeland Security Committee informed me, "On the House floor under each desk, we used to have the previous day's congressional record. Now we have gas masks under there. In front of the Capitol you'll see benches with seats. They're full of emergency kits and gas masks. It's very sobering around here to think about what could have happened."

Each member's office is equipped with emergency kits and gas masks. The halls of the office buildings across the Hill are equipped with cabinets containing quick gas masks for visitors to the nation's Capitol. Additional "cabinets" test the air for dangerous biochemical or nuclear agents. The mail slots lining the halls that were once so convenient for staffers and visitors alike are now sealed off and provide no function at all. Green concrete bollards line the Capitol and the office buildings to provide an additional barrier against possible truck bombs. The windows now have a coating that will prevent glass from shattering inward in an explosion.

Additional improvements in security involve screening. Visitors to the Capitol have passed through magnetometers for decades, but since 2001 Capitol Police have severely restricted the visitor entrances to the Capitol. In the aftermath of these terrorist attacks, members of Congress demonstrated a renewed commitment to the Capitol Visitor Center—a further mechanism for improving screening of Capitol visitors and limiting access to the building. One senior Democratic member on the House Appropriations Subcommittee on Homeland Security noted changes by Capitol Police, stating: "I think that physical barriers and metal detectors and security has improved. It is 100 times more than what it was. The buildings are very heavily secure. You must have experienced that. We also get drills. Growing up in the nuclear era where we had drills, we had to crawl under our desks."

Not only do security measures include screening visitors, but also all mail coming into the Capitol Complex now undergoes screening and chemical irradiation at an off-site location before being sent to the members' offices. While this process has led to many other changes in Capitol culture that will be discussed elsewhere, the relevance to this analysis is the increased screening endemic to Hill culture.

While most of the perceived threat and thus security protocol surrounds visitors, several security measures directly involve members and staff. Several roads surrounding the Capitol have been closed to through traffic. In addition, cars entering the parking garages of the Capitol office buildings must pass through security. Capitol Police use mirrors to search for explosives hidden underneath incoming vehicles, and bomb-sniffing dogs are also available to provide assistance. Inside the buildings, staff must display identification badges at all times. Before 2001, these badges were only required for entry into the Capitol Building itself. Even members are required to wear their pins of identification. The Capitol Police have questioned those members failing to do so. In 2006, for example, Representative Cynthia McKinney (D-GA) was the subject of much media scrutiny for assaulting a Capitol Police officer who questioned her identity upon entering the Capitol. Capitol Police have warned members against displaying license plates identifying themselves as members of Congress. As a Republican member in leadership suggested:

I was already aware of some of the elementary steps. I had adopted habits that are reasonable. Even before 9/11, I didn't have congressional tags.

After 9/11, they told us you shouldn't do that, but you can still get them.
. . . It's better not to wear congressional pins off the Hill. You shouldn't
leave your little tag ID in the car. They're common sense things, but they
weren't recommended till after 9/11. . . . There are probably a lot more
security measures that could be taken; there is a lot of deference given to
members. They are not searched, for example.

While members are allowed some liberties, in general they have had to
abide by much more stringent codes of behavior than were required before the terrorist attacks of 2001.

All of these measures have led not only to heightened security but
also to the heightened visibility of security. As a Democratic member on
the House Homeland Security Committee remarked, "Prior to 9/11, they
tried to keep the police force hidden, but now you see the whole special
operations team. Now it's common. 9/11 took our innocence."

The visibility of security and the frequency of security threats have
led to a heightened sensitivity among those who work on the Hill. While
several aspects of daily congressional activities have been altered in the
name of security, what seems to be the biggest change is the climate itself.
A Republican member on the House Homeland Security Committee
provided this observation: "There have been other tangible changes. The
mail gets X-rayed. The main thing is just a general sense of insecurity. It's
funny—the real threats—there are lots of people who would like to blow
us up, probably lots of domestic political people [laugh]. . . ."

During the summer of 2006, an incident in the Rayburn Office
Building garage led to a lockdown of the House side of the Capitol for
nearly six hours. According to a CNN report, "Armed officers searched
'the old-fashioned way,' Schneider [spokeswoman for the Capitol Po-
lice] said, going door to door checking the 50 acres of office space in
the 169 suites in the building."[55] Subsequently, *The Hill* reported that a
noise due to construction work on the elevators was misconstrued as
a gunshot and led to a staffer in the garage alarming Capitol Police.
Those interviewed in the aftermath of this event pointed to it as a prime
example of the general climatic change around the Hill since 2001. A
Democratic member on Homeland Security, reflecting on the incident,
stated: "They've been doing work on elevators for a year. I'm not saying
that people should know better, but it wasn't even a question of whether
'oh my god,' but OH MY GOD!!!! If something really did happen. . . .

Urgent these days is like somebody leaves something in the hall. It's a tragic comedy, if you will. There's a funny energy. . . . It's unpredictable." Similarly, a Republican member in the House leadership summarized the feeling around Capitol Hill: "9/11 ushered in an era of awareness of very heightened vulnerability. This is a very vulnerable place. We are a sought after target here at Capitol Hill. We feel as though . . . have a sense as though we are a desired target. The London bombings were all part of it. There is a sense that we are very vulnerable. It made us aware of that again. You learn how to live with an added threat level, with a certain level of vulnerability."

Looking to the Future

Perhaps the greatest change to Hill security will be felt by the more than 3 million annual visitors to the Capitol—nearly 10,000 visitors a day. On December 2, 2008, the Capitol Visitor Center opened its doors. It now serves as the only entrance to the Capitol for visitors. The Architect of the Capitol's Web site offers details on the historic addition to the Capitol Complex: "From its inception, the Capitol Visitor Center has been conceived as an extension of the Capitol that welcomes visitors to the seat of American government. At nearly 580,000 square feet, the CVC is the largest project in the Capitol's 212-year history and is approximately three quarters the size of the Capitol itself. The entire facility is located underground on the east side of the Capitol so as not to detract from the appearance of the Capitol and of the grounds designed by Frederick Law Olmsted in 1874."[56]

While members of Congress first envisioned a Capitol Visitor Center in the mid-1970s with a report by the Architect of the Capitol entitled: "Toward a Master Plan for the United States Capitol," they did not invest in conceptual planning and design until 1991.[57] The plan was revisited and updated to include additional security after the 1998 shootings of two Capitol Police officers, but funds were not fully appropriated for construction until after the events of 9/11. As a member of the Democratic leadership suggested: "I don't think it would have been done but for 9/11. It had been talked about, but 9/11 kick-started it." The Capitol Visitor Center (the focus of chapter 5) is a major facet of the institutional changes introduced to the Hill after 9/11.

In the end, the events of 2001 are just the most recent set of attacks on the Capitol. They denote the culmination of a long history of events threatening the Capitol facilities and those who work in them. In response to these threats, the institution has adjusted the resources available to assist in Capitol security. These resources have taken a variety of forms, including additional manpower, weaponry, the latest technology, restricted access, and even additional construction.

Even given the ever-growing investment in Capitol security, the Capitol Complex is far from secure. As a senior staffer for a Democratic member on the House Homeland Security Committee remarked: "The Capitol Police are wonderful, but it is not as safe as we think it is. . . . If you go downstairs, one level down, you see a line of tourists going on Capitol tours. Just the way they funnel through one specific location seems to amplify the threat." In large part, this is due to the philosophical purpose of the building and its members. As Felicia Bell of the U.S. Capitol Historical Society reflects, "When I think about the United States Capitol, I think about a structure that represents freedom and democracy in all its architectural beauty. The Capitol . . . is the most recognized symbol of democratic government in the world."[58] Similarly, Turpin Bannister, a leading architectural historian of the twentieth century, states: "The Capitol of the United States is today the best known building in the world. Just as it physically dominates [architect Pierre Charles] L'Enfant's majestic vistas, it has become a commanding symbol of democratic faith and power. To students of American history in all its phases, it recalls multitudinous associations that intimately illuminate the evolution of our common culture."[59]

Those who are charged with protecting such an important place are simultaneously burdened with the task of preserving all the auspices of openness for which it stands. Representative Eleanor Holmes Norton, who represents Washington, D.C., warned after the 1998 Capitol shootings: "We've got to look at security, improve it, but we must not overreact so that the people's house is no longer that; so that we are barricaded. We must not have the Pennsylvania Avenue reaction, close down Pennsylvania Avenue, it's been a terrible inconvenience to all concerned. . . . We do not want to make the people's house a fortress."[60]

Nonetheless, the current climate is one of heightened security. While much of the change is warranted, given the importance of the building and the people who inhabit it, there is concern on Capitol Hill that the place is losing some of the character that serves to differentiate it from the rest of the world. One senior Democratic member on the House Appropriations Subcommittee on Homeland Security, describing the climate on Capitol Hill after 2001, suggested: "There are greater security barriers, multiple layers. . . . It feels more like being in the former Soviet Union than in America, being up here, because of all the armed guards. . . . Turkey's government is inaccessible—on a hill like a fortress. The government of Hong Kong sits up with mansions rather than with ordinary people. The U.S. embassy was built underground in Beruit, Lebanon. If [America] has to live underground, she will not prevail."

Conclusion

From these observations it appears that the events of 2001 did have both a tangible and intangible effect on the Hill. From the actual security measures used to protect the Capitol Complex and its inhabitants to the psychological disposition of members and their staffs, these events served to shape the institution in meaningful ways. Summarizing the evolution of Capitol security over the last half century, Manuel Roig-Franzia suggests: "The House floor looks much the same as it did in 1954. But there are subtle signs that this is a place far more attuned to danger than it once was. Behind the leather backs of the members' chairs, there are sturdy metal plates to ward off bullets and impede the spread of a bomb blast. Beneath the chairs, in the brass cubbies once used for copies of bills, there are 'escape hood' gas masks, constant reminders of what happened on September 11, 2001, and what could happen in the future."[61] While the changes themselves are unique, the dynamic of change is no stranger to Capitol Hill. The history of the Capitol has been marked by both actual and perceived security threats and evolving security measures to meet them. Security protocol has increasingly limited access both to visitors and to staff, altered facilities and institutional resources, and increased screening procedures. Consequently, security has become increasingly more visible across the Capitol Complex, altering both the appearance and reality of the democratic openness of the nation's Capitol.

A senior member of the Republican staff for the House Veterans' Affairs Committee summarized the changes in Hill security occurring over the last few decades. "It's been an evolutionary process in security. When I came, there was no magnetometer, no barriers. You could take a visitor in and out of the Capitol. It changed security and sensitivity considerably." A senior Republican member of the House similarly lamented the permanent loss of openness around the Capitol: "The lasting effect you can see all around. There's a type of armament, the vests they're wearing, the roads are blocked, the gas masks in the halls. . . . Everything you see is gonna be around. . . . Used to be, go back 25–30 years ago, you didn't want to get into Big Brother's watching you. Did you see all those [history of the Capitol] pictures they put up? Isn't it amazing there was no security, no barricades? I had the benefit of coming here in 1981, of living here when it was not an issue."

In sum, the practical implication of this analysis is that the culture of Capitol Hill will never be the same. If liberty and security are viewed at opposite ends of a spectrum, when compared to the pre-9/11 era, the Hill now falls more heavily on the side of security. Yet Capitol Police recognize the fundamental importance of using the least restrictive means possible to accomplish the goal of securing the Capitol. As a representative of Capitol Police explained: "Frustrating is not the way to describe it. It is more of a challenge every day to keep Congress open so people can come and visit their member of Congress. It is their right and privilege. We must ensure safety while keeping an open society."

This chapter illustrates that much of what takes place in the U.S. Congress is best understood within rich historical context. Capitol security has evolved over more than two hundred years. While the events of 2001 did pose a major threat to the institution and did result in major security adjustments, they were just that, adjustments. They were adjustments to a system that had been developed over time in response to environmental changes such as new threats, technological advancement, and newly available resources.

Some have suggested, however, that the security changes of the past are mild compared to the post–September 11 Capitol. "Now the building is almost an armed encampment, buffered from attack by tasteful, yet imposing, barriers to prevent car bombings. Police roam the halls. Lines form behind checkpoints. Everything, everyone is suspect."[62] While extensive resources have been expended to adequately balance security measures with public access to the Capitol Complex, this analysis suggests that security and liberty have yet to be reconciled. As Representative Paul Kanjorski (D-PA), a man who witnessed firsthand the shootings of 1954, attests, "If you take the effect it has on the openness of the system, it has been very destructive."[63] Only time will tell how successfully a balance between the two is reached. The next chapter focuses on the impact of terrorism on the average office workings of members of Congress.

ENUNCIATORS AND BLACKBERRYS

Congressional Office Administration Post 9/11

The Capitol Police, the janitors and maintenance workers, the grounds crews, the people who serve food, the secretaries, the Parliamentarians, the clerks, the young pages, our legislative and our committee staff, our field and caseworkers, and all the other dedicated and courageous people who make this place and our government run all deserve our thanks and our praise. With tears in their eyes, with sadness and with fear in their hearts, but with indomitable courage they came right back to work to serve this country we all love.
—Representative Brian Baird (D-WA)

On September 11, 2001, a massive coordinated terrorist attack on the United States threatened the Capitol Complex. All federal office buildings in Washington, D.C., were evacuated; Reagan International Airport was shut down; the Pentagon was ablaze; all monuments were barricaded; and rumors of bombs at the State Department, the White House, and the Capitol proliferated. As one *Washington Post* reporter suggested: "The news of the attacks and evacuation of federal buildings sent hundreds of office workers into the streets and created a frenzied atmosphere downtown. . . . Fire engines roared down streets, dozens of office workers milled in Farragut Square and K Street was jammed with cars at a time when most of establishment Washington usually would be in their homes."[1]

On that day, members of Congress as well as the thousands of support personnel evacuated to safety. They returned to work the next day as the dust from the attacks was just beginning to settle. It later became apparent that the Capitol Complex possibly was spared from major devastation by passengers of United Airlines Flight 93, which crashed in Pennsylvania en route to Washington, D.C.[2]

In the fall of 2001, approximately 30,000 legislative employees worked on Capitol Hill. Covering approximately 274 acres, the Capitol Complex incorporates several important buildings, including: the Cannon, Longworth, and Rayburn House Office Buildings; the Dirksen, Hart, and Russell Senate Office Buildings; three Library of Congress buildings; two House annex buildings; and several others. On October 15, 2001, just one month following the 9/11 terrorist attacks, a congressional staffer opened a letter containing anthrax spores in Senator Tom Daschle's (D-SD) office. Anthrax was also discovered in the Longworth building as well as the Ford Building, which is responsible for distributing the mail. According to the *Congressional Record,* 6,000 legislative employees were tested for anthrax exposure, and 28 tested positive. More than 1,000 employees were given a sixty-day supply of Cipro, an antibiotic used to treat anthrax exposure; as a precautionary measure the various House office buildings were closed for seven to nineteen days, and the Senate office building closures ranged from six to ninety-six days.[3]

These events introduced dramatic structural and cultural changes to the U.S. Congress and the staff supporting it. This chapter explores the impact of environmental factors such as national crises on the institution of Congress, its members, staff, structure, and processes. Congressional staff suggest that post-9/11 security measures have focused on improving the physical safety of members and congressional staff. In the process, these measures also have directly impacted Capitol Hill communications, office coordination, staff responsibilities, constituent responsiveness, and staff job satisfaction.

Legislative Staff

Research regarding legislative staff previously has been limited to a few primary areas: types of staff, staff characteristics, staffing reform, and staff influence.[4] Early staffing studies focused on the descriptive characteristics of congressional staff, including demographics and tenure.[5] Research on staff soon turned to the influence of congressional staff on legislative output,[6] on member decision making,[7] and as manifested through partisanship.[8]

Other studies dissect the individual offices of members of Congress, exploring the ways in which staff are utilized. Attention has been paid to the organization of staff in congressional offices[9] as well as to the allocation of staff resources to legislative responsibilities, such as constituency responsiveness and policy development.[10] Research has also focused on staff communication networks, paying particular attention to the informational exchanges in the legislative process as well as interoffice communication.[11] While the centrality of legislative staff to the policymaking process is undisputed, surprisingly few studies focus on the administrative behavior of staff in personal offices of members of Congress.[12]

In terms of its staffing patterns, Congress as an institution does respond (even if in a gradual fashion) to external and internal stimuli. For example, through multiple legislative reorganizations, legislative staffing has expanded to meet the growing workload and institutional complexity of Congress.[13] In addition, members have utilized staff differently to meet constituency expectations and demands.[14]

To a large degree, political scientists treat congressional staff as appendages facilitating the goal-driven behavior of members of Congress.[15] Staff respond to constituents to facilitate member reelection; staff develop portfolios of issue expertise to facilitate member policymaking; and staff advertise office accomplishments and activities to promote member institutional power. While some attention has been paid to staff motivations, such as personal career goals,[16] it is with a focus on involvement in the legislative process. The impact of staff on legislative institutions has been well documented, but very little work addresses the impact of legislative institutions on staff.

Of critical importance to the present chapter is the idea of Congress as an administrative organism responsive to external stimuli. While the broader question of this book concerns how external crises impact the corridors of Congress, the specific focus of this chapter is how external crises particularly impact staff and the administrative workings of member offices. Do member offices adjust to meet new demands, new challenges, and new administrative responsibilities introduced by crisis? If so, how does this impact the professional careers and office duties of congressional staff?

Staff Remember the Terrorist Attacks of 2001

While most staff agreed that the anthrax attacks were more physically devastating to the Hill, several recalled the emotional toll of the events on Tuesday, September 11, 2001. A House communications director noted:

> Jets kept flying around and breaking the sound barrier, and people thought we were under attack. On 2nd Street in front of the Mall, about twenty cameras set up looking at the Capitol. . . . Streets were filled, but everything was silent because everyone was in shock. There were Secret Service with shotguns walking down Constitution Avenue. It was something out of a science fiction movie—martial law. . . . We all went to the Capitol Police, and they were screaming at the top of their lungs, "Get the hell outta here!" They were petrified because the whole legislative branch of government would be wiped out [if attacked]. . . . We called family right away, but within an hour no one could get through. It was days till phone service was back to normal.

One legislative director for a House leadership office at the time of the attacks recalled a lighthearted comment made by Capitol Police during the course of the evacuation of the Hill on 9/11. He noted: "I saw one of the Capitol Police gathering members up. He said, 'If you see one out on the street, grab it!'"

Of particular note was the lack of credible information. Most people on the Hill relied entirely on the television coverage of the terrorist attacks to gauge the danger to their personal safety. Once evacuated from the buildings, people turned to radio coverage. One staffer suggested that "the craziest thing about it was the lack of information. No one knew what was going on or what to do. The amount of false information was ten times more prevalent than the actual information that was out there."

A chief of staff for a House leadership office suggested that while work returned to normal the next day, there was very little normal about it: "We were back in the office the next day on the 12th. Nothing had closed. Incredible things had happened. . . . The glass [windows] in the Capitol and in the offices around Capitol Hill were just paper thin, and that was really frightening. Days after, it was hazy and foggy. . . . Do you remember just watching TV and crying? It was the first time we ever watched terror and destruction, and it wasn't a movie . . . and we watched it over and over and over and over again."

The feeling of staffers who returned to work the following day was largely one of fear. Nevertheless, staff were responsible for the physical location and mental state of their bosses—members of Congress—who were a target of the terrorists and were very anxious to get out of the city: "Members were so tired," the chief of staff said. "No plane flew for four days. You've got people [members of Congress] who are used to going home. There were no cars to rent. People rented Ryder trucks and got in the back. There was a real need for people to touch and lay eyes on their loved ones. It was very scary for them. We had been attacked. It's like the resolve of the English after the subway attacks. 'We will not back down.' But it was not known for a little while who it was who attacked us. We simply hated and feared fear . . . but didn't know who to hate or who to fear."

Anthrax

The terrorist attacks of 9/11 led to dramatic changes in national homeland security and challenged Capitol Police to revisit several policies concerning emergency evacuation protocol. The anthrax attacks of October 2001, however, led to a complete shutdown of the Capitol Complex, the thorough decontamination of several Capitol buildings, and the overhaul of mail processing and distribution. It was in many respects a continuation and exacerbation of the havoc 9/11 wreaked across the Hill. A member of Congress summarized those eventful months in the fall of 2001 this way:

> Just as we were calming people down, three weeks after, anthrax letters started arriving. It felt like the extension of 9/11. It was part of a scary fall; it felt like no end in sight. Our confidence was shaken. It was so drawn out. There was no mail for weeks. We were buying rubber gloves for staff and evacuation kits called GO-packs. And then staff were standing in line to get Cipro. . . . Anthrax had a more profound effect. People who worked on the Hill realized that it was a target and the importance of our work that made us a target. We felt that we were part of the American federal government that is having war waged against it. We're on the team. It added a sense of weight to [our] responsibility and a sense of pride.

A House press secretary who had firsthand experience with the anthrax treatment stated:

They set up military doctors to administer Cipro. With Q-Tips, it was this long jam down the throat and then the other end. They'd say, "We'll let you know in a week," and would give you a week's worth of Cipro. . . . Daschle's office went home with contaminated clothes. They had to have their whole house quarantined. There were guys in space suits at the Hart Building. There was film over everything and a gritty, sour smell. It was from the chemical used to disinfect the building. Newspapers that were left inside [during the evacuation] were all yellow and crumbled. . . . A continuation plan was then at the top of the list in the event of an attack. They were digging up all parts of the Capitol.

A chief of staff for a House leadership office described the impact of the anthrax attack of 2001 on the Hill and the dramatic scene observed by those first to return to the buildings weeks later.

Anthrax was crippling to us because we didn't know if it was foreign or domestic. Should everybody get vaccinated? A course of Cipro is very hard on your body. It's like penicillin; if you don't need it, you don't take it. But there were a bunch of employees that you would see in line. . . . Then we evacuated. . . . We thought we were about at the end of this. . . . We had been out of the office for about two weeks. October 14th plus two weeks later. . . . People left our staff when we evacuated after anthrax. . . . When they said we could come back, there was a designated person [from each office] who came in. I had lists of things to get. I was one of the first people in there. There were mice running everywhere. It was then sort of like a twilight zone . . . like life had stopped on that day. Someone had left a Caesar salad on the desk, and there was a mouse in it. I had faced al Qaeda, anthrax, but I was screaming over this fuzzy little mouse.

While anthrax and 9/11 were separate events, they had the cumulative effect of "lifting the veil of innocence" across the Hill, as one staffer noted. He continued: "The difference between anthrax and September 11th was that anthrax was likely to affect me, but as a nuisance. September 11th was less likely to affect me, but its consequences were much more severe than anthrax."

Through the course of these separate yet equally potentially devastating emergencies, several elements of Hill security were found lacking. Prior to the attacks, to track down a member of Congress you would need to call his or her office and the staff would locate the member. There was no public address system in the Capitol or in the House and Senate office buildings. A legislative director for a House leadership office stated: "It was evident we needed a more upgraded communication system—a central way to contact people."

In addition, several aspects of office organization and communication were inadequate to deal with the challenges associated with dislocation from the Hill as the result of an evacuation. The same staff recalled: "What threw me off more was anthrax. We had to abandon the building for three or four weeks. We were up at GAO [Government Accounting Office]. I couldn't get what I wanted on the computer. There was a shuttle service. You couldn't get anything done. You couldn't get any control over it. I got the strong sense that [my congress member] was going to retire. In October I left." These inadequacies became the focus of congressional administrative reform in the months and years following the 9/11 and anthrax attacks. In general these changes can be categorized in terms of Capitol communications, coordination, and security.

Changes to the Hill Affecting Congressional Staff

Overall, a number of changes were introduced to the Hill after 2001 to increase preparedness for future emergencies. A communications director for a House member described the widespread nature of these changes, stating:

> Things that have changed, hmm. . . . Roadblocks, enunciators—because they freak me out, "quick hoods" or gas masks. . . . They only last for a few hours. We try to lighten the mood by taking pictures [with them on]. In the wooden boxes in the halls are quick hoods [for the public]. There is an emergency coordinator now that we check in with downstairs. They check in with the police. . . . In terms of the Capitol, now there are lines, and they check IDs. You can't take liquids or other things in your purse. . . . We have BlackBerrys. We get e-mail shortly after [an evacuation or drill] on our BlackBerrys. . . . A few weeks ago, we got a call from the FBI about questionable material—a suspicious package. . . . The mail is just slow; it takes two to four weeks. . . . They check our cars with mirrors. On major occasions, they have police dogs out sniffing. When big whigs are on the Hill, there are choppers.

In the following pages, this laundry list of changes is organized into those changes affecting Capitol communications, coordination of personal office emergency response, and Hill security. The impact of these changes on staff office responsibilities and job satisfaction is then evaluated.

Communications

Perhaps the changes most directly affecting office administration on the Hill are those involving communications. After 9/11, several tools were introduced to improve internal communications throughout the Capitol Complex, including BlackBerrys, a public address system through the use of enunciators, and remote access to the server in case of displacement. In addition, several offices adapted their protocol to improve external communications, more heavily utilizing technologies such as fax and e-mail.

One of the most visible changes to the Hill was the proliferation of BlackBerrys. While one would be hard pressed to find a staffer without a cell phone prior to 9/11, relatively few staffers carried BlackBerrys. On 9/11, cell phones proved unreliable. As Doug Heye, the communications director for Representative Richard Pombo, suggested, "On September 11, this technology [the BlackBerry] was often the only way I could communicate. . . . When the House buildings closed recently, I could not have done my job without it."[17] After the terrorists' attacks, demand for BlackBerrys surged, and several more base stations were installed across the Hill. These devices are "no longer seen as a fun gadget but as an essential communications tool, especially in times of crisis."[18]

Further changes introduced to the Hill in the months following 9/11 included the installation of enunciators in every member office. Enunciators are radio devices used to communicate security threats through a public address system. Capitol Police have utilized this communications system over the last few years to notify members and congressional staff of several security breaches, including the ricin threat in Senator Bill Frist's office on February 4, 2004, the unidentified airplane of June 9, 2004, and the nerve gas scare and evacuation of the Senate's Russell Office Building on February 9, 2006.

In my interviews, staff identified communication as one of the biggest changes in security directly impacting offices across the Hill. A communications director on the House side, when asked about changes since 9/11, commented: "So much has changed. Has anybody told you about the enunciator system? There are two or three around the office. When it goes off, you grab the walkie-talkie. They'll say, 'unidentified plane—you have three minutes till impact.' We have places we go to." Similarly, another House communications director stated: "We have enunciators. They shoot to volume #7 with a woman screaming, 'Air threat! Air threat! Not a drill!' People just start running. We get the threat, and everybody runs out . . . and then everyone is in one place."

Several offices reported frustration over the lack of specificity when the enunciator system is used to warn of an impending threat. In response, Capitol Police suggested: "The point has been raised numerous times that we need to decide the nature of the threat and determine whether we keep everyone inside or outside. We have very little information at the time when the decision needs to be made whether or not to evacuate. The way it should be looked at is that if it's an incoming plane, and imminent risk, then we should get people to safety. . . . The enunciator is another tool that we have to use to warn people that we're sworn to protect. It seems to work out fairly well."

On October 17, 2001, two days after the anthrax-laced letter sent to Senate Majority Leader Tom Daschle's (D-SD) office had been opened, the Hart Senate Office Building was evacuated and closed indefinitely. Eventually all of the office buildings across the Capitol Complex were closed for environmental testing, but Hart was closed for the longest period of time. The experiences of the senators and staff displaced from Hart—some for over three months—suggest the impact of the anthrax event on Capitol Hill. Senator Daschle recounted the responses of his colleagues to this evacuation.

> Most displaced senators . . . began making do without complaint. By that afternoon, makeshift offices were set up all over the Capitol, as staffers with cell phones and laptop computers began working in whatever spaces and on whatever surfaces they could find. Chuck Schumer took his work home to his Capitol Hill town house.
>
> John Edwards arranged himself on a bench in the hall outside the Senate chamber. Barbara Mikulski told a reporter, "If you see me at a Starbucks with a yellow legal pad, it could be the Veterans, Housing, and Urban Development budget." And she wasn't joking.
>
> Over the next forty-eight-hour period, fifty senators and thirteen committees from the Hart Building were relocated. This extraordinary feat—which involved, among other things, setting up temporary offices at a new building, connecting 600 new telephone lines and 650 new LAN lines, setting up 73 new routers, and connecting over 700 PCs and 100

printers to them—was accomplished because of the tireless efforts of the staffs of the sergeant at arms and the Senate Rules Committee. . . .

By that Wednesday evening, we would all be finding alternate office space, at least for the next few days, as the Russell and Dirksen Senate Buildings, as well as the Rayburn, Longworth, and Cannon Buildings on the House side, were shut down for environmental testing. . . .

There was a light aspect to this, and a real sense of camaraderie, as members ad-libbed to create working space. Storerooms and conference rooms became headquarters for some. Dianne Feinstein and Barbara Boxer converted their Capitol "hideaways" into staff offices. Chuck Hagel made room in his Russell Building suite for several members, including Ben Nelson, whom Hagel had defeated in their 1996 race for the Senate. Debbie Stabenow greeted constituents and visitors in a refitted storage room next to a loading dock.[19]

In the aftermath of this attack, offices had to revise communications both with individual constituents and the district at large. On the whole, members' personal offices were encouraged to restructure their Web sites to address the war and to prepare for possible displacement. The Congressional Management Foundation (CMF) conducted a study of member Web sites and found that offices were keeping current statements by members posted to the Web sites, but were not providing substantial information for constituents on available government services for those affected by military deployment, information on the war, and preparation for terrorist attack, among other things.[20]

Offices also realized the utility of Web sites and Internet resources for keeping congressional office staff connected in the event of an evacuation. In the weeks following the anthrax attacks of 2001, offices were displaced to satellite locations, such as the Postal Square Service, the Library of Congress, the Congressional Research Service, the Capitol basement hallways, cars, and member and staff homes in the surrounding area.[21] Most offices sent all but critical staff home to wait for the Hill to return to normal. Unfortunately, a mere 5 percent of offices had the capability to update their Web sites remotely.[22] Most offices lacked remote access to office files and e-mail as well.

This event demonstrated the real possibility for displacement and the necessity of an emergency communications plan. After 2001, the Congressional Management Foundation encouraged members to utilize the capabilities of the Internet for staff communication, stating: "Online communications can help you keep in touch with your constituents and staff even when you lose access to your office. Now is the time to set up contingency procedures and capabilities so that you and your staff are prepared should an emergency situation arise."[23]

Similarly, the CMF suggested in a special report on anthrax: "Sept. 11 changed America and Congress' priorities. But another date may have a greater effect on how the Congress operates—Oct. 15. That is the day a letter with anthrax was discovered in Sen. Tom Daschle's office. The anthrax contamination did more than threaten employees' safety and disrupt the legislative process, it also demonstrated that the most reliable, safe, and effective means to communicate during this crisis was via Web-based systems."[24]

When asked about changes since 2001, staff frequently mentioned an increased reliance on e-mail as a preferred mode of constituent contact. When anthrax hit the Congress in October 2001, mail facilities were shut down. A new irradiation process was established to screen mail bound for government offices. Staff expressed universal frustration with the quality of this process. One press secretary stated: "The mail goes to Ohio, and they fry it for a week. Now it just crumbles. We rent a P.O. Box down the street, and discourage people from sending mail here. FedEx and UPS couriers are not allowed in anymore. They must be met outside." Yet according to a chief of staff, this has not cut down on constituency responsiveness: "Constituency contact has changed, because we do not receive much 'snail mail' anymore. We ask for faxes or e-mails. This has actually caused constituency contact to escalate dramatically. Whatever 9/11 and the anthrax scare had caused to decrease has been offset by the Internet. We go through 5,000–6,000 e-mails a month."

According to one member's office, the volume of constituent e-mail increased by 400 percent in the weeks following the anthrax attacks of 2001.[25] While this increase was dramatic, it merely offset the loss of traditional mail. Having reviewed changes in office communication, the next section traces changes introduced to emergency coordination. The next chapter treats in great detail the significant changes to constituent correspondence introduced by the anthrax attacks of 2001.

Coordination of Office Emergency Response

On the day of 9/11, congressional offices lacked any centralized information on the unfolding national security threat and lacked any familiarity with protocol for responding to such emergency situations. In fact, the lack of coordination would prove to be a major complaint of staff and weakness of Capitol security during the fall of 2001. Staff consistently suggested that it was unclear on 9/11 whether offices were supposed to contact the Speaker's office, the Capitol Police, or some other entity altogether. Similarly, it was unclear to the Capitol Police who should make the final call concerning security. Though dialing 9-1-1 on the Hill connected directly to Capitol Police, this force reported directly to the Speaker of the House prior to 9/11. Not only was there a lack of direction or preparedness, but the attack at the Pentagon just five miles from the Capitol remained unknown for many Hill personnel until media coverage of the event appeared. In hindsight, it seems that United 93 most likely was headed for the Capitol. Considering the extreme lack of emergency coordination on the Hill, an attack of this nature would have devastated the U.S. Congress.

Some personnel clearly understood what was at stake on 9/11. As a chief of staff, one is responsible for the whereabouts of his or her own member and office staff. One chief of staff for a House leadership office who was unable to locate her boss at the time of the terrorist attacks commented, "There was no central emergency plan—no mass communication system. Three F-whatevers [fighter planes] were up. I thought 'something has happened . . . I've killed a congressman!'" Consequently, individual offices made independent decisions concerning evacuation on 9/11. In fact, some members refused to evacuate their offices altogether and kept staff on the Hill with them. Executive staff in offices choosing to evacuate gave orders for staff to leave cell phones on and evacuate immediately; however, no clear direction was given by Capitol Police concerning accessible evacuation routes or alternative means of communication. In fact, many routes were closed to through traffic, particularly those arteries surrounding the Pentagon. Once evacuated from the Hill, staffers wandered the streets and congregated throughout downtown D.C. in a confused daze. The next day, as members and staff returned to the Capitol, there was a general consensus concerning the chaos of the evacuation of the Capitol Complex. This consensus led to a subsequent call for a coordinated emergency protocol.

Some have suggested that coordination on the Hill has improved. One legislative assistant stated: "Communications from top down is better. The top really is the Capitol Police. We have an evacuation drill or a real one once a month." Capitol Police also claim that responsibility in emergency situations was clarified in the aftermath of 9/11. A representative from Capitol Police, for example, stated:

> 9/11 opened peoples' eyes. It was a new thinking to be put in place . . . thinking ahead, putting plans in place. There are plans and ideas of where certain people need to be. Our job up here, our whole mission, is to protect Congress members and the institution. We report directly to Congress. In life or death situations, discretion has to be put aside. The best choices have to be made in terms of protection of life. We work directly for Capitol Police. We know what our function is. When a decision has to be made quickly, everyone knows there is no time to pass along information. Decisions have to be made immediately based on the information we have received. We do the best we can.

Other sources, however, suggest that responsibility over Hill security has not been entirely centralized. According to the "Member's Handbook" published by the Committee on House Administration, for bomb threats or "physical threats" employees should contact the House sergeant at arms, while for removal of unwanted office visitors employees should contact Capitol Police.[26]

Individual offices have emergency response coordinators, and these individuals are responsible for appraising the office of evacuation protocol in case of an emergency and supervising the evacuation of the office during these events. Evacuation is organized and facilitated by Capitol Police on the Hill, but once outside of the office buildings, office emergency response coordinators are responsible for designating a meeting place for the office. This person is assigned to meet with the Capitol Police for training and information gathering on new emergency management procedures. While entirely at the discretion of each office, this duty appears to be normally assigned to legislative assistants and executive assistants within congressional offices. It appears that most offices do not have regular emergency management meetings, but emergency coordination issues are discussed as needed in weekly staff meetings. On the House side, the Speaker supervises the Office of Emergency Preparedness and Operations. According to a representative from Capitol Police, "each side has its own [office] in terms of training. The Senate does several trainings a year. This is to accommodate the huge influx of people."

Staff repeatedly noted problems with coordination in Capitol Hill emergency response. From the perspective of the Capitol Police, it is possible that this lack of coordination is to some degree due to the generally fragmented nature of law enforcement coordination in Washington, D.C. A Capitol Police representative painted this picture of security around the Capitol Hill complex: "We are the only federal police department that falls under the legislative branch of government. We are unique in that sense. The Supreme Court police department only falls under the judicial branch of government. We have a great relationship with surrounding [law enforcement] agencies. I've heard they include upwards of sixty-three departments."

Overall, perceptions of coordination effectiveness differ widely across the Hill. While some fear that not much has really changed since 9/11, others feel more confident in the newly established protocols. At the end of the day, however, it is not certain whether these or any other changes could lessen the impact of a devastating attack in the future. A senior legislative assistant, critical of the evacuation protocol introduced after 9/11, pointed to inevitable pitfalls in emergency coordination: "How helpful is that to tell you to 'run'? You know we have a staffer in a wheelchair [as he gestures to a special access desk next to his]. What are we supposed to tell him, you know? 'Hit the turbo button on your wheelchair.' If you have ninety seconds to evacuate the Capitol, depending on where you are, you're probably not getting out. And think about the Capitol Police." Beyond the changes to office communications and emergency coordination, there are other changes that seem to have directly or indirectly impacted congressional staff as well.

Hill Security and the Physical Reminders of 2001

There are several physical reminders of the dangerous nature of work at the Capitol Complex. Both inside and outside the office buildings, Hill staffers are aware of the increased importance of security. One chief of staff was concerned about returning to work on the Hill following the anthrax scare, but said: "While I was worried about coming back, since returning I have not considered leaving. The security measures, like the 'football' package [GO-packs], definitely impacted my decision to remain on the Hill. [But] during the airplane incident, our office was the only one that brought the 'football' pack with them."

While no specific number of Capitol security breaches since 9/11 is readily available, in discussing the threat of biological agents Capitol Police did suggest that some level of threat is present on a daily basis:

"If there's a suspicious item or substance, we send out hazardous material teams and devices units. Some [items] are smaller or not as much of a concern, and we just restrict traffic. That happens daily. Then if it's possibly anthrax or ricin, it does cause a more serious threat. Staff on both sides should be aware. They have information and know what they should do."

Staff are keenly sensitive to the heightened security awareness that pervades the post-9/11 environment. A Senate communications director permitted me to interview him in one of the interior overhanging hallways of the Hart Building. As we visited, he noticed something out of the corner of his eye and interrupted the interview to say: "See that bag there? . . . Somebody will be checking that out here pretty soon. . . . It's so much lost productivity, but it's good to be careful. . . . There's the issue of dirty bombs. It's horrible to think about. It's probably unlikely that they would get anywhere close enough."

One of the major changes that members and staff illuminated is the introduction of additional security measures throughout the Capitol Complex. First, the Hill has been equipped with resources for offices and staff in case of an emergency. These resources include, for example, gas masks in the corridors, individual offices, and even on the floor of the House.[27] In addition to the physical resources available to offices in the event of evacuation, Hill staffers are also reminded of the dangerous nature of their job through the additional drills, evacuations, and physical alterations to the buildings since 9/11. A legislative assistant summed up some of these physical changes, stating:

> You see a lot of aesthetic differences. On some of the walls there are stainless steel panels. They used to be public mail slots, but now they are sealed. That didn't happen till anthrax. Then they temporarily sealed them off, and then riveted steel panels on them. Have you seen the furniture about the size of a cabinet base? Those are gas masks available for the public. The [personal office] mail slots used to be outside. Now they have to be placed inside the door. The cabinets with vents on the side just circulate the air, detecting chemical [and] biological agents for nuclear, biological, and chemical preventions. . . . There's a lot of security people don't see. There is film over all of our windows. It looks like clear laminate on the inside to prevent the glass from blowing in on us. The trick is finding us security, but not scaring the hell outta everyone trying to come up here . . . finding the balance between security and openness.

In addition, security measures are always undergoing revision and improvement. For example, a year after 9/11 and anthrax hit the Hill, the Congressional Office of Compliance released a report raising concerns over the number and reliability of the gas masks or "escape hoods" available to workers and visitors in the event of an attack on the Capitol Complex.[28] The same office illuminated health hazards associated with the irradiation processes used to neutralize congressional mail since the anthrax attacks of 2001. Staff have had to regularly adapt to the changes introduced in response to congressional oversight. One legislative assistant noted: "You tend to get complacent. But people around here have stayed pretty vigilant. They're always changing something . . . one new little rule that we have to follow. But the footprint of security is not imposing on visitors or staff."

In the end, staffers are universally aware of the changes introduced by 2001. Even though work continues as normal, there is an ever-present awareness of the security threat. A press secretary who came to the Hill after 2001 but who works for a senior member of Congress suggested how this threat impacts staff life both on and off the Hill:

> I can only imagine being here was a dramatic event and those here having real fear. I remember bursting into tears [on 9/11] because my dad's a pilot. From my mom especially, I remember her saying, "When an alarm goes off, get out of the building and ask questions later. When the Capitol Police tells you to get out of the building, you get out. . . ." When the alarms went off the last time we evacuated, the Capitol Police told us to take off our [high-heel] shoes and run. We ran all the way to 395 and looked behind us, and there was nobody else there. My friend told me later that he said, "I think they're in Virginia by now." . . . You have to always pay attention. You have to be on alert because of all the things. Just pay attention, and not only when you're on Capitol Hill.

For those hired after the 9/11 and anthrax attacks, heightened awareness of the need for security is central to employment on the Hill. There is no desirable alternative to constant vigilance.

For those who have worked on the Hill for more than a decade and who have witnessed the dramatic changes introduced across the Capitol campus as a result of security breaches, the current dynamic is less desirable. Some staff noted and even expressed frustration over the increased security present since 2001. These frustrations centered on lack of access previously afforded to staff, lack of personal privacy, and changes in the overall atmosphere or feel of the place. Additionally, even with all of the increased attention to security, several staff find vulnerabilities in the current security system.

In terms of access, several staff bemoaned the current environment. Areas that were previously open to Hill staff now have very limited access. As one communications director summarized: "You can't talk your way in [to the office buildings] on the weekend without your ID anymore . . . same thing in the tunnel. White House tours are not issued through tickets. You have to reserve a spot six months before, only in groups of ten, and only in the morning . . . but no guided tours anymore. You also have to provide security information five days prior for a background check on anyone over fourteen years old."

Some staff expressed dismay over the increased security inside and around the Capitol. A legislative director for a House leadership office in 2001 reminisced over the way things were before 9/11. "Nothing was the same after that. The Capitol first of all . . . one of the joys of leadership is that you get the keys to historic rooms. Now you couldn't even pause walking through. Even if you worked in the building, you had to keep moving. No tours."

Not only did security inside the Capitol drastically change, the streets outside the Capitol were also closed to through traffic. Before 9/11, one could drive down either side of the Capitol on Constitution and Independence Avenues. After 9/11, Capitol Police blocked both streets. In addition, they closed the streets around the Senate and House office buildings. Staff were funneled into a few specified routes to office garages. One legislative director working on the House side noted: "I live North of the city. They started closing roads around the Capitol. Whereas it would take me twenty-five minutes to get to the Senate side from home, it would take another twenty minutes to get ten more blocks. I guess they figured they [the terrorists] would be coming back someday." Fluctuating with the level of threat, barriers continue to be raised and lowered around the Capitol Complex. In response to intelligence on al Qaeda in August 2004, for example, Capitol Police introduced fourteen vehicle checkpoints around the Capitol and closed down First Street, a main thoroughfare between two of the Senate buildings.[29]

Not only do staff bemoan the changes in Hill security that have limited their access to the Capitol, but they also find that new security measures introduced since 2001 invade their personal privacy. In particular, staff communicated frustration over excessive intrusion into the personal effects of staff entering the House parking garages. A communications director for one member of Congress stated: "We [are] very naive. They [Capitol Police] don't have a right to go through your trunk. Recently, they've been back there a little longer. Ask Capitol Police what constitutes something peculiar. Ask them what they have to do to investigate that. Do they have to have a search warrant?"

Beyond street closings and additional security measures, in the months following 9/11 the climate around Washington, D.C., changed dramatically. Members and staff alike expressed dismay over the environmental shift caused across the Capitol specifically and Washington, D.C., generally. One member of the House leadership described the ironic post-9/11 milieu introduced in Washington, D.C., a city symbolizing democratic government to the rest of the world: "Capitol Hill Police are some of the nicest guys, and they were standing next to national guardsmen in full gear. . . . You could go past the national monuments and there were missile batteries parked there. And those were just the ones we saw. It was like a scene from Red Dawn. Heavy artillery was coming down from the Armory. There was a tank in front of Banana Republic. It was an odd image for us to see." In a PBS special aired on April 6, 2004, Tom Bearden noted the increased physical symbols of security in what he called "Fortress Washington": "In response, streets are closed down, checkpoints are up. Heavily-armed patrols can be seen above ground, and below, in the Washington subway. Surface-to-air missile batteries in and around Washington have been in place for some time."[30]

The shift immediately following 9/11 and anthrax was particularly severe. The current climate does not include missile batteries and heavy artillery, but it does provide constant small reminders of the impact of terrorism on normal office operations. In describing the more subtle changes to Hill life, a House communications director suggested: "Anything that's catered has to have been cleared. When you have take-out, you have to meet them on the corner. . . . Flowers are no longer delivered; you have to meet someone on the corner. . . . If you're bringing in a package, you have to have your ID."

From daily security breaches, to the accessibility of gas masks in every hallway and office, to the duffel bags provided in the event of an evacuation, the workplace is different for congressional staff today than it was for them before the terrorist attacks of 2001. One chief of staff poignantly summarized these internal and external changes in Hill security and the important reason for them: "Everyone was issued a badge, and they have to have their car checked before parking. They have to go through security to get into the building. Many roads are shut down, and the Capitol is not as accessible. My family and I realize that Washington, D.C., is the number one target in the free world. The issuing of gas masks made that even clearer." Yet others suggested that security is still quite lax. A Senate legislative assistant, in discovering I had an appointment to visit with Capitol Police, offered a few questions of his own: "One question that I have is that there is a real discrepancy in security measures in place for visitors and staff. There are so many ways that we [staff] can get into the building. Security for staff is lacking, especially getting into the parking garages." The security threats introduced by 9/11 and anthrax increased sensitivity and awareness of the real threats to personal safety associated with congressional employment. How are staff coping with the added stresses of working on the Hill since 9/11?

Impact on Staff Job Satisfaction

Crisis introduces a number of new organizational and performance-related issues offices must consider. After the events of the fall of 2001, congressional offices were forced to address a number of crisis-related issues. The Congressional Management Foundation released a report in 2005 delineating the specific issues for congressional offices that arise as a result of crisis. CMF argued that offices should address the questions presented below to develop a plan in case of crises like those experienced in 2001.

1. What goals or priority activities should be delayed or dropped as a result of the crisis?
2. What, if any, issues or activities now deserve much greater office attention?
3. What changes should the office make in staffing to accommodate these changes in the environment? (E.g., shift legislative assistant or caseworker assignments to ensure the workload is equitably balanced; hire a new staff person; hire a part-time or short-term person to deal with an emerging need.)
4. How will this crisis affect our external communications practices over the next several months?

5. How will this national crisis affect the boss's schedule over the next few months? (What events will she and won't she now participate in?)
6. How will the office communicate these changes in priorities and/or responsibilities and activities to our staff?[31]

These events might be expected to hold implications for staff stress, job satisfaction, and tenure. When questioned about job satisfaction, the staff I interviewed offered a variety of responses. It should be noted that all of these interviews were of congressional elite who did not choose to leave the Hill in the aftermath of the terrorist attacks of 2001 or subsequent security threats. Nevertheless, several of them expressed a newfound fear associated with their job, and some suggested that this environmental change was responsible for the departure of certain friends and colleagues from the Hill after 2001.

A House legislative assistant noted: "I was in the army, so you know. . . . If they're gonna come take me, I'm gonna take a few of them down with me. When I come to work, I don't take the metro, so I don't have to look over my shoulder." A press secretary expressed similar resolve, suggesting: "It did affect people, but not me. I didn't want to cheat myself out of the experience. When we are all evacuating, running four blocks from the Capitol and looking to the sky, we joke that we should get hazard pay. Down the hall, they had a group of girls down at Bono's office, and they started crying."

It might be expected that staff tenure would decrease following the events of 2001. Nevertheless, congressional reports suggest that the terrorist attacks of 2001 and tenure are unrelated. A study of congressional staff tenure reported that the average years in Congress of House staff from 1994 to 2004 remained fairly constant across the period (see figure 2.1). The same study suggests that staff tenure in Senate offices was notably low in 2001, yet it appears that this level represents a decade-long trend rather than an episodic event (see figure 2.2).[32] In sum, staff tenure and the events of 2001 seem to be unrelated. If anything, tenure has increased in the House since 9/11, and the trend in the Senate is due to forces at work prior to 9/11.

While the terrorist attacks of 2001 seem not to have directly affected staff tenure, they may have raised the level of stress on Capitol Hill. As Senator Frist (R-TN) suggested in his extended remarks on the Senate floor on February 14, 2003:

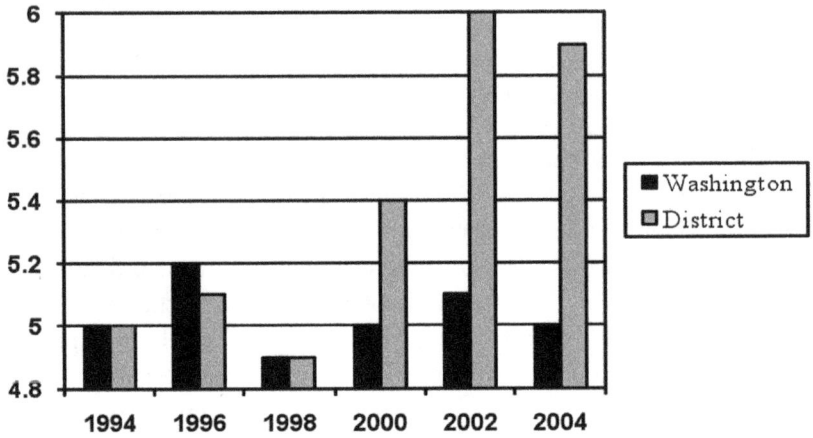

Figure 2.1: Years in Congress of House Staff. Adapted from Congressional Management Foundation, "2004 House Staff Employment Study" (Washington, D.C.: Congressional Management Foundation, 2005).

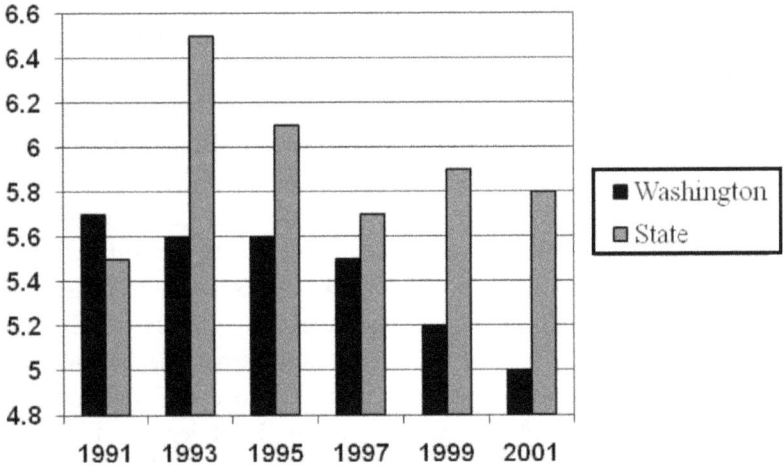

Figure 2.2: Years in Congress of Senate Staff. Adapted from Congressional Management Foundation, "Senate Staff Employment Study—Salary, Tenure, and Demographic Data: 1991-2001" (Washington, D.C.: Congressional Management Foundation, 2005).

I could not be prouder of the many fine women and men who make up this institution. Yes, I have mentioned the Senators, but I also include the thousands of individuals who come to this building and surrounding buildings on Capitol Hill to support the activities of what goes on in this body and in this room as we debate and amend and pass legislation. Through very difficult, long, and hard hours so many have demonstrated to this fine city and to the Nation that life must go on in times of threat and increased alert. . . .

It is important at this time of heightened awareness and vigilance that we also maintain the right perspective. As I have talked to people throughout Tennessee and family members who are not here in Washington, they have watched on television gas masks being put on, duct tape being put up; they see artillery with the Capitol in the background. I am speaking mainly to families at this standpoint. We have to be very careful because with 24-hour news cycles 7 days a week, every 30 minutes the news cycle being repeated, with the potential use of germs, microbes, bacteria, chemical agents, all of which are new in this arsenal of terrorism—new in terms of the weapons of mass destruction we traditionally think about being nuclear 50, 40 years ago, now we are thinking about little viruses and bacteria—it is easy to overstate, and all of a sudden the pain and paralysis you begin to feel inside, if you are mesmerized by that television set, seeing these images come again and again, we have to be careful. We all know these visual images are put on television to capture your attention. We know this captures our emotion and attention because we have that inner fear that we do not want that little virus to hit us.

Again, we have to be careful as we look at television, as we look at media today, not to let it feed our paralysis and fear. I am a parent. I have two high school boys; they are still children. I do not want them sitting there every day watching what is, yes, real, but in terms of perception, if you just watch television, you say: This risk is huge; that virus or bacteria is going to hit tomorrow; and there is nothing I can do about it. I am helpless, and things are out of control, and I don't know what is going to happen to my parents or kids. . . .

Let me comment on one last thing and then I will close. This is a time of stress. In talking to my colleagues and their families, I sense that when we go to this high alert—and as a physician I know this—there is a sense of stress that may or may not be talked about or noticed. I have to put my physician hat on for one second, because it can be reflected both physically and emotionally. I think it is important at least to be aware of it.

People do not sleep as well. Some people eat more; some people eat less. Some people develop tummy aches or belly aches. Some people develop back pain. That is sort of the physical and emotional manifestations: irritability, detachment, periods of depression, feeling blue, being on edge, waking up in the middle of the night.

That is normal. The body is remarkable. We are truly remarkable. The fact that we have this response, it is physiologic but it has an emotional component; it has a mental component and a physical component. The important issue is how one deals with it. When we go to these elevated stress levels or heightened threat levels, which correlate with stress levels, it is important to realize that everybody feels it to a certain extent. It is not just you. You are not alone.[33]

Several staff noted the stressful environment created by 9/11 and anthrax. One legislative assistant suggested that staff on the Hill have come to realize the great risk to personal safety inherent in their job. Consequently, staff are more aware and more critical of the security measures in place. He elaborated:

I was here on 9/11. It was absolute and total chaos. Nobody knew what the hell was going on. My wife was calling from home telling me what was going on. "You know the Pentagon is on fire. You need to think about our five-week-old daughter." For those on staff, you suddenly realized it was not as safe a place as you thought it was. Absent the heroics of people on the plane, it would have crashed into the Capitol. You can look out this window, and it's not hard to imagine the impact. Now the focus is a little more on our own sense of personal safety. One out of every six weeks, we get a warning. They [Capitol Police] have now made it easier [for an attack] putting everybody outside. So unless I can teleport myself, it's not going to work. You are more conscious of where you are and where you work. You keep track of your keys, cell, and BlackBerry. You have a communication plan with your family. They would meet me far from the Capitol. You think, "Wow, coming to work is not inherently safe."

Not only is the necessity of a detailed office and family emergency plan in case of an attack an additional stress on staff at the Capitol, the procedures for carrying out this plan are stressful. The same legislative assistant communicated the anxiety related to the evacuation protocol for staff and Capitol visitors in the event of an attack.

The Capitol Police are wonderful, but it is not as safe as we think it is. We go through mask training. There is no more stark reminder of what is different now than before than having to put that mask on. [I think to myself] what if what is in here isn't sealed enough to keep it from my goofy lips? What if I'm not calm enough to put it on? If you think about that, you go—oooh, that is serious. I can't imagine being a visitor and having to put it on. They haven't been trained. You would hope staff would help. If there's forty people in the Capitol, who's gonna show them how to put them on? If you go downstairs, one level down, you see a line of tourists going on Capitol tours. Just the way they funnel through one specific location seems to amplify the threat.

Conclusion

The events of 2001 critically impacted the culture of Capitol Hill. Those most directly affected by these events were members of Congress and their staffs. This chapter began with a twofold purpose: first, to present the stories of those public servants who experienced the terrorist attacks of 2001 on the Hill, and second, to identify the major changes introduced to the Hill as a result of this experience. It appears that some of the deepest changes to Hill culture are in the areas of internal and external communications, coordination of personal office emergency response, staff responsibilities, and Hill security.

In terms of internal communications, offices have incorporated enunciators, BlackBerrys, and remote access to the Internet server in case of displacement. Offices also have had to make major adjustments in external communications to maintain constituent responsiveness. Scheduling requests are largely handled via fax; constituent concerns are largely handled via e-mail. In terms of coordination, individual offices have appointed emergency response coordinators and have established evacuation plans in case of an emergency. In terms of Hill security, there are significant physical reminders both inside and outside the Capitol office buildings of the importance and urgency of emergency preparedness.

These changes hold important implications for staff efficiency and job satisfaction. While staff tenure has not decreased in the House since 2001, it appears that staffers do feel the heightened stress of their job. BlackBerrys allow them constant access not only to their phone but also to their e-mail. Similarly, remote access has brought the office home for congressional staff. In addition to greater access, changes since 2001 have led to greater responsibility. Legislative correspondents are responsible for much greater volumes of mail due to the heavy reliance since 2001 on e-mail as the preferred mode of constituent communication. The office staff member holding the position of office emergency response coordinator is responsible for frequent briefings and training on emergency preparedness as well as office coordination in the event of evacuation.

Universally, staff have assumed more responsibility for Hill security. They are required to be more conscious of their surroundings and standing protocol and to be better prepared to protect themselves and visitors to the nation's Capitol Complex in the event of an emergency. Finally, staffers have the additional stress of an extended commute to and from the Hill. With greater security both on and off the Hill, the average day is even longer for the congressional staffer.

Representative David Dreier (R-CA) addressed Congress on September 22, 2004, concerning the need to develop a plan for the continuation of government in the event of another attack on the nation's Capitol. What follows is an excerpt of his remarks:

> Mr. Speaker, since the District of Columbia became the permanent seat of our government, the United States Congress has been unable to use the Capitol for an extended period only once. That occurrence, of course, was during the War of 1812 when the Capitol was burned, as we all know. Nonetheless, the enduring threat of the last century, the Cold War, forced the Federal Government to plan for its continuity in the event of a catastrophe.
>
> Some people assumed, however, that after the Cold War this kind of planning could stop. We all know that 3 years ago this past September 11, not only did that tragic event put that notion to rest, but it changed our thinking and our planning for the continuation of representative government, representative democracy as we know it.
>
> Indeed, we saw smoke rising from the Pentagon and later heard of the bravery of the passengers on Flight 93 as they cried, "Let's roll." Many of us shared a feeling of having just missed a bullet, a bullet that could have hit this Capitol itself.
>
> We share the additional responsibility for our very institutions, for our individual Members, for our staff and for the thousands of people who visit the Capitol every single day.
>
> Following September 11 and the subsequent anthrax and ricin attacks, our continuity learning curve has been very, very steep. However, the good news is that we have worked hard and have implemented a number of measures that improve the continuity of our Congress.

Indeed, we have taken the advice of one of our great Framers of the Constitution, Alexander Hamilton, who in Federalist 59 said, "Every government ought to contain in itself the means of its own preservation." Let me say that again. "Every government ought to contain in itself the means of its own preservation." Those are Alexander Hamilton's words.

Toward that end, in the last 3 years, the Speaker has focused the United States House of Representatives on three core areas for our overall continuity: number one, upgrading the physical security of both our D.C. and our constituency offices; number two, preserving our continuity of operations here in Washington, D.C.; and number three, addressing the continuity of our form of government itself through debating how to deal with catastrophes that result in large numbers of Members being killed or incapacitated.[34]

From the comments so graciously provided by both members and their staffs, it appears that Congress is an institution that is responsive to its environment. Further, it is an organization with a unique culture created and re-created by those who compose it. The staffers who served members of Congress during the fall of 2001 were critically impacted both personally and professionally by the terrorist attacks from the sky and through the mail. Those who have joined the Hill since 2001 are impacted on a daily basis by the environmental changes to processes and procedures introduced by heightened Hill security. Overall, feelings are mixed concerning security. Some staff appreciate the far-reaching changes that have been implemented to increase physical security on Capitol Hill. Other staff express dismay over current security measures. Capitol security is criticized as both inadequate as well as invasive. Staff criticize the impact of security measures that decrease access to facilities, that invade the personal privacy of congressional staff, and that change the environment of Capitol Hill.

Previous scholarship on reform efforts involving legislative staff have focused on changes to staff size and changes in staff allocation.[35] This chapter examines reform efforts that change administrative protocol and office operations. It illustrates that reform can target the culture, norms, and responsibilities of congressional staff. Further, those responsible for instituting reform can include not only members of Congress or political parties but also administrative personnel, such as congressional staff or Capitol Police. This work charges us to move beyond a treatment of staff as appendages of members, facilitating their goals and decision making. Similarly we should move beyond an understanding of the Hill as a conglomeration of autonomous member offices or partisan caucuses. Congress is more than a policymaking body. Staffers are more than cue-givers. The Hill is a unique place with a community life of its own. As an institution, Congress adapts in response to partisan regime change as well as nonpartisan critical events, such as the terrorist attacks of 2001.

3

IS WRITING A LETTER TO YOUR MEMBER OF CONGRESS A THING OF THE PAST?

Congressional Office Communication and Accessibility

Now the mail is sent out to be zapped somewhere. You never know what condition it's going to be in. . . . The anthrax scare shows how easy it is to disrupt this place. It's a little scary in that sense. We've had wars and everything, and terrorism and anthrax are the only things to shut Congress down. They tried to set up temporary offices everywhere, but it was very different. With computers it is easier. If it had been earlier, we really would have been disrupted. The change in the mail system is disruptive. They do something to the paper. The constituents can't be as close to their representatives as they used to be.
—Former member of Congress

In response to the events of 2001, the Capitol Police introduced several new operational norms on the Hill. Some of the most significant changes involved congressional office communications and accessibility to constituents. For example, mail is now sent to a processing facility where it is "cleaned" or irradiated to decontaminate it. The process delays the mail, and often the chemical treatment practically disintegrates letters by the time they reach the congressional office. Members have responded by instituting a number of office-level policies to accommodate the new security-driven protocol. These changes hold significant implications for constituent responsiveness and representation.

This chapter examines the impact of the anthrax attacks on congressional communications and accessibility. After reviewing the anthrax attacks of October 2001 and the changes introduced to the postal system, this chapter traces the literature on representation and responsiveness and particularly the role of constituent mail in facilitating representation. The chapter then examines the evidence concerning member preferences in handling constituent mail in the post-anthrax environment. It appears that a supermajority of members offer e-mail as a viable mode of constituent contact, and a sizable portion of members emphasize e-mail over postal mail as a preferred mode of contact. Congressional elite attribute this shift to changes in institutional protocol for handling office correspondence since 2001. Members are reluctant to simply comply with operational norms (instituted by the Capitol Police for the purposes of security), because the process for screening the mail is too time-consuming and destructive and thus inhibits constituent responsiveness. In addition, there are significant differences in member preferences, driven largely by electoral concerns as well as institutional memory. This case speaks to the evolutionary nature of congressional operational norms, the role of historical context in shaping the representational relationship, and the tension between security and liberty in a democratic institution threatened by terrorism.

October 15, 2001

On October 15, a letter containing anthrax spores was opened in the office of Senate Majority Leader Tom Daschle (D-SD). A second letter had been sent to Senator Patrick Leahy (D-VT) but was misdirected to a mail room and was not discovered until November 2001. These letters marked a second wave of anthrax attacks nationwide. The first wave occurred a week after 9/11 when a series of anthrax-laced letters were sent to a variety of news media outlets. The anthrax contained in the first wave of letters was a brown granular form of the substance known to cause skin infections and referred to as cutaneous anthrax. By contrast, the anthrax sent to the Senate was a fine, white, powdery form of the substance, a lethal form referred to as inhalation anthrax. The FBI provides a picture of the envelope of the contaminated letter sent to Senator Daschle. The return address does not represent an actual place, though the letter was postmarked from Trenton, New Jersey.

The FBI also provides a picture of the actual letter sent to Senators Daschle and Leahy. The timing as well as substance of the letters suggests a connection to the 9/11 terrorist attacks. The first wave of letters was postmarked one week after 9/11, and the second wave was postmarked exactly three weeks after that (on October 9). Both grades of the anthrax included in the letters matched a strain produced at the U.S. Army Med-

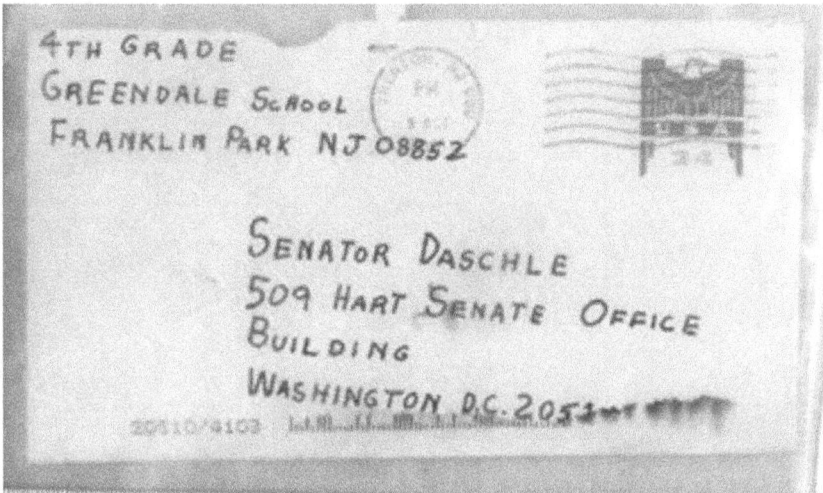

Envelope sent to the office of Senate Majority Leader Tom Daschle. (Courtesy of the Federal Bureau of Investigation of the U.S. Department of Justice.)

ical Research Institute of Infectious Diseases (USAMRIID) in Fort Detrick, Maryland. This strain was distributed to laboratories across the country as well as overseas, and an internal report produced by the U.S. Army indicated that "27 biological samples went missing in the 1990s."[1] Both of these factors made it very difficult to track the specific source of the letters, although the FBI focused its efforts on making a case against Steven Hatfill in the months after the attacks. Hatfill had been a researcher at USAMRIID and had criticized our government's unpreparedness for biological attack.[2] The authorities never were able to muster enough evidence to implicate Hatfill, who ultimately received a $4.6 million settlement in court for the disparagement to his reputation caused by the investigation.[3]

In the summer of 2008, new developments in the anthrax investigation became public when a senior microbiologist working at USAMRIID committed suicide. Bruce E. Ivins had worked for the federal government to develop vaccines against potential biological weapons, including anthrax, since 1980. In fact, he was one of the scientists tasked by the FBI with initially examining the anthrax spores taken from the mail attacks of 2001. Recent advances in genotyping made identification of the "signature" of the anthrax used in these attacks possible. This signature pointed to Ivins, who mixed anthrax spores obtained at USAMRIID

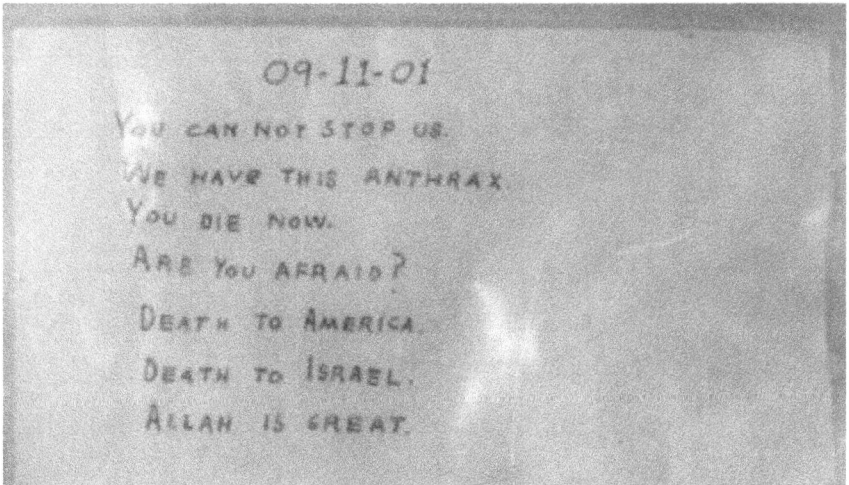

Letter sent to Senator Tom Daschle and Senator Patrick Leahy. (Courtesy of the Federal Bureau of Investigation of the U.S. Department of Justice.)

with spores from the Army's Dugway Proving Ground in Utah.[4] With Ivins's death, however, the country may never know with certainty the culprit or the motives behind this attack.[5]

As suggested by figure 3.1, the anthrax letter sent to Senate Majority Leader Daschle was processed through several postal facilities before ultimately arriving at his congressional office. The letter sent to Senator Leahy was also processed through this same route but was intercepted before delivery. Originally postmarked in Trenton, New Jersey, these letters were sent to the Hamilton Processing Facility in New Jersey, to the Carteret Hub and Spoke Facility in New Jersey, and then to the Brentwood Mail Facility in Washington, D.C. The Brentwood Facility is a 700,000-square-foot distribution center responsible for processing most mail sent to federal buildings throughout the District of Columbia. In fact, the CDC flowchart depicted in figure 3.1 suggests that Brentwood processed mail for 177 federal agencies and 56 U.S. Postal Service facilities across the region.

From here, the Daschle letter traveled to the P Street Mail Sorting Facility, the Dirksen Senate Office Building mail room, and then to Daschle's office in the Hart Senate Office Building. Investigative units discovered environmental samples testing positive for anthrax, most likely due to contamination by this letter, at two Capitol sites receiving mail

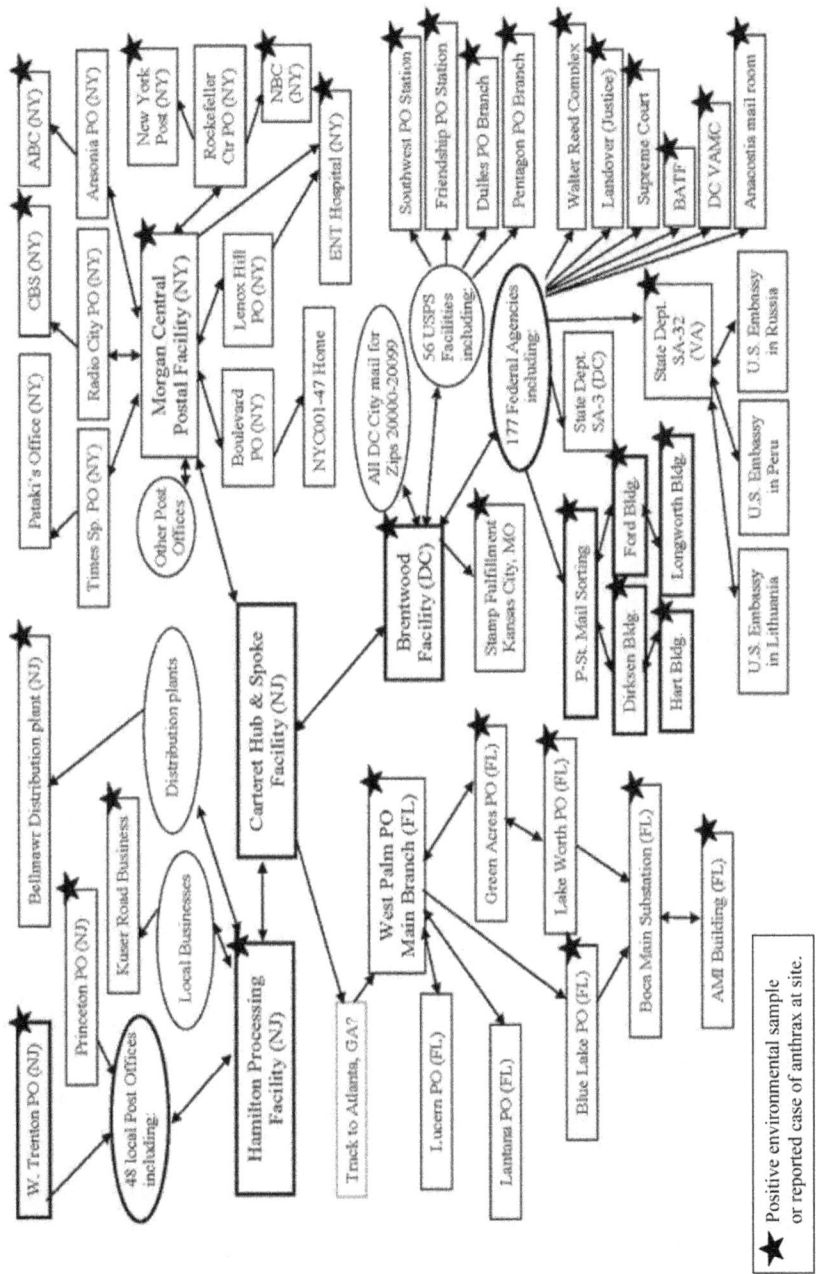

Figure 3.1: Mail Flow in Florida, New Jersey, New York, and Washington, D.C. *Source:* "Mail Flow in Florida, New Jersey, New York, and Washington, D.C.," Centers for Disease Control and Prevention, U.S. Department of Health and Human Services, November 7, 2001.

from the P Street Mail Sorting Facility. The Ford Building houses the central mail room for the House of Representatives. Ford produced positive samples on Saturday, October 21, 2001. The Longworth House Office Building houses 251 member offices and produced positive samples on the following Friday, October 26, 2001.

Ultimately, investigators discovered positive samples at multiple governmental sites across Washington, D.C. The chart compiled by the Centers for Disease Control notes that anthrax was detected at Walter Reed, the Justice Department, the Supreme Court, the Bureau of Alcohol, Tobacco, and Firearms, and the District of Columbia VA Medical Center. A case of anthrax was reported at one of the State Department's mailing facilities in Virginia, State Annex SA-32. USPS facilities throughout the area produced positive samples, including the Southwest PO Station, the Friendship PO Station, the Dulles PO Station, and the Pentagon PO Branch.

To begin to understand the impact of these attacks on Congress, table 3.1 presents a timeline of events on Capitol Hill related to anthrax. The substance was first discovered in Senate Majority Leader Tom Daschle's office in the Hart Senate Office Building. Senator Daschle was in his Capitol office when members of his staff opened the anthrax-laced letter in the sixth-floor-office mail room. When the letter was opened, thirteen people were present in the room. Daschle vividly recounts the events of that morning in his book *Like No Other Time.*

> In the regular course of sorting and opening mail, Grant Leslie (an intern) opened a letter, noticing it was from a New Jersey elementary school class. Contrary to later media reports, the letter was not heavily taped and didn't appear unusual in any way. She cut about an inch into the envelope, and a fine white powder, much like talcum powder squeezed out of its container, accompanied by a cloud of white dust, spilled out. Powder landed on her skirt and shoes, on the clothes of Bret Wincup, the intern standing next to her, and on the floor.
>
> Grant realized immediately what this might be and sat frozen, trying to keep the envelope closed.[6]

Over the next few days, the movements of Daschle staff after the envelope was opened became the focus of intense scrutiny, as the anthrax incident in Hart seemed to spark a chain reaction of contaminated spaces throughout the Capitol Complex.

I remember October 15–17, 2001. As an APSA Congressional Fellow serving in a House leadership office, I experienced these days as a staffer. The anthrax was discovered on Monday, October 15. The real impact was felt the next day, when the tests on the substance found in the letter came back positive for anthrax. This day was Tuesday, October 16, marking exactly five weeks since 9/11.

Senator Daschle's office sent staff home with prophylactic antibiotics Monday afternoon. By Wednesday, hundreds of congressional staff had persevered through lines outside the Capitol for nasal swab testing. One reporter for the BBC, who found himself in the midst of the contamination, recounted his experience with the testing: "The line took three and a half hours. Then there was form-filling and we were handed a tipped swab, alarmingly long, which a young naval technician inserted up the nose till the eyes watered. And we moved on to listen to the advice of a naval pharmacist, who handed us six days' supply of the Cipro. Just a precaution, he said, until you get your results at the weekend, which, he implied, would probably be negative."[7] With thirty-one people testing positive for anthrax exposure, Speaker Dennis Hastert (R-IL) announced in a press conference that the House would close for environmental testing. Senate Majority Leader Daschle (D-SD), initially refusing to close the Senate, reluctantly did so by the end of the day.

Table 3.1: Timeline of Anthrax Attacks on Capitol Hill

10/9	Contaminated letters addressed to Senator Patrick Leahy and Senator Tom Daschle are postmarked in Trenton, N.J.
10/12	The two letters are processed at the Brentwood Facility.
10/15	The contaminated letter addressed to U.S. Senate Majority Leader Tom Daschle is opened by a staffer in the Hart Senate Office Building. It is later traced through the Dirksen mail room, which is also found to be contaminated.
	Environmental sampling begins in Hart.
10/17	Staff in exposed areas of Hart undergo nasal swab testing and are given a supply of Cipro to serve as a prophylactic antibiotic.
	The Hart Senate Office Building is closed. Hundreds of Senate staffers are displaced to off-site locations.
	On Capitol Hill, thirty-one people test positive for exposure to anthrax. Speaker Dennis Hastert (R-IL) announces that the House will close for testing. Later, Senate Majority Leader Tom Daschle (D-SD) announces that the Senate will close as well.

Table 3.1: Timeline of Anthrax Attacks on Capitol Hill (cont'd)

10/19	Brentwood postal worker is admitted to the hospital with suspected inhalation anthrax.
10/20	Two postal workers in Washington, D.C., die from inhalation anthrax.
	CDC (Centers for Disease Control and Prevention) team visits Brentwood.
	Traces of anthrax are found in the Ford Building, housing a mail room of the U.S. House of Representatives.
10/21	The Brentwood Road Mail Processing Center in Washington, D.C., is shut down for anthrax decontamination. Postal workers undergo nasal swab testing and treatment.
10/22	Another postal worker in D.C. tests positive for inhalation anthrax.
	The Capitol Building is reopened.
10/23	Anthrax is found in an off-site White House mail facility.
	CDC and U.S. Postal Service contractors begin extensive environmental sampling of Brentwood postal facility.
10/24	Six Washington, D.C., postal workers are hospitalized for suspected anthrax.
	The Russell Senate Office Building is reopened.
10/25	Anthrax is discovered in additional spaces in Hart Senate Office Building.
	Cannon and Rayburn House Office Buildings are reopened.
10/26	Dirksen Senate Office Building is reopened.
11/5	Longworth House Office Building is reopened except for three member offices where trace amounts of anthrax were detected.
11/6	Portions of the Ford House Office Building are reopened.
11/17	Dirksen and Russell Senate Office Buildings are closed after contaminated letter to Senator Patrick Leahy (D-VT) is discovered in quarantined congressional mail.
11/19	Dirksen and Russell Senate Office Buildings are reopened after environmental sweeps for anthrax produce negative results.
12/1	Fumigation begins in Hart Building.
12/16	Hart is fumigated again.
1/22	The rest of the Ford House Office Building is reopened. The basement mailroom remains unoccupied.
1/23	The Hart Senate Office Building reopens after tests confirm decontamination.
4/3	Daschle and his staff are allowed to return to his office in Hart Senate Office Building.

On Saturday, traces of anthrax were found on the House side of the Capitol Complex, in the Ford Building, which includes a central mail

A sample is inserted into a vial in the Hart Senate Office Building. (Courtesy of the Environmental Protection Agency.)

room for the House office buildings. Though the Capitol was reopened on Monday, October 22, the office buildings surrounding it remained closed. On the House side, office buildings were reopened by the end of the week, but the Longworth House Office Building remained closed until November 5 due to positive tests for anthrax in three member offices located in the building. On the Senate side, Russell and Dirksen were reopened by the end of the week, but they were closed again on November 17 for a brief period after the letter addressed to Senator Leahy was discovered in quarantined congressional mail. The Hart Senate Office Building remained closed for three months. Finally, after multiple rounds of fumigation and testing, Hart reopened on January 23, 2002.

The employees at the Brentwood Facility and the Hart Senate Office Building felt the public health impact of the anthrax attacks most directly. According to one study, "It was recommended that approximately 2,743 people from the Brentwood population and 600 people from the Hart building take at least 60 days of antibiotic prophylaxis based on a presumed high risk for inhalation anthrax."[8] Four employees at Brentwood were diagnosed with inhalation anthrax, and for two of these employees the exposure was fatal. Though the Hart population initially was thought to be more at risk and several staff did test positive for anthrax exposure, not a single person developed inhalation anthrax from the incident in Daschle's office.

Because public health officials treated Senate employees more aggressively than they did Brentwood employees, charges of racial and economic discrimination surfaced in the days following the October 15 attack. A team of scientists used focus groups of employees at Brentwood and Hart to study the perceptions and responses of these affected populations toward public health information. The Brentwood participants cited the media as the most common initial source of information on the anthrax attack, whereas the Senate workers cited "internal channels of communication."[9] Nevertheless, "participants at both sites felt that the information they did receive was unclear, inconsistent, and in many cases, inaccurate."[10] These feelings resulted in mistrust among both groups of primary sources of information, including the CDC. For the Senate, the primary concern expressed was the "inconsistency of information and poor organization of the public health representatives responsible for communication."[11]

In addition to the public health impact, the anthrax attacks had a significant economic impact. The Environmental Protection Agency was tasked with the Capitol Hill anthrax cleanup and was authorized to use Superfund program funding. While the statutory limit for "removal actions" or governmental cleanup of contaminated sites is set at $2 million, the EPA increased this cost estimate six times based on new information. A report by the General Accounting Office[12] in 2003 set the final cost for the decontamination project at approximately $27 million. Part of the uncertainty associated with the cost of cleanup stemmed from the unprecedented nature of the project. Since the anthrax attacks of 2001 marked the first time the substance had been used as a weapon of terrorism in this country, the "EPA had not addressed anthrax contamination in buildings previously and protocols for responding to contamination by anthrax or other biological agents did not exist."[13] The EPA had limited knowledge of the tools to fight anthrax, the costs of competing methods of cleanup, or the health risks associated with anthrax contamination.[14] Confounding these factors, the U.S. Capitol was the site of the contami-

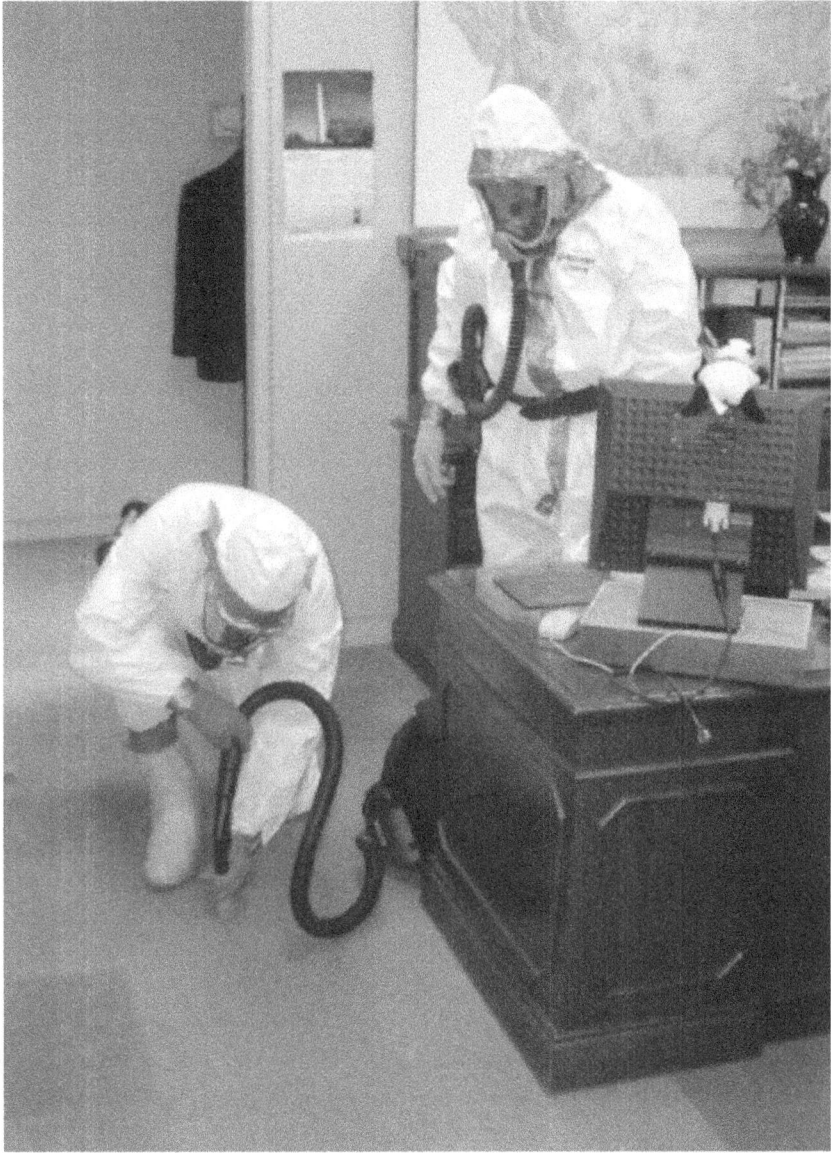

Cleanup personnel use a HEPA vacuum in a congressional office. (Courtesy of the Environmental Protection Agency.)

Cleanup personnel prepare duct work for air sampling in the Hart Senate Office Building. (Courtesy of the Environmental Protection Agency.)

nation. Lawmakers clamored for use of congressional office space, pressuring the EPA to work "around the clock, 24/7, for months."[15] In the end, the anthrax attacks of 2001 wreaked havoc on the public psyche, significantly disrupted the political process, and cost exorbitant amounts of money and time devoted to decontamination. While the cost of the Capitol cleanup alone is staggering, officials report that the total cost of cleanup of all affected facilities is in the hundreds of millions of dollars.[16]

Anthrax and Congressional Mail

Chapter 2 briefly describes the impact of the anthrax attack on congressional office administration, including the handling of mail. This section pursues the implications of this impact on constituent responsiveness. Perhaps most significantly, the anthrax attacks of 2001 led to a rapid transition from "snail mail" to e-mail. There is no doubt that this transition would have been made without the intervening events of 9/11 and anthrax. Nonetheless, countless members and their staff, when asked about the greatest impact of terrorism on Hill operations, noted the influence of this period on the mail system. Many offices seem to appreciate the speed and efficiency that e-mail has brought to the representational relationship between members and their constituents, but some see it as an inadequate substitute for more traditional forms of communication. A Senate committee staffer criticized the new dynamic:

> Now, the emotion of the moment becomes an e-mail to a member, and the person expects a response. I think e-mail is pathetic. The people don't even know what they're sending. It requires more staff to respond to these ridiculous e-mails. Offices adopt a policy to send e-mail responses, and then you have staff who become nothing but glorified letter writers.

I'm a bit anachronistic in this approach. If you come here and your whole experience is e-mail, then responding to 6,500 e-mails is great. But if you want to come to D.C. and be an expert on policy and have staff as experts, then e-mails are a poor measure of policy positions. It used to be different, but we've lost something. [My] concern is over constituent responsiveness and representation.

These changes perhaps hold even greater and more lasting implications than the broader "War on Terror" for representation and the legislative process. As a member of Democratic leadership noted, "The response to 9/11 was inconvenient for members, but anthrax affects the constituents." While the physical threat posed by both 9/11 and anthrax was significant, the lasting repercussions of anthrax for the entire mail system were possibly more severe.

Representation as Responsiveness

"Representation . . . means acting in the interest of the represented, in a manner responsive to them."[17] According to Bryan Jones, responsiveness only exists when two conditions are met: "First, the representative must correctly perceive his constituency's attitudes on relevant political issues. Secondly, he must act in accord with his perceptions of his constituency's preferences."[18]

Heinz Eulau and Paul Karps identify four components of representation as responsiveness: policy, service, allocation, and symbolic responsiveness. They warn us against limiting our focus on representation to electorally driven behavior, suggesting: "Anyone who has the least sensitivity to the representative process recognizes that representatives are influenced in their conduct by many forces or pressures or linkages other than those arising out of the electoral connection and should realize that restricting the study of representation to the electoral connection produces a very limited vision of the representational process."[19]

While all four components of Eulau and Karps's typology of representation as responsiveness are involved in constituent communication, service responsiveness and symbolic responsiveness are the most at stake if the system becomes inefficient. Service responsiveness "involves the efforts of the representative to secure particularized benefits for individuals or groups in his constituency." These activities include member action on constituent concerns and requests for tours and casework.[20] The importance of this type of responsiveness cannot be overestimated:

"Members and their staff sincerely believe that with the increasing complexity and scope of government involvement in the daily lives of citizens, the Congressman serves as one of the few remaining links between the individual and a depersonalized state. . . . Most of the mail involved in the service function is from those who either do not know where to go for information, or are unsatisfied with the response from a government agency."[21] In elections, members of Congress are not only evaluated on their policy positions. They are also evaluated on their service responsiveness.[22] Increased activity of the service sort has earned members the label "errand boys" and has led to speculation about the implications for legislative behavior and policy development.[23]

It is understandable then that members of Congress would react to changes in the mail system. These changes directly impact the ability of members and their offices to respond to constituent concerns and requests. Scanning the Web sites of members of Congress provides evidence that representatives are not content to simply follow the mail-handling protocol established by the Capitol Police. Several member Web sites discourage constituents from sending mail to their Washington offices because of the involved screening process and lengthy delays. They encourage those who would attempt to contact them to send mail directly to their district offices, thus bypassing the security protocol altogether. The two Web pages below provide just a few examples.

These examples illustrate two points about member preferences concerning constituent contact. First, as both images suggest, members recognize the frustrations posed to service responsiveness by security protocols concerning handling of the mail. They highly encourage e-mail as an efficient mode of contact and often attribute this preference directly to heightened security. Second, members utilize interactive electronic forms to solicit constituent contact and process constituent requests. It is debatable whether e-mail and electronic forms constitute the same caliber of correspondence as handwritten or typed letters sent through the postal system.

Scholarship on organizational communication has explored the relative value of different modes of communication. There are significant differences across modes of communication, including the cues they provide, the amount of information they carry, and the social presence they convey. According to D. Rutter, as the cues provided by a communication mode decrease, so does the "psychological closeness" between those at-

Offices of Congressman Zach Wamp

Email me and receive a timely response!

Chattanooga District Office	Oak Ridge District Office	Washington D.C.
900 Georgia Avenue Suite 126 Chattanooga, TN 37402 (423) 756-2342 (423) 756-6613 fax **Map It**	200 Administration Road Federal Building Suite 100 Oak Ridge, TN 37830 (865) 576-1976 (865) 576-3221 (fax) (800) 883-2369 toll free **Map It**	Please do not send mail to my D.C. office. It will reach me much faster in TN. My office is in room 1436 of the Longworth Building. (202) 225-3271 (202) 225-3494 (fax) **Map It** **Directions**

Contact Information for Representative Zach Wamp (R-TN). (Adapted from the official Web site of Representative Zach Wamp, "Offices of Congressman Zach Wamp," http://www.house.gov/wamp/contact_offices.shtm.)

Contacting Me

*** IMPORTANT NOTICE ***

Due to increased security measures, all mail service to Congressional Offices is delayed due to security screening procedures. Because of these procedures, the best way to contact me to share your opinion is via e-mail or by filling in the form below

If you would like to receive the Berkley Bulletin, please click here and fill out the form.

Washington Office
The Honorable Shelley Berkley
U.S. House of Representatives
405 Cannon House Office Building
Washington, DC 20515-4708
Phone:(202) 225-5965
Fax: (202) 225-3119
Toll free: (877) 409-2488

Las Vegas District Office
The Honorable Shelley Berkley
2340 Paseo Del Prado, Suite D-106
Las Vegas, NV 89102
Phone:(702) 220-9823
Fax: (702) 220-9841
Map

First Name: [   ]   Last Name: [   ]

Comments: [Place Comments Here]   Submit

Contact Information for Representative Shelley Berkley (D-NV). (Adapted from the office Web site of Representative Shelley Berkley, "Contacting Me," http://berkley.house.gov/contact/index.html.)

tempting to communicate.[24] Media richness involves the degree to which the communication mode is able "to transmit multiple communication cues, provide instant feedback, and offer a personal focus to communication."[25] In addition, communication modes diverge in terms of "social presence." As Christopher Sullivan summarizes, social presence refers to the perceptions and evaluations of the communication mode rather than the capabilities of it. "Social presence refers to characteristics of the channel that offer 'psychological closeness,' are 'people oriented,' or allow rich interpersonal involvement."[26]

In drawing from these concepts, it seems that e-mail is rather low in terms of the verbal and nonverbal cues it provides, and is rather high in terms of media richness. Its social presence is debatable. The degree to which citizens find e-mail to provide psychological closeness may depend on situational factors related to the digital divide. Certain demographic groups are still significantly less likely to use the Internet, including the elderly, the uneducated, the poor, and disadvantaged minority populations.[27] Even among Internet users, there is a significant digital divide based on broadband access and Internet activity that corresponds with age, education, and minority status.[28] Politicians themselves are influenced by their own exposure to the Internet as well as constituency considerations related to the digital divide.[29] The way in which digital divides alter political behavior holds ramifications for the character of service representation offered to constituents.

The second major type of responsiveness suggested by Eulau and Karps that is possibly impacted by changes in congressional mail is symbolic responsiveness. This type of responsiveness "involves public gestures of a sort that create a sense of trust and support in the relationship between the representative and the represented."[30] In fact, "symbolic satisfaction with the process of government is probably more important than specific, instrumental satisfaction with the policy output of the process."[31] Sending a constituent letter and receiving a member letter in response may lack policy substance but indicates on some level symbolic responsiveness. If e-mail replaces the traditional system of letter correspondence, this might have implications for symbolic responsiveness. Automated e-mail messages might not provide the same degree of symbolic satisfaction with government as an official letter on congressional letterhead. After reviewing the types of responsiveness involved in representation, it is useful to examine possible factors leading members to be more or less concerned with responsiveness.

Factors Leading to Responsiveness

A large body of congressional scholarship suggests that members are driven by reelection concerns. As David Mayhew suggests, members are "single-minded seekers of reelection."[32] Other goals may also figure into legislative behavior, such as policy and power concerns, but reelection is the proximate goal.[33] To achieve reelection, members engage in a number of D.C. and district-based activities. In this way reelection concerns directly impact responsiveness.

Each member of Congress develops a unique representational relationship with his or her district. This relational style includes the way in which members allocate their scarce resources, present themselves to their constituents, and explain their Washington activity. Members may alter their "home style" to facilitate greater responsiveness for a number of reasons. These reasons may include changes in the district, such as a change in the demographic composition of the constituency. They may also include personal factors, such as member age, ambition, or ideology.[34] Finally, strategic factors such as electoral circumstance might also influence members to adjust their "home style."[35]

Some of these changes follow the natural cycle of a member's career. During the early or *expansionist* stage of a legislative career, a member may emphasize activities to build a reliable reelection constituency. In the later or *protectionist* stage of a legislative career, a member is less likely to be concerned with self-promoting activities.[36] Regardless of career stage, however, members who are electorally vulnerable or "marginal" are likely to emphasize activities thought to convey constituent responsiveness and to increase efforts on constituency contact and casework.[37] Responsiveness to constituent mail is one means by which members can attempt to measure and address constituent concerns.

Responsiveness and Constituent Mail

In an indirect democracy it is the job of representatives to keep in touch with their constituents. It is important that they understand the concerns of those they represent. When congressmen are asked where they receive information about their constituents' attitudes, many times they answer, "From the mail."[38] Warren Butler emphasizes: "Most Members would subscribe to the re-election advice reportedly given by Speaker William B. Bankhead to an incoming freshman in 1939: 'It is a simple secret. Give close and prompt attention to your mail. Your votes and speeches may make you well known and give you a reputation, but it's the way you handle your mail that determines your re-election.'"[39] Constituents use mail for a multitude of reasons: "to complain about a service, to report problems, to pay a compliment, to seek information, or to make suggestions."[40] These inputs are very important to organizations, especially to representative organizations, because they can be a source of information as well as "provide early warning signs about problems, opportunities, and trends."[41] In this way mail serves to facilitate dialogue between members of Congress and their constituents.

Changes in the handling of congressional mail can be viewed as individual-level and aggregate-level phenomena. At the aggregate level, a shift to e-mail has happened across congressional offices. Nevertheless, members vary in the degree to which they emphasize e-mail correspondence. E-mail was first used by seven members in the House in the 103rd Congress (1993–1994) as part of a pilot program.[42] By 1996 nearly every House office and nearly two-thirds of Senate offices had e-mail.[43] Today, while e-mail has not replaced more traditional modes of communication, every member's office struggles to keep up with the expectations created by this vehicle for constituent contact.[44]

On the individual level, members differ in the amount of attention they pay to constituent mail. In fact, older members tend to be less concerned with constituent mail.[45] This behavior could be because older members have greater familiarity with the concerns of their constituents. Alternatively, older congressmen could neglect the mail because of busier congressional schedules and competing demands on their time and resources. Even further, older members could enjoy added electoral security, thus insulating them from individual constituent concerns. In contrast, young members driven by less certain electoral circumstance are the most readily concerned with responding to constituent inquiries.[46]

Another form of constituent connectedness is provided through member office Web sites. Considering Web sites as an extension of member "home style," E. Scott Adler, Chariti Gent, and Cary Overmeyer find partisanship, age, and district affluence to be related to investment in

Web site development. They further find that partisanship and electoral safety are related to utilization of home pages by members to solicit case-work.[47] A member who finds himself or herself in an uncertain electoral environment might be expected to "utilize all possible communication outlets, including high-technology forms of contact for shoring up his or her reelection prospects."[48]

In the end, responsiveness is important to the representation relation-ship. One mode of responsiveness involves member handling of constitu-ent mail. Several factors might affect member investment in constituent responsiveness. As Butler suggests: "A Member's seniority, legislative re-sponsibilities and committee assignments, the location, population and area of his state or district, the needs and demands of his constituents, his political vulnerability and ambitions, the quality of potential staff available to him and the staff's own view as to proper office procedure, contribute to this divergence of approach. . . . Allocations of time and work, as well as the delegation of responsibility to staff members, de-pends, in the final analysis, on the preferences and inclinations of the individual Senator and Representative."[49]

While individual-level factors shape member responsiveness and attention to constituent mail, aggregate-level factors can also shape this dynamic. The shift to e-mail in the late 1990s and the emphasis on e-mail correspondence following the anthrax attacks of 2001 has caused an aggregate shift in congressional office communications. Evidence at the time of this shift suggested that constituents did not find congressional responsiveness to this mode of contact adequate. According to Kathy Goldschmidt et al., "Growing numbers of citizens are frustrated by what they perceive to be Congress' lack of responsiveness to e-mail."[50] Part of the problem is caused by the impact of e-mail on public expectations. Be-cause e-mail is a media-rich mode of communication permitting quick response, those who use it expect timeliness in correspondence. Yet con-gressional offices are overwhelmed by the steady growth in e-mail from citizens both inside and outside of their districts and have lacked the resources to accommodate the increasing demands caused by e-mail. In sum, this dynamic "fails to meet the needs of citizens who expect greater responsiveness from their elected officials."[51]

The relationship between modes of contact and representation is also shaped by the perception of users of the imbedded value across modes of communication. In other words, how valuable a mode of communication is perceived to be impacts the quality of correspondence through that medium. Returning to the concept of "social presence," if congressional offices do not see e-mail as a mode of contact that is just as legitimate, substantive, and valuable as a letter mailed through the postal system, then this holds consequences for representation of the constituent interests expressed through e-mail. In 2001, a study of congressional office communications revealed that most offices did in fact underestimate the value of e-mail correspondence from constituents. According to this study, "The general assumption is that e-mail messages are just quick notes or uninformed thoughts. Offices figure that constituents will take the time to call or send a longer letter about issues that deeply concern them."[52] Given this perception, congressional offices often gave less attention to e-mail than letters and phone calls.

If citizens share this perception of the value of e-mail, believing it to be less meaningful than letters or phone calls, then they should expect different treatment for utilizing e-mail as their mode of communication with congressional offices. Unfortunately, this does not appear to be the case. Survey responses of constituents using e-mail as early as 1999 suggest that this mode of communication is preferred by some and is overwhelmingly intended to be treated equally with other more traditional forms of correspondence.[53]

From this discussion, it appears that changes in the mail have caused significant burdens on congressional offices that hold implications for the quality of representation members provide. E-mail has made constituent communication easy and has opened new avenues for outreach and timely dialogue on important issues facing Congress. At the same time, it has opened the floodgates of access to congressional offices by citizens and groups outside the boundaries of members' geographical districts. Advocacy groups blanket offices with e-mail "spam" and encourage their membership to do the same. Frustrated with the volume of e-mail in their in-boxes and the constraints imposed on their time, congressional staff must prioritize among modes of contact and among groups of constituents.

Overall, does this trend hold positive or negative implications for the representativeness of our democratic institutions? If the problem is simply one of office technological capability, then Congress can adapt. Members can and have utilized software programs that permit data collection on constituent e-mail contact, generate automated messages to acknowledge receipt of e-mail, and provide automated responses across issue domains to save office time and resources. If the problem involves negative perceptions of e-mail as a legitimate mode of contact within congressional offices, then, as the digital divide narrows and more and more citizens "go paperless," it is reasonable to expect these perceptions to change. If, however, the problem is one of e-mail abuse by special interests or others who seek the attention of congressional offices, then the situation is less remediable. Members operate on limited budgets, and e-mail is causing greater and greater demands on the attention of staff. This can lead to two possible scenarios. On the one hand, the quality of attention and time devoted to any one constituent concern proportionately can decrease. On the other hand, staff can respond only selectively to office inquiries via e-mail. The next section examines the possible factors influencing member preferences for specific modes of constituent contact in a post-anthrax environment and further explores the implications of these preferences for representation.

Examining the Evidence

To assess the modes of constituent contact preferred by members of Congress in light of the heightened security environment created by the anthrax attacks of 2001, I surveyed the Web sites of all members of the House in the fall of 2006. I coded the information available from each member's office Web page dedicated to contact information. Along with this information, I also recorded information concerning the member's party, gender, and seniority. A member's position on the House Homeland Security Committee was noted, as well as whether the member entered Congress before or after the events of 2001. Finally, information was also gathered on the electoral vulnerability of the member, as well as the distance between the member's district and Washington, D.C. A member receiving less than 55 percent of the vote in the last electoral cycle was treated as electorally "vulnerable."

In the fall of 2006, members of the House suggested different preferred modes of constituent contact on their personal office home pages (see figure 3.2). While the majority of members provided both postal addresses and means for e-mail contact (57 percent), a quarter of member offices emphasized e-mail as the preferred mode of contact, and 9 percent specifically suggested anthrax as the reason for this preference.

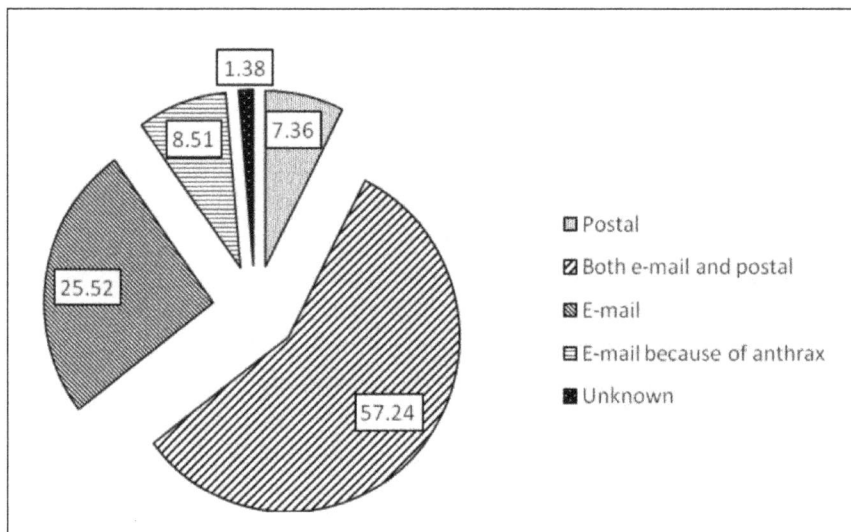

1.38
7.36
8.51
25.52
57.24

☐ Postal
▨ Both e-mail and postal
▧ E-mail
▤ E-mail because of anthrax
▦ Unknown

Figure 3.2: Preferred Mode of Contact for Members of Congress

Less than 10 percent emphasized postal addresses on their homepage as the preferred mode of contact.

For the sake of readability, only a summary of the statistical analysis follows.[54] The results of this analysis reveal that a few factors are significantly related to member preferences concerning constituent contact. Electoral vulnerability is significantly associated with preferred mode of contact. Members in tough seats are more likely to emphasize e-mail as part of their office contact information than are electorally safe members. This is because electorally vulnerable members are extremely concerned about appearing to be responsive to constituent concerns and requests. For these members, e-mail may provide a more immediate mode of communication than "snail mail." There is also a meaningful connection among how electorally vulnerable a member is, when he or she entered Congress, and what mode of contact he or she prefers. Electoral vulnerability and year of congressional entry combine to influence the member's preferred mode of contact. Electorally vulnerable members elected before 2000 are four times more likely to emphasize e-mail as a preferred mode of contact and to mention that this preference is due to the security concerns introduced by the anthrax attacks of 2001 than are their other colleagues.[55] Members elected since 2000 and the anthrax attacks of 2001 are less likely to restrict contact preference to e-mail. Once again, however, electoral safety is a key factor. Electorally vulnerable members elected since 2000 are about 20 percent more likely to emphasize e-mail than are their electorally safe colleagues.[56]

Table 3.2 illustrates the relationship between electoral vulnerability and a member's preferred mode of constituent contact. Perhaps the most significant observation is that electorally vulnerable members do not prefer to receive "snail mail." While 8 percent of electorally safe members provide their postal address as the primary means of contacting the office, 0 percent of electorally vulnerable members provide the same. In addition, a greater proportion of electorally vulnerable members (13.5 percent) mention anthrax as the justification for e-mail correspondence than do safe members (8.2 percent). It is reasonable to surmise that members who are less certain of their electoral fate feel they need to be in closer contact with their constituents than the new mail system can facilitate.

Table 3.2: Cross-Tabulating Preferred Mode of Contact and Electoral Safety

Safe Members	Valid Percent (N)
Postal	8.2 (32)[a]
Both Postal and E-mail	57.9 (227)
E-mail	25.8 (101)
E-mail because of Anthrax	8.2 (32)
Vulnerable Members	
Postal	0.0 (0)
Both Postal and E-mail	59.5 (22)
E-mail	27.0 (10)
E-mail because of Anthrax	13.5 (5)

[a] In this particular case, p values are inappropriate indicators of the significance of these associations. The data are drawn from a population eliminating the concern for generalizability. When cross-tabulating the variable measuring the preferred mode of contact for members of Congress with others, cell values are at times too low to permit the calculation of a chi-square statistic. In addition, the preferred mode of contact variable is not dichotomous, precluding the calculation of a Fischer's exact test of significance. The appropriate statistic in this case is a measure of effect size. Consequently, the values of Cohen's d and effect size r are reported here. The effect size is small between the variables in this table (Cohen's $d = -.2731$, effect size $r = -.1353$).

Statistical analysis further illuminates an interesting interaction between preferred mode of contact and year of congressional entry. Cross-tabulating these two member characteristics suggests that members elected before 2000 have somewhat different preferences than those elected since 2000 (see table 3.3). Members who remember office operations under the old mail system are more likely to prefer e-mail (27 percent compared to 23 percent) and are more likely to mention anthrax as a reason for this preference (10 percent compared to 5 percent). Members initiated into the new mail system during their first term and those elected since its establishment are more likely to include both sets of contact information, postal and e-mail addresses (65 percent compared to 55 percent). They are also less likely to mention anthrax when describing their preferred mode of contact. Newer members may not feel the need to mention anthrax because they were not habituated into congressional life under the old mail system. It is also possible that without experiencing the psychological impact of the event firsthand, these members do not feel the visceral need to mention it.

Table 3.3: Cross-Tabulating Preferred Mode of Contact and Entry

Members elected prior to 2000	Valid Percent (N)
Postal	7.7 (23)[a]
Both Postal and E-mail	55.2 (165)
E-mail	27.1 (81)
E-mail because of Anthrax	10.0 (30)
Members elected in or after 2000	
Postal	6.9 (9)
Both Postal and E-mail	64.6 (84)
E-mail	23.1 (30)
E-mail because of Anthrax	5.4 (7)

[a] In this particular case, p values are inappropriate indicators of the significance of these associations. The data are drawn from a population eliminating the concern for generalizability. When cross-tabulating the variable measuring the preferred mode of contact for members of Congress with others, cell values are at times too low to permit the calculation of a chi-square statistic. In addition, the preferred mode of contact variable is not dichotomous, precluding the calculation of a Fischer's exact test of significance. The appropriate statistic in this case is a measure of effect size. Consequently, the values of Cohen's d and effect size r are reported here. There is a large effect size in the association between the preferred mode of contact of members elected before 2000 and members elected in or after 2000 (Cohen's $d = .9703$, effect size $r = .4365$).

When considering both electoral vulnerability and congressional entry, there are subtle differences in the behavior of members due to both electoral security and institutional memory (see table 3.4 and figure 3.3).

Approximately 8 percent of members who are electorally safe regardless of the timing of their first term in office are likely to prefer postal correspondence with constituents. Contrastingly, no members who are electorally vulnerable regardless of the timing of their first term in office are likely to prefer postal correspondence with constituents. The greatest proportion of safe members provides both postal and e-mail information but indicates no preference between the two modes of contact. In fact, more safe members elected in or after 2000 provide both types of contact information (62 percent) than do those safe members elected before 2000 (56 percent).

The largest group to indicate no preference, however, is electorally vulnerable members elected in or after 2000 (75 percent). It appears that these members respond to their vulnerability by encouraging all forms of contact from constituents. By contrast, electorally vulnerable members elected before 2000 are not nearly as likely to readily offer both postal and e-mail addresses to constituents (31 percent). Instead, the greatest proportion of this group prefers e-mail as the primary mode of constituent contact (39 percent). They are also the most likely to mention anthrax as the justification for preferring this type of communication (31 percent).

Is Writing a Letter to Your Member of Congress a Thing of the Past?

The vast majority of those I interviewed about the impact of the terrorist attacks of 2001 on Hill culture suggested that the mail marked the largest change in congressional operations. Their comments centered both on the impact to the postal system and the rise of e-mail correspondence. While these changes largely appear to have become institutionalized, they nonetheless have implications for the quality of constituent contact and member correspondence, and thus the representation possible in a post-anthrax environment.

As a legislative director for a Republican senator suggested, members and staff "really don't remember what it was like before." While immediately after the anthrax attacks, some constituents expressed frustration with the inefficiency of the postal system, this staffer suggested that "people are getting used to it." Since 2001, the process of screening mail sent through the postal system has improved somewhat. On occasion

Table 3.4: Cross-Tabulating Preferred Mode of Contact Considering Both Electoral Safety and Entry

Elected Prior to 2000	Valid Percent (N)
Safe Members	
Postal	8.0 (23) [a]
Both Postal and E-mail	56.3 (161)
E-mail	26.6 (76)
E-mail because of Anthrax	9.1 (26)
Vulnerable Members	
Postal	0.0 (0)
Both Postal and E-mail	30.8 (4)
E-mail	38.5 (5)
E-mail because of Anthrax	30.8 (4)
Elected in or after 2000	
Safe Members	
Postal	8.5 (9)
Both Postal and E-mail	62.3 (66)
E-mail	23.6 (25)
E-mail because of Anthrax	5.7 (6)
Vulnerable Members	
Postal	0.0 (0)
Both Postal and E-mail	75.0 (18)
E-mail	20.8 (5)
E-mail because of Anthrax	4.2 (1)

[a] In this particular case, p values are inappropriate indicators of the significance of these associations. The data are drawn from a population eliminating the concern for generalizability. When cross-tabulating the variable measuring the preferred mode of contact for members of Congress with others, cell values are at times too low to permit the calculation of a chi-square statistic. In addition, the preferred mode of contact variable is not dichotomous, precluding the calculation of a Fischer's exact test of significance. The appropriate statistic in this case is a measure of effect size. Consequently, the values of Cohen's d and effect size r are reported here. Two associations have a large effect size in this table. There is a large effect size between the preferred mode of contact of electorally safe and electorally vulnerable members of Congress elected before 2000 (Cohen's $d = -.8026$, effect size $r = -.3724$). In addition, there is a large effect size between the preferred mode of contact of electorally vulnerable members elected before 2000 and electorally vulnerable members elected after 2000 (Cohen's $d = 1.0175$, effect size $r = .4534$).

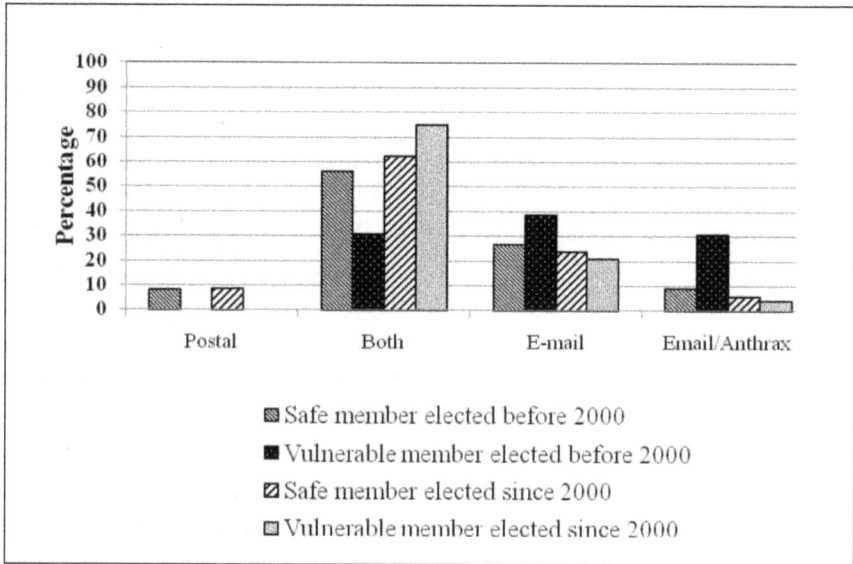

Figure 3.3: Members' Preferred Mode of Contact Considering Electoral Safety and Year of Entry

mail will take up to two months to reach a member's office, but more often than not mail reaches congressional offices within three weeks. Nonetheless, the majority of constituent contact now comes to member offices via e-mail, and members largely suggest that they prefer to be contacted through this medium.

Changes in the mail hold important implications for the quality of communication possible between members and their constituents. As a member in the Democratic leadership summarized: "The anthrax scare in many ways was more destructive to the legislative process than 9/11 because so much of what we do up here values the contact with and response to constituents. Anthrax redefined that. It's difficult to maintain the kind of relationships we had in the past. We have a hard time getting constituents to understand that it is better to contact us at our home offices. They think if we serve them in D.C. they should contact us in Washington." While the popularization of e-mail most likely has been associated with an appreciable decline in constituent letter writing, members and their staff point to heightened security measures as being primarily responsible for the decline in postal correspondence. Reflecting on the changes brought about by 9/11 and anthrax, a Republican member of Congress commented, "There's been a noticeable decline of handwritten letters; more individuals e-mail."

Part of this change in constituent correspondence might be due to the preferences of members themselves. The same Republican member suggested that after anthrax the office "really pushed for e-mail; [they] sent letters out telling people not to send letters but to write e-mails." Another senior legislative assistant noted that because "the mail has been slowed down and everything is pre-opened, lost occasionally, and damaged, constituents are encouraged to use fax, e-mail, and Web sites to communicate." Part of this change in constituent correspondence is most likely due to the preferences of constituents as well. With the popularization of e-mail over the past several years, constituents find this mode of communication to be fast, easy, and inexpensive.

There are dangers associated with limiting modes of constituent contact. The legislative director for a Republican senator stated: "We don't discourage mail. Older constituents like sending mail; they can't use e-mail. Lots just call to chat." Restricting slower modes of contact could discriminate against the elderly, who lack technological proficiency, or the poor, who lack technological resources. Second, while e-mail is much more efficient than "snail mail," it is also subject to abuse. As one Democratic member commented, "e-mail is so easy that groups do it." Offices can be blasted with mass e-mails. Interest groups, for example, blanket member offices with impersonal e-mails to gain attention for their cause. Further, this mode of communication prohibits certain types of correspondence. Offices must "make alternative arrangements for mail that can't go through the irradiation process, such as videotapes and electronic devices," according to a chief of staff for a Republican senator. Finally, this medium carries the potential of changing the character of member response. While some staff suggested that "just because we receive letters via e-mail doesn't mean we respond via e-mail," it is reasonable to expect that, as the sheer volume of e-mail increases, so will the strain on member staff and resources.

Conclusion

In sum, mail is an integral part of the communication process between members of Congress and their constituents. Considering Hanna Pitkin's definition of representation as being responsive, constituent communication is key to a healthy democratic system.[57] Over the last few years, the protocol for receiving mail has changed dramatically. While in years past, it was something special to write a letter to your member of Congress, the findings of this chapter indicate that most House members do not currently emphasize this mode of contact. In fact, more than 50 percent of members indicate no preference between postal or e-mail constituent contact. What has changed over the years, however, is the proportion of members preferring postal correspondence. At just under 8 percent, those members who prefer postal mail are a disappearing breed.

If advancements in technology started this institutional shift toward electronic mail, then the anthrax scares in late 2001 secured these changes. Some members and staff claim that this transition hinders the personal nature of constituent communication and thus hurts the quality of democratic politics. Others, however, believe that this change has narrowed response time, which they claim has enhanced the quality of legislative responsiveness.

Overall there is diversity across members concerning their preferred mode of constituent contact. Electorally vulnerable members clearly are most likely to prefer any mode of contact necessary to ensure communication with their constituents. Older members in tough seats, however, are more likely to prefer e-mail and to mention the anthrax experience as a justification for this preference. Perhaps this is because these members actually had to change their correspondence policies to address the threat posed by biohazardous materials such as anthrax. The fact that older, electorally vulnerable members are the most likely group to mention anthrax tells us that they may feel the need to justify restrictions in their policies.

While this chapter examines the impact of 9/11 and anthrax on the culture of the Hill from one very specific vantage point, it illuminates a unique change in legislative behavior. The mail system dramatically changed to accommodate necessary security. This change resulted in a subsequent change in office policy concerning the preferred mode of constituent contact. To date, these changes have not been uniform, but they do correlate significantly with member electoral vulnerability and entry into the institution. It is possible that in the near future postal mail will be replaced almost entirely by electronic mail. Future research should explore the ramifications of such a change for the quality of correspondence between members and their constituents. The next chapter turns to changes introduced to the committee system by the events of 2001.

4

TERROR WARS AND TURF WARS

The Homeland Security Committees

> Later on today, we will vote to create a Select Committee on Home-
> land Security. Members of this select committee will oversee the
> creation of the Department of Homeland Security to make certain
> that the executive branch is carrying out the will of the Congress.
> This select committee will be our eyes and our ears as this critical
> department is organized. The standing committees of the House will
> maintain their jurisdictions and will still have authorization and
> oversight responsibilities. The House needs to adapt to the largest
> reorganization of our executive branch in 50 years, and this select
> committee will help us make this transition.
> —Speaker Dennis Hastert (R-IL)

In the aftermath of the terrorist attacks of 2001, the executive and legislative branches took several drastic steps to alter the structure of the federal
government to provide improved administration and oversight of homeland security. In the executive branch, these steps included the creation
of a Department of Homeland Security, adding a fifteenth department
to the federal bureaucracy of President George W. Bush's administration. The creation of this department led to significant reorganization
of the jurisdictions of the existing bureaucratic agencies. A member of
the House Republican leadership summarized the institutional changes,
stating:

> There is a historical expansion of federal government structure after cri-
> sis. The FBI changed forever. Before it only reacted to a criminal event.
> Now it is an agency that is primarily charged with preventing domestic
> acts of terrorism. There has also been institutional change in terms of the

relationship between intelligence agencies like the FBI and CIA brought about by the Patriot Act. . . . There is a Director of National Intelligence over the intelligence community. The creation of the Department of Homeland Security is permanent and positive. The House Committee on Homeland Security is permanent because a department needs oversight. There was a permanent effect of what we did after 9/11.

This legislative reorganization constitutes an important piece of the institutional change brought about by the terrorist attacks of 2001 because of its relative uniqueness in the history of congressional committees. While numerous committees have been added to the institutional roster to process legislation more efficiently over our nation's history, the trend of the last fifty years has been a reduction in the number of committees and a streamlining of committee jurisdiction.

Committee Reform

The modern committee system dates to the late 1940s, when the Congress passed the Legislative Reorganization Act of 1946. This act led to many changes, including the reduction in committees on the House side from forty-eight to nineteen and on the Senate side from thirty-three to fifteen. In addition, committee jurisdiction was clarified through chamber rules. Since this time, remarkably few adjustments have been made to the committee system. The Legislative Reorganization Act of 1970 focused on a more open committee process, increases in committee staff, and transformation of the Legislative Reference Service into the Congressional Research Service. Later in that same decade, Congress created committees in both the House and the Senate to review the president's budget proposal and draft a federal budget. Also, a temporary Joint Committee on the Organization of Congress was established in 1993 to review the committee system. This committee made several recommendations, some of which were adopted by the newly elected Republican Congress in 1995. Under the leadership of Speaker Newt Gingrich, the new Republican majority further eliminated three House standing committees in 1995: the Committee on the District of Columbia, the Committee on the Post Office and Civil Service, and the Committee on Merchant Marine and Fisheries.

All of these reforms were introduced in light of a perceived institutional threat, a new partisan majority, or internal partisan cleavages. The

Legislative Reorganization Act of 1946, for example, was in response to a perceived institutional threat. In light of the growing dominance of the executive branch due to congressional deference provided to President Franklin D. Roosevelt during the Great Depression and World War II, Congress sought to reclaim institutional power and prestige through reforms that would encourage efficiency and effectiveness throughout the legislative process. Walter Kravitz highlights the uniqueness and magnitude of these changes: "Never before had Congress, in a single stroke, made such broad changes in its organization, administration, procedures (both committee and floor), resources, and workload, in relations between its houses, and in its relations with the executive branch. Never before had Congress so radically restructured the committee systems in both houses, and never before had the House of Representatives and Senate done so cooperatively and simultaneously."[1]

The Legislative Reorganization Act of 1970, by contrast, grew out of internal discontent within congressional membership. The large classes of freshmen members elected in the late 1960s (seventy-one Democrats in 1964 and fifty-nine Republicans in 1966) voiced protest over the authoritarian leadership styles of senior southern Democrats serving as committee chairs and the lack of recourse provided to rank and file membership or members of the minority party. The ensuing reforms dealt less with committee structure than process but did lead to adjustments in staff allocations.

The committee reforms introduced by the new Republican majority in 1995 were intended to centralize power in the party leadership. Committee chairs were limited to three terms (or six years). The seniority system often was ignored. Instead, committee assignment and leadership decisions were based on party loyalty. In addition, special task forces were utilized to bypass the committee system altogether. As part of this reform package, the Republican leadership cut the number of full committees, subcommittees, and committee staff and eliminated the use of joint referrals.

From these examples, it is clear that committee reforms can be introduced by a number of environmental changes. Over the last half century, however, almost all of the trigger events leading to committee reform have been instigated by political circumstances within government. Perhaps there is one notable exception to this general pattern. A reform to the committee structure closely resembling the recent addition of Homeland Security would be the creation of the House Un-American Activities Committee (HUAC). This committee originated as a special committee in 1938 and actually survived in some form until its elimination in 1975. For thirty years, this committee enjoyed permanent status investigating suspicious activities of groups on U.S. soil, including those of the Nazis, the KKK, and various communist sympathizers. It is interesting to note that the House changed the name of the committee in 1969 to the House Committee on Internal Security. In more ways than one it appears that HUAC bears a unique resemblance to the House Homeland Security Committee.

From this discussion, it seems that the House committee system does adapt to its environment. Nevertheless, major reform is infrequent and major restructuring of standing committees even more rare. The recent reforms to the committee system to include a new standing committee in the House on homeland security and a newly restructured committee in the Senate to include homeland security mark a critical moment in congressional history. The following few pages trace the history of these reforms and evaluate factors affecting the legislative productivity and oversight of these committees. The chapter ends with an assessment of the potential future of the committees in the upcoming years.

History of Homeland Security Committees

Prior to the creation of a standing committee on homeland security, the House established a select committee and directed it to provide recommendations to the Congress concerning committee organization and oversight of homeland security. A standing committee is a permanent committee (it "stands" from one Congress to the next) that typically considers bills through hearings and markups, recommends funding levels for government operations and programs, refers legislation to the floor, and performs oversight. Examples of standing committees in the U.S. Congress include: the House Committee on Education and Labor, the House Committee on Armed Services, and the Senate Committee on the Judiciary. By contrast, a select committee is a temporary committee. Sometimes it is referred to as a "special" committee or "ad hoc" committee. A select committee's responsibilities typically are investigative rather than legislative in nature. While a select committee can be renewed, it generally dissolves after completing its tasks. Other examples of select committees include the House Select Committee on Assassinations (94th–96th Congresses) and the House Select Committee on Energy Independence and Global Warming (110th–111th Congresses).

While the issue of appropriating funds to the Department of Homeland Security (DHS) fell squarely on the shoulders of the Appropriations Committee, the issue of legislative authority over homeland security was less clear. One list of the committees holding principal jurisdiction over policies directly affecting DHS at the time of the select committee's review included: "Agriculture, Armed Services, Energy and Commerce, Financial Services, Government Reform, International Relations, Judiciary, Science, Transportation and Infrastructure, and Ways and Means, and the Permanent Select Committee on Intelligence."[2] Many of these committees not only held jurisdiction over policies involving DHS but also played key roles in homeland security issues outside the purview of the department.[3]

The 9/11 Commission provided specific recommendations to the Congress concerning improvement of homeland security. Among the commission's recommendations was a charge for both the House and the Senate to create an independent homeland security committee. In response to the recommendations, the House created a separate full committee to focus on homeland security. While it was initially formed as a select committee in 2002, once the Department of Homeland Security was created, the committee was given permanent status as a standing committee at the beginning of 2005.[4] As suggested on the committee Web site, the House created this committee in the aftermath of September 11, 2001. It is made up of six subcommittees: Subcommittee on Border, Maritime, and Global Counterterrorism; Subcommittee on Intelligence, Information Sharing, and Terrorism Risk Assessment; Subcommittee on Transportation Security and Infrastructure Protection; Subcommittee on Emerging Threats, Cybersecurity, and Science and Technology; Subcommittee on Emergency Communications, Preparedness, and Response; and the Subcommittee on Management, Investigations, and Oversight.

For some on Capitol Hill, the creation of the committee was a relatively minor adjustment to the existing system of authorization and appropriation. One senior staffer of a Democratic member of Congress stated: "There is a new committee—Homeland Security and Governmental Affairs, but there hasn't been a fundamental restructure. The committee structure proved pretty durable. The appropriations subcommittee changes are pretty remarkable. I would have thought that would have been the hardest to change."

In the Senate, the issue of homeland security and the creation of a new department impacted the committee structure, although not as drastically as on the House side. Whereas the House created an altogether new standing committee, the Senate restructured a pre-existing committee, the Senate Committee on Governmental Affairs. Reflecting on chamber differences, a senior committee staff member on the House side stated: "The Senate loves traditions and customs. It's not always as flexible as the House."

The Senate voted in the fall of 2004, during the second session of the 108th Congress, to broaden the jurisdiction of the Governmental Affairs Committee to include homeland security.[5] The restructured committee took on the name of the Senate Committee on Homeland Security and Governmental Affairs at the beginning of the 109th Congress in 2005. The House mirrored this organizational change by giving its Homeland Security Committee permanent status as a standing committee at the beginning of the 109th Congress as well.

Two ad hoc committees of the Senate Homeland Security and Governmental Affairs Committee handle the bulk of the issues surrounding the Homeland Security Department. The Ad Hoc Subcommittee on State, Local, and Private Sector Preparedness and Integration has jurisdiction over certain Homeland Security Department functions related to state and local emergency preparedness. The Ad Hoc Subcommittee on Disaster Recovery has jurisdiction over information sharing and agency coordination for disaster recovery. When the Democrats took control over Congress, Senator Mary Landrieu was named chair of this subcommittee. Her home state of Louisiana had suffered one of the largest disasters in U.S. history in the aftermath of Hurricane Katrina, making this issue one of Landrieu's top priorities.

Jurisdictional Battles

Perhaps the greatest impediment to both the legislative productivity and effective oversight of the House Homeland Security Committee and the Senate Homeland Security and Governmental Affairs Committee has been the constant and continuing jurisdictional warfare among rival committees over policy concerns related to homeland security. Part of this conflict stems from a deeper definitional battle over the meaning of "homeland security." In summarizing the recommendations and witness testimony received by the House Select Committee on Homeland Security, Michael Koempel suggests, "*homeland security* is a continuum of international and domestic initiatives and activities, all of which are essential to reducing the likelihood and potential impact of terrorist attacks against the United States."[6] While this definition broadens rather than narrows the focus of homeland security, it also suggests the interconnectedness of the issue with other policy areas. Koempel further asserts: "For transportation policy, agricultural policy, public health policy, trade policy, and so on, homeland security is one component of the policy area. Even if homeland security is now recognized as a critical component, some policymakers see the need for homeland security policy to mesh with the specific policy area and to be made within the context of the specific policy area."[7] Airline security, for example, should be considered within the broader context of mass transportation. A senior Democratic staffer summarized: "It is a substantial new responsibility, but it is lumped on top of everything else. Other committees that think they have jurisdiction are not going to give up easily. Those committees want to play a role."

The U.S. House of Representatives

Several of those I interviewed on the House side noted the role of jurisdictional disputes in delaying committee productivity and effective oversight of the Department of Homeland Security (DHS). A chief of staff for one member serving on the committee, when asked to evaluate the effectiveness of homeland security in the post-9/11 environment, suggested: "[My member] toured the Homeland Security Department because he wanted to see where these people worked. There wasn't any vision. It was created as a knee-jerk reaction. It is the largest civilian department. It is incredibly diverse, and dealing with it is a living hell. They're afraid of making decisions. Part of it is Congress's fault. To pick up votes, they [party leadership] gave to rural, small-town districts. . . . Homeland Security still hasn't passed a bill [as of 2006]. The committee is still fighting for jurisdiction. Appropriations won't give it up. Judiciary won't either. The infighting and backbiting is typical." Why has there been such a problem with establishing the jurisdiction of the Homeland

Security Committee? The same staff person explained that "you can't create a new committee without changing all the committees. It affects both authorization and appropriations for justice, commerce, armed services, interior, government oversight. . . ."

With the fight over jurisdiction continuing years after the creation of the House Homeland Security Committee, it is reasonable to ask if all the effort is well spent. The committee has been designated as a permanent or standing committee of the House. Once jurisdiction is ironed out, is it likely that this committee will be a critical feature of the committee structure of future congresses? The general consensus among those with whom I spoke was that this committee is in fact here to stay. One senior House staffer noted, "Homeland Security Committee has to be long-term. We can't have a country at war and bombings around the world and not put an emphasis on it." Just as each department was created in response to the political environment, Homeland Security has been created "because there was a national need for recognition of the importance of these matters."

Many argue that the creation of the Homeland Security Department *required* the creation of a Homeland Security Committee. Those serving on the initial House Select Committee on Homeland Security pointed to the ongoing congressional oversight required by the institutional reorganization of the executive branch. One member of this initial committee noted: "The committee may have been titled 'Select,' but it was always the goal for it to be a free-standing authorizing committee." For certain members, the most significant and enduring change to the Congress introduced by the events of 2001 was the change to the committee structure. One member of the House Republican leadership who simultaneously served in a prominent role in the development of the House Homeland Security Committee reflected on changes introduced after 9/11 and anthrax:

> First we have a new committee. . . . We were tasked with making recommendations to Congress with regard to permanence of the committee. We did make a recommendation that it be permanent. The main reason was as an oversight mechanism for the department. The goal is to start the process of concentration of oversight of the department and testimony of officials as well as concentration of focus of time. It's very hard to create significant primary jurisdiction. There is nothing tougher than when you are dealing with turf wars. We ended up creating shared jurisdictions.

The goal is that there will be incremental increase or assumption of jurisdiction. But it's better to create an imperfect structure than none at all. It's
been a frustrating two years.

An overarching consensus among those interviewed is that the future
of the House committee is still uncertain. The jurisdictional reorganization has been extremely contentious, and the fate of Homeland Security's
jurisdiction largely depends on the effectiveness of other committee
chairs in fighting to retain their turf. A Democratic member reflecting on
the extent of the structural changes to the committee system suggested:
"It's hard to know [how the structure has changed]. The Homeland Security Committee is now a standing committee, but it has less than complete jurisdiction. There are still jurisdiction fights going on among the
committees. So the outcome is yet to be known. It's impossible to predict
how long it will take. The jurisdiction battles between chairs are intense.
It has to do with the powers of people. Take for example the Commerce
Committee. [John Dingell (D-MI)] was a usurper of jurisdiction successfully. They have astonishing jurisdiction in terms of homeland security.
Science, for example, doesn't have complete jurisdiction over space." In
these comments, it is clear that the personality of the committee chair is
central to committee integration and effectiveness.[8]

The U.S. Senate

The decision to create a venue for homeland security in the committee
structure was met with controversy in the Senate as well. The major jurisdictional battles over the restructuring of the Senate Committee on
Governmental Affairs took place among members of the existing committee as well as among members of the Judiciary, Commerce, Budget,
Science, and Transportation committees. In the end, the vote by the full
Senate on S Res. 445, the bill to restructure the Senate Governmental Affairs Committee, was 79–6. While the size of the vote majority suggests
widespread bipartisan consensus on the restructuring, the six senators
voting against the resolution included Governmental Affairs Chair-
woman Susan Collins (R-ME) and ranking member Joseph Lieberman
(D-CT).[9] Battles over restructuring the committee eroded much of the
homeland security jurisdiction intended for the newly restructured Senate Homeland Security and Governmental Affairs Committee. According to one depiction of the jurisdictional fight:

Things only got worse for Collins and Lieberman on the floor, where rival committees seemed to gang up on Governmental Affairs to reclaim jurisdiction. For starters, the Senate ordered jurisdiction over the Secret Service and immigration policy to be returned to the Judiciary Committee, while Commerce easily repelled a bid by Collins, Lieberman, and John McCain, R-Ariz., to claim jurisdiction over TSA [the Transportation Security Administration]. Then, on Oct. 9, the Budget Committee piled on, winning a 50–35 vote to claim sole jurisdiction over the congressional budget process. Currently, the Governmental Affairs and Budget committees share jurisdiction, and it was no small irony that the Governmental Affairs panel wrote the 1974 law that established the modern congressional budget process and created the Budget Committee in the first place.[10]

When the dust settled from the amendment activity to S Res. 445 on the Senate floor, the committee's leadership felt that they lacked the necessary authority to provide effective oversight of governmental agencies and programs related to homeland security.

Hurricane Katrina perhaps posed the first real test of the ability of the House Homeland Security Committee and the Senate Homeland Security and Governmental Affairs Committee to provide meaningful oversight of the Department of Homeland Security. While both committees have produced little legislative activity due to jurisdictional battles, this event provided an opportunity for immediate action on an issue with widespread public concern. In the House, however, consensus was nowhere to be found. According to Patrick Yoest, "the chairman of Homeland Security, Peter T. King of New York, sparred for months with fellow Republican Don Young of Alaska, chairman of the Transportation and Infrastructure Committee, over a proposed overhaul of FEMA."[11]

With new Democratic leadership, it is uncertain what the future holds in the area of homeland security. Speaker Nancy Pelosi (D-CA) promised major changes in homeland security at the beginning of the 110th Congress, claiming that House Democrats will "make America safer by the first day" of the new Congress. Her focus on better implementation of the 9/11 Commission's recommendations involves possibly revisiting committee jurisdictions over homeland security and intelligence.[12] While it is certain that Democrats will push for greater oversight, it is by no means clear that they can better overcome the turf wars that have plagued these committees since their creation.

Productivity

In terms of productivity, the committees have been a disappointment to the rank and file membership in the House. Beyond the limitations to legislative productivity created by competing jurisdictional claims, a second issue affecting productivity involves committee prestige. One chief of staff of a member on the House Homeland Security Committee suggested, "What can you do? Prestige is inexorably linked to what the committee can achieve. The jury is still out. They [the House Homeland Security Committee] haven't passed a damn bill!"

When pushed to reflect on the reasons for Homeland Security not counting as a prestigious assignment, he continued, "House leadership is not interested in having this be a powerful committee." To counteract the negative implications of lack of prestige, "the committee needs a strong chair and bipartisan cooperation." But without clear jurisdiction, any chair is strapped in terms of what can practically be accomplished. Those in power to clarify jurisdiction have neglected to take an aggressive, proactive role in this battle. The same staff person suggested, "The leadership is not interested in taking jurisdiction away or a political hassle. The committee has been just for show thus far. We still have to see what they can achieve."

This comment highlights the role of the parties and presidential support in structuring the committee system and its role in the oversight function of Congress. This role is particularly significant in times of unified government, when one party controls both the White House and Congress. Summarizing the centrality of partisanship to legislative productivity and effectiveness, the House chief of staff stated, "The party is the milieu in which everything occurs. It is so much a part of everything. It's hard to separate out honest differences and partisanship. And these [members of Congress] are national class at appearances."

Once the committees' jurisdictions are solidified, the fate of the committees' productivity rests on other factors, such as the leadership style of the committee chairs. The same staff person concluded: "It depends on who's involved. Personalities are different. Committee chairs have other responsibilities as well. Some are more forceful or brighter. They honestly differ over goals and conclusions." Another legislative assistant responsible for homeland security issues for a Democratic member noted: "What committees do is contingent on the strengths of the chair. If there is a chair that looks at a bill and doesn't like it, no matter how many members like it, the chair can just sit on it. When it's a select committee, it's too large, and it has too many chairs and ranking members from other committees who want to keep an eye on their territory. That was quite the battle. It's now a little smaller, which has helped." From this assessment, the early problems in the House with committee effectiveness stemmed partly from the temporary nature of the select committee, partly from the sheer size and composition of the group, as well as partly from the distinct personalities composing the initial panel.

The activity of congressional committees is further related to their legislative authority. The House Homeland Security Committee and the Senate Homeland Security and Governmental Affairs Committee are authorization rather than appropriation committees, which holds implications for their legislative productivity. As one member of the House Republican leadership suggested: "The jury's still out whether the committee will be able to produce a reauthorization bill for the department that could actually become law. But most of authorizing committees don't produce actual law. Most appropriations bills become law; that's where a lot of legislating occurs because it has to fund government. Bills that do pass every year are appropriations bills."

Finally, beyond leadership and legislative authority, the direction of the committees will be somewhat dictated by the institutional agenda. Within the issue domain of homeland security, there exist several possible policy directions. From transportation security to emergency management and preparedness to border security, the broad purview of the two committees leaves those responsible for them open to criticism from a number of fronts. The charge of one Republican member provides insight on this point: "Chris Cox [R-CA] and Homeland Security [Committee] have done a good job getting set up and organized. The next chair needs to push forward a real plan to secure the Southern border and secure ports. We've done a good job so far securing the airline industry and continuing to. . . . But hell, man. We gotta get on the border! We gotta get defense!"

Beyond these factors, some of the disappointment with the House committee's productivity may stem from unique characteristics of the chamber. As a chief of staff for a senior Republican member suggested: "Members of Homeland Security on the Senate side bleed over to other committees that have other jurisdictions. They have a greater interest than this [one issue]. On the House side, members of Homeland Security have a narrower interest than this. It gives them a greater ability to dig in on any of those issues. A couple of members become experts. They can reach a critical mass talking to a handful of others. The large numbers make it easier to be more fluid and active in some ways." The comments of this staffer reflect the thesis of Richard Hall in his book *Participation in Congress.*[13] Members do not participate equally. On any given issue, only a select few participate in meaningful ways. Due to the extreme division of labor in the House chamber, this principle holds important implications for the productivity of the committee. Depending on the organizational climate and cohesion of the committee, as Richard Fenno suggests, the committee can be expected to be more or less successful in its legislative efforts.[14] In this case, the personalities recruited from other standing committees to serve on Homeland Security in the House have longstanding careers of service and expertise on related issues and deep institutional loyalties to committees with previous jurisdiction over security issues. These commitments have frustrated committee cohesion on the House side and served to severely limit productivity at least during the early years of committee organization.

Legislative Activity

One of the only early major legislative initiatives of the House Homeland Security Committee was its authorization bill for DHS (HR 1817) for fiscal year 2006. Mirroring President Bush's budget request for DHS, the bill called for $34.2 billion to target hiring Border Patrol agents, refining the color-coded terror alert system, and addressing problems with intelligence.[15] Chairman Christopher Cox (R-CA) argued for the authorization bill for DHS—which represented the fifth-highest discretionary budget in the federal government. During consideration of the bill, Cox's main concern was establishing the legitimacy of the standing committee. To avoid jurisdictional conflict, Cox fought to limit amending activity in committee, thus keeping controversial legislative language to a minimum and increasing the likelihood of support for the bill by other committee chairs once the bill reached the floor.

In 2006, the House Homeland Security Committee and House Appropriations Subcommittee on Homeland Security put forward a similar authorization bill. On the floor, the bill (HR 5441) was met with dozens of amendments. The authorization proposed a 6 percent increase from the FY2006 levels.[16]

The Senate Homeland Security and Governmental Affairs Committee did not draft a Homeland Security authorization bill during the 109th or 110th Congress. With a Democratic Congress and the leadership of Chairman Joseph Lieberman (D-CT), it remains to be seen whether the committee will take up this task in the future. According to a committee staffer, "We feel like we've done pretty well without it, but it's definitely something he [Lieberman] thought should happen at one point. . . . The question is whether it's needed and it's a good use of our time."[17]

Reflecting on the committee changes brought about by the events of 2001, a senior Republican senator noted: "We're a lot better than we were, but I'm not sure that if there was an alarm right now . . . I'm just not sure. . . . Everyone is cognizant of what could happen, but, after the authorization, committees don't want to give up turf, so it's especially hard to pass a bill."

According to the Republican senator, the performance of the committee has been limited not by leadership but by jurisdictional battles and early membership decisions. He commented: "Lieberman and Sue Collins did a good job in putting together the best bill possible after the arm wrestling contest when people were transferred over to Homeland Security. We didn't send the best and brightest; it has taken some time to firm up. But I think we have made rather remarkable progress."

Resource Allocation

One of the common themes stemming from the interview data concerns the geographic distribution of Homeland Security resources. Several members and staffers bemoaned the uneven and unreasonable allocation of funds by the Homeland Security committees. Funds have been unevenly distributed within states. They have also been unevenly distributed across states. Some question the prudence in granting appropriation dollars to states not located on a border, not housing a critical commercial port, or not claiming a major city or airport. The controversy over resource allocation revolves around the fact that Congress mandated that the initial grant formulas consider equitable distribution both across states as well as across populations. As one staffer for a senior Republican member from Florida summarized: "Wyoming gets the same money as

New York per person [because of Senate representation], but doesn't have the same threat level." A brief foray into the funding formulas is necessary to understand the real criticism posed by members reviewing the activities of the department and committees responsible for Homeland Security appropriations.

In Steven Maguire and Shawn Reese's examination of grant allocations from the Department of Homeland Security (DHS) to states and local governments from FY2003 to FY2006, they specifically target seven grant programs: the State Homeland Security Grant Program (SHSGP), the Urban Area Security Initiative (UASI), the Law Enforcement Terrorism Prevention Program (LETPP), the Emergency Management Performance Grant Program (EMPG), the Metropolitan Medical Response System (MMRS), the Citizen Corps Program (CCP), and the Critical Infrastructure Protection Program (CIP).[18] The total budget for these seven programs in FY2006 was $1.85 billion.

Four of these seven programs are new since the terrorist attacks of 9/11. Prior to 2001, states and localities could obtain the State Domestic Preparedness Program (SDPP) grant (now SHSGP) from the Department of Justice, the EMPG from the Federal Emergency Management Agency, and the MMRS from the Department of Health and Human Services. After 2001, these programs were transferred to DHS, and four new grant programs were created to augment homeland security.[19] Provisions of the Patriot Act specified the purposes of these grant monies and, through the appropriations authorization for FY2002 through FY2007, set a minimum state allocation of 0.75 percent of the total grant appropriations per year for five of the programs.[20] The other two programs target urban areas, and DHS maintained sole discretion over resource allocation for these initiatives.

Though Congress gave DHS much discretion over grant allocation, the 0.75 percent minimum state allocation advantaged small states. Even after DHS allocated the remaining funds in FY2003 through FY2005 by state population, small states enjoyed a disproportionate advantage, as did states with low levels of risk (see table 4.1). In FY2006, DHS changed its allocation scheme to reflect risk and the ability of states to "effectively use federal homeland security assistance."[21] This new funding formula met with its own round of criticism. Not only did the vast majority of states receive less funding under the new scoring system, but the element of state proposal "effectiveness" as a criterion for receiving Homeland

Security dollars raised several questions. "What is unclear to many is whether there exists a risk threshold where effectiveness would be irrelevant."[22] In other words, what would happen if a high-risk area submitted an ineffective plan? Would the area at high risk of a terrorist attack or natural disaster not receive Homeland Security funding? Additional criticisms concern the disproportionate allocation within states to urban centers. See table 4.2 for a presentation of the distribution of resources in Florida, for example. One senior aide for a Republican member from the Florida delegation suggested: "We have a specific Florida issue—the urban area security initiative. Miami got all the money and didn't share with Ft. Lauderdale and Palm Beach. We have two ports. We have been active in trying to bulk up security. The city of Miami is responsible in the urban area, but each city is involved. We are trying to separate to become our own urban area."

Table 4.1: Per Capita Distribution of State Homeland Security Grant Program Funds across Selected States: FY2003–FY2006

| State | Total for SHSGP (in millions) | Per Capita Amount (in millions) | | | | |
		FY2003	FY2004	FY2005	FY2006	Percent Change[a]
Alaska	$45.12	$25.69	$22.92	$14.24	$6.68	-74.0%
California	$430.44	$4.70	$3.78	$2.36	$1.32	-72.0%
Florida	$227.01	$19.27	$15.63	$9.88	$5.61	-70.9%
Idaho	$56.06	$15.76	$12.62	$7.83	$4.68	-70.3%
Kentucky	$86.99	$8.03	$6.51	$4.07	$2.52	-68.6%
Maine	$53.27	$16.18	$13.08	$8.21	$3.32	-79.5%
Montana	$49.57	$21.25	$17.19	$10.73	$4.80	-77.4%
New Hampshire	$53.01	$16.40	$13.23	$8.27	$3.30	-79.9%
New York	$252.37	$5.04	$4.10	$2.56	$1.43	-71.7%
North Dakota	$48.62	$28.69	$23.43	$14.68	$9.85	-65.7%
Vermont	$49.40	$29.39	$23.86	$14.97	$11.59	-60.6%
Wyoming	$45.44	$35.29	$28.61	$17.89	$8.68	-75.4%

[a] In some instances, the beginning year for calculating percentage change is a fiscal year later than FY2003.

Source: Adapted from Steven Maguire and Shawn Reese, "Department of Homeland Security Grants to State and Local Governments: FY2003 to FY2006," Congressional Research Service, Order Code RL33770, December 22, 2006, 21–56.

Table 4.2: Urban Area Security Initiative Grant Allocation to
Florida Urban Centers: FY2003–FY2006

City	Total for USAI (in millions)	Amount Allocated (in millions)				
		FY2003	FY2004	FY2005	FY2006	Percent Change[a]
Ft. Lau-derdale	$9.98	$0.00	$0.00	$0.00	$9.98	NA
Jackson-ville	$16.15	$0.00	$0.00	$6.88	$9.27	34.7%
Miami	$64.14	$13.18	$19.15	$15.83	$15.98	21.2%
Orlando	$18.21	$0.00	$8.77	$0.00	$9.44	7.6%
Tampa	$31.62	$5.77	$9.28	$7.77	$8.80	52.5%

[a] In some instances, the beginning year for calculating percentage change is a fiscal year later than FY2003.

Source: Adapted from Steven Maguire and Shawn Reese, "Department of Homeland Security Grants to State and Local Governments: FY2003 to FY2006," *Congressional Research Service,* Order Code RL33770, December 22, 2006, 26.

One of the reasons for the state minimum allocation factor stems from the interest primarily among those members of the Senate Homeland Security and Governmental Affairs Committee in maintaining access among small states and inland states to Homeland Security grants. Examining the membership of the committee since its creation illuminates the interests at play in this issue domain (see table 4.3).

It appears that the membership of this Senate committee did not change much during its transition from Governmental Affairs to Homeland Security and Governmental Affairs. Before the change in committee jurisdiction, there were no senators from the most populous states that were thought to face the greatest risk of a terrorist attack, such as New York, California, and Florida, and there are no senators from those at-risk states now. While there originally were senators on the committee from large states with major urban areas, such as Illinois and Pennsylvania, it should be noted that a good number of states represented on the committee seem to be at a remarkably low risk of a terrorist attack. Take Connecticut, Montana, and Arkansas, for example. Senate representation on the committee from these low-risk states ensures that the 0.75 percent minimum state allocation of Homeland Security grant monies will persist as a central feature of the funding formula. This fact continues to frustrate those representing at-risk constituencies seeking additional funding.

Table 4.3: Membership during the Senate Committee Transition from Governmental Affairs to Homeland Security and Governmental Affairs: 108th Congress–111th Congress

		108th Congress 2004–2005	109th Congress 2005–2006	110th Congress 2007–2008	111th Congress 2009–2010
		Governmental Affairs	Homeland Security and Governmental Affairs	Homeland Security and Governmental Affairs	Homeland Security and Governmental Affairs
Democrats		Joseph Lieberman (CT) RM[a] Carl Levin (MI) Daniel Akaka (HI) Dick Durbin (D-IL)[c] Thomas Carper (DE) Mark Dayton (MN) Frank Lautenberg (NJ) Mark Pryor (AR)	Joseph Lieberman (CT) RM Carl Levin (MI) Daniel Akaka (HI) Thomas Carper (DE) Mark Dayton (MN) Frank Lautenberg (NJ) Mark Pryor (AR)	Joseph Lieberman (1-CT) C Carl Levin (MI) Daniel Akaka (HI) Thomas Carper (DE) Mark Pryor (AR) Mary Landrieu (LA) Barack Obama (IL) Claire McCaskill (MO) Jon Tester (MT)	Joseph Lieberman (1-CT) C Carl Levin (MI) Daniel Akaka (HI) Thomas Carper (DE) Mark Pryor (AR) Mary Landrieu (LA) Claire McCaskill (MO) Jon Tester (MT) Roland Burris (IL) Michael Bennet (C)
Republicans		Susan Collins (ME) C[b] Ted Stevens (AK) George Voinovich (OH) Norm Coleman (MN) Arlen Specter (PA) Robert Bennett (UT) Peter Fitzgerald (IL) John Sununu (NH) Richard Shelby (AL)	Susan Collins (ME) C Ted Stevens AK George Voinovich (OH) Norm Coleman (MN) Arlen Specter (PA) Tom Coburn (OK) Lincoln Chafee (RI) Robert Bennett (UT) Pete Domenici (NM) John Warner (VA)	Susan Collins (ME) RM Ted Stevens (AK) George Voinovich (OH) Norm Coleman (MN) Tom Coburn (OK) Pete Domenici (NM) John Warner (VA) John Sununu (NH)	Susan Collins (ME) RM Tom Coburn (OK) John McCain (AZ) George Voinovich (OH) John Ensign (NV) Lindsey Graham (SC)

[a] RM denotes ranking member.
[b] C denotes chair.

From the vantage point of representation theory, this scenario speaks to the fundamental tension between representatives acting as delegates and representatives acting as trustees. Acting as delegates, senators would protect the interest of their own states, making sure to bring home grant monies for homeland security. Acting as trustees, however, senators would protect the interests of the public at large, making sure to allocate federal dollars for homeland security based strictly on assessments of risk.

Oversight Activity

The Homeland Security committees in both the House and the Senate have struggled to provide effective oversight of DHS. Reasons for this struggle abound. First, the creation of DHS and the corresponding congressional oversight committees happened at a time of unified government. With homeland security serving as the foremost issue on President George W. Bush's policy agenda, it is no wonder that party loyalty perhaps served to limit meaningful oversight in this area. As one senior staff member of a Democratic senator suggested: "There has been a failure of oversight of all committees. We have a Republican administration and Republican committee chairmen. Before, they were responsible to the Senate; now we see loyalty to party and leadership and the administration. It's very difficult to run executive branch agencies *and* hold them in account" (emphasis added).

Second, the significant reorganization of security-related agencies to form the new department created a nightmarish jurisdictional battle among congressional committee chairs. This infighting served as a major distraction from effective oversight. Finally, the lack of seniority and established expertise on the new House committee somewhat leveled the playing field among rival personalities jockeying for the chairmanship helm left vacant by Christopher Cox in the fall of 2005—just two years after the creation of the fledgling committee. With disparate constituencies and concerns, these members dug in their heels on important issues, such as the reorganization of FEMA in the aftermath of Hurricane Katrina, and further inhibited expeditious and effective oversight. One Democratic member summarized the less than desirable result:

> The Department is a disaster. Democrats say it out loud; Republicans whisper it; but we all know it's true. Ridge is an affable man, but a terrible administrator. It's shameful how in some areas nothing has happened. . . .

Mass transit needs a plan. They never have gotten the plan. . . . It's really haphazard. It's a joke, and that's what we have. It's an administrative problem, not legislative. Homeland Security ought to be focused on prevention of terrorism in the U.S. and protection of our infrastructure for those elements to minimize terrorists' ability to deliver a crushing blow to the United States, whether biological, chemical, cyber, or infrastructure.

While the atmosphere immediately following 9/11 was one of unusual bipartisanship, some members suggest that the climate soon reverted. This shift was accompanied by increased concern among Democrats over the lack of effective oversight of the newly created Homeland Security Department—now housing several critical components of disaster preparedness (see table 4.4). When asked about the period of bipartisanship in 2001, a senior staffer for a Democratic member suggested: "It has dissipated. One reason was over the decision to go to war in Iraq, with the administration using 9/11 somewhat speciously as an excuse to go after Hussein—mischaracterizing and misusing intelligence for its own purposes. There have been missteps. TSA has not been very successful. The massive reorganization by [Michael] Chertoff was not quite right the first time around. Most would acknowledge that the department was set up as a political tug-of-war. It was rushed through here and became a real political football in off-year elections. There is a lot of resentment over that."

As suggested by the previous account, an early focus of oversight was transportation security. Due to the form the terrorist attack on 9/11 took, the immediate concern following the event was airline security. The Transportation Security Administration became the target of new legislation, including "research and development programs on security, missile defense, and the security that we now have in place," according to a prominent Republican member in this policy domain. The need for an expedited response following 9/11 led to poor oversight and ineffective implementation. The same member noted: "What Congress mandated was that we have screening immediately. That's costly in manpower and dollars. It performs poorly. We had the system tested. It was disastrous for checked baggage screening. It was not able to detect problems. The technology is not that effective. Dogs are probably the most effective. We have spent money on manpower rather than technology. We are trying to do that now."

Table 4.4: Organization and Function of Department of Homeland Security

Major Organizational Unit	Function
Directorate for National Protection and Programs	Responsible for risk reduction in physical and virtual threats, including protection of the nation's cyber and communications infrastructure; responsiveness to attacks, natural disasters, or other emergencies; coordination with state and local governments; and standardization of risk management and analysis.
Directorate for Science and Technology	Responsible for research and development to provide federal, state, and local officials with technology and capabilities necessary for security.
Directorate for Management	Responsible for budget, appropriations, expenditures, accounting, procurement, human resources, information technology systems, facilities, and development and tracking of performance measures.
Office of Policy	Responsible for developing and integrating department policies, planning, and programs.
Office of Health Affairs	Responsible for developing and supporting a biodefense and health preparedness architecture to protect the United States from health hazards.
Office of Intelligence and Analysis	Responsible for collecting, analyzing, and disseminating information related to homeland security threats.
Office of Operations Coordination	Responsible for deterring, detecting, and preventing terrorist acts by coordinating the information and operations of state and local governments.
Federal Law Enforcement Training Center	Serves as an interagency training organization for more than eighty federal agencies and provides services to state, local, and international law enforcement agencies.

Table 4.4: Organization and Function of Department of Homeland Security (cont'd)

Major Organizational Unit	Function
Domestic Nuclear Detection Office	Responsible for detecting and reporting unauthorized use of nuclear or radiological material against the United States.
Transportation Security Administration (TSA)	Responsible for securing the nation's transportation systems for people and commerce.
U.S. Customs and Border Protection (CBP)	Responsible for protecting national borders to prevent terrorist activity and protect the flow of legitimate trade and travel.
U.S. Citizenship and Immigration Services	Responsible for administering immigration and naturalization adjudication functions and establishing immigration services, policies, and priorities.
U.S. Immigration and Customs Enforcement (ICE)	Responsible for monitoring the nation's border, economic, transportation, and infrastructure security and protecting national security by enforcing customs and immigration laws.
U.S. Coast Guard	Responsible for protecting the public, the environment, and U.S. economic interests in ports and waterways, along the coast, on international waters, or in any maritime region required for national security.
Federal Emergency Management Agency (FEMA)	Responsible for emergency preparedness, management of response and recovery efforts, and administration of the National Flood Insurance Program.
U.S. Secret Service	Responsible for protecting the president and other dignitaries and for investigating counterfeiting and other financial crimes, identity theft, computer fraud, and other computer-based attacks on our financial, banking, and telecommunications infrastructure.

Source: Adapted from Department of Homeland Security, "Department Subcomponents and Agencies," http://www.dhs.gov/xabout/structure/#1.

When examining the partisan climate around Capitol Hill following the terrorist attacks of 2001, other members contended that the return of partisan fervor was isolated to general debate and media accounts rather than actual committee activity. Policy experts placed on the House Homeland Security Committee may have resented the jurisdictional reorganization caused by the creation of the committee, but they were not embittered with partisan difference. A senior Republican member with decades of experience in this policy domain remarked: "Partisanship is mostly from media accounts. Most issues relating to security are not that partisan. There are just constraints on the dollars and a little bit different philosophies, different priorities. There is a lot of emphasis on cargo security. That has been a priority issue, and that's somewhat philosophical. We are better at pinpointing and targeting. There is much more profiling. But only 10 percent of members have seen classified reports. The rest just stand up and mouth off. They're mostly shooting from the hip."

A specific factor frustrating oversight activity in the Senate concerned a jurisdictional battle over restructuring the Senate Governmental Affairs Committee to house homeland security. Opting to add homeland security to a preexisting committee rather than to create an independent committee led to a severely handicapped Senate Homeland Security and Governmental Affairs Committee at the start of the 109th Congress in 2005. To build consensus over the new committee structure, the Senate entertained numerous amendments to the committee design—all introduced with the intent of stripping the committee of its jurisdiction over homeland security. An article written at the beginning of the 109th Congress to survey the committee organization of the Senate suggested: "The panel will have to oversee the Department of Homeland Security (DHS) without exercising jurisdiction over immigration, U.S. Customs and Border Protection, the Secret Service, the Transportation Security Administration, the Coast Guard and the Federal Law Enforcement Training Center. DHS components that have been added to its jurisdiction include directorates on Information Analysis and Infrastructure, Science and Technology, Management, and Emergency Preparedness and Response. . . . The panel lost its share of jurisdiction over measures affecting the congressional budget process to the Budget Committee."[23]

Without jurisdiction over the Transportation Security Administration and the Coast Guard, the Senate Homeland Security and Governmental Affairs Committee was ultimately left with little actual authority

Table 4.5: Senate Homeland Security and Govermental Affairs Committee Jurisdiction

Department of Homeland Security

Investigations concerning:
(1) The effectiveness of present national security methods, staffing, and processes as tested against the requirements imposed by the rapidly mounting complexity of national security problems;
(2) The capacity of present national security staffing, methods, and processes to make full use of the nation's resources of knowledge and talents;
(3) The adequacy of present intergovernmental relations between the United States and international organizations principally concerned with national security of which the United States is a member;
(4) And legislative and other proposals to improve these methods, processes, and relationships.

Exclusions	Committee with Jurisdiction
• Coast Guard	Commerce, Science, & Transportation
• Transportation Security Administration	Commerce, Science, & Transportation
• Federal Law Enforcement Training Center or Secret Service	Judiciary
• U.S. Citizenship and Immigration Service	Judiciary
• Immigration functions of U.S. Customs and Border Protection, U.S. Immigration and Custom Enforcement, and Directorate of Border and Transportation Security	Judiciary
• Functions related to customs revenue	Finance
• Commercial function or operation of Bureau of Customs and Border Protection or Bureau of Immigration and Customs Enforcement, including matters relating to trade facilitation or trade regulation	Finance
• Other related functions exercised by the U.S. Customs Service before Homeland Security Act of 2002 became effective	Judiciary
• Jurisdiction of other committees over National Flood Insurance Act of 1968 and other related functions of the Federal Emergency Management Agency	Banking Environment & Public Works

Source: Adapted from "Committee on Homeland Security and Governmental Affairs: Full Committee and Subcommittee Jurisdictions for the 111th Congress," http://hsgac.senate.gov/public/index.cfm?FuseAction=AboutCommittee.Jurisdiction; and Paul S. Rundquist and Christopher M. Davis, "S. Res. 445: Senate Committee Reorganization for Homeland Security and Intelligence Matters." Congressional Research Service, Order Code RS21955, October 15, 2004, http://digital.library.unt.edu/govdocs/crs/permalink/meta-crs-5772:1.

Table 4.6: House Homeland Security Committee Jurisdiction

Department of Homeland Security

Investigations concerning:
(1) Overall homeland security policy;
(2) Organization and administration of the Department of Homeland Security;
(3) Functions of the Department of Homeland Security related to the following:
  (A) Border and port security;
  (B) Customs;
  (C) Integration, analysis, and dissemination of homeland security information;
  (D) Domestic preparedness for and collective response to terrorism;
  (E) Research and development;
  (F) Transportation security

Exclusions	Committee with Jurisdiction
• Coast Guard	Transportation and Infrastructure
• Immigration and non-border-related policy	Judiciary
• Transportation safety	Transporation and Infrastructure
• Customs revenue	Ways and Means
• Natural disasters and other emergencies	Transportation and Infrastructure

Source: Adapted from Judy Schneider, "Committee System Rules in the House, 109th Congress," Congressional Research Service, Order Code RS22018, January 5, 2005, http://digital.library.unt.edu/govdocs/crs/permalink/meta-crs-7463:1.

over the personnel of DHS. Michael Bopp, a Republican staff director for the Senate committee, recalls the floor debate on the resolution to reorganize the committee. He suggests that it was "by far the ugliest and the lowest point of my career on the Hill." Given that this committee overhaul constituted the largest reorganization in thirty years, the negotiations were rather unusual. "It was like no other bill," says Bopp. "The coalitions were completely different. They weren't geographical, or partisan, or any of the normal ways that Congress divides up. It was purely about committee jurisdiction."[24] See tables 4.5 and 4.6 for a presentation of the jurisdiction of the Senate Homeland Security and Governmental Affairs Committee and House Homeland Security Committee as well as those areas related to homeland security retained by other committees.

The impact of this jurisdictional web is that DHS must now report to a litany of congressional panels responsible for oversight. When asked for suggestions on improving the workings of the department, Tom Ridge, the former secretary of Homeland Security, encouraged Congress to take a hard look at the number of committees with jurisdiction over the department. "'I think we could be even more effective in what we're doing,' he began, 'if there was some means of reducing, frankly, the multiple layers of interaction that we encounter every single day.'"[25] In fact, during the 110th Congress alone, DHS representatives provided more than 5,000 briefings to congressional offices and attended more than 370 congressional hearings. Although the sheer volume of requested appearances is staggering, the real work is in the preparation. On average, according to DHS estimates, testimony for a single congressional hearing requires approximately sixty hours of preparation.[26] The new secretary of Homeland Security, Janet Napolitano, summarized the attitude of DHS officials in a response to Representative Peter King (R-NY) at one such congressional hearing. "'While it would be presumptuous of me to recommend to Congress how it be organized,' she said, 'I think that's a fact that is relevant.'"[27] A further consequence of shared committee jurisdiction over homeland security issues is that the Department of Homeland Security is spread quite thin trying to accommodate requests for information from multiple congressional sources.

Perhaps a final element inhibiting effective oversight of the new Department of Homeland Security concerns the department itself rather than the congressional committees. A former Republican member of Congress reflected: "[Effective oversight] doesn't depend on the status of us being at war. It has to do with a lot of things being dumped into [DHS]. Homeland Security has a lot of jurisdiction. All of these agencies have their own cultures, traditions, and styles. It requires a melding that doesn't happen easily. It is a big ball of wax that was put under Homeland Security." This same member shed an interesting light on the jurisdictional battles that have so significantly curtailed legislative activity by the Homeland Security committees. According to the retired Republican member, part of the problem is that you have a number of members who have "devoted a lot of life to trying to understand the issues now handled by [DHS]. This expertise they had developed is now of no value to them." The resistance provided by these members was no match, however, to the feeling of party leadership "that in order to really coordinate all the disparate parts, we

needed one committee to really oversee [DHS]." While this strategy theoretically makes sense, it will take some time before the old experts develop
new interests and the new members of the Homeland Security committees
develop general issue expertise. Until then, there will be disgruntled members of Congress on committees fraught with internal discord.

Predicting the Future

One of the interesting implications of the homeland security environment on Capitol Hill initiated by the fall of 2001 involves the strategies
of members and special interests in trying to gain attention for their pet
issues and projects. A senior staffer for the Senate Intelligence Committee suggested: "Someone who wants to shove some pieces of pork into the
budget is going to tie it to Homeland Security. The thinking on K Street
is that if you can link to Homeland Security, you got a better chance, but
I don't think that's the reality. Everybody's got their Homeland Security
widget that they're trying to sell. It's pathetic. Some members probably
think that they have a really good project, but at the same time members
play the political game." It is not so much that the people pressuring the
system have changed, but rather the messages couching political causes
have changed. The same Senate committee staffer noted, "There is a new
set of concerns because of the Patriot Act, but they're the same people."
Similarly, a member of the House Republican leadership suggested, "The
interest in the topic leads to interest in the committee. The media is interested. It gets a lot of coverage and that might increase interest."

Perhaps some of this emphasis is driven by the electoral incentive.
Rank and file members are paying more attention to issues of intelligence
and national security as well as special interests. This holds implications
for the productivity of the Homeland Security committees. Unlike other
less prestigious committees, with specialized members and staff enjoying
autonomy over niche jurisdictions, the Homeland Security committees
lack the prestige or the obscurity to claim autonomy over their legislative
agenda. This dynamic has plagued the committees since their creation
and has been perpetuated by the ongoing War on Terror. As a member of
the House Republican leadership suggested:

> Members take their role in national security and intelligence far more se-
> riously than in the past. We've slipped some, but clearly we are more aware

and sensitive to our role in world access to sensitive information. Before, we had a small clique of members who specialized in national security. The rest specialized in other things. But today we still have specialists, but we don't abandon what's going on in national security and intelligence. . . . Voters acknowledge that also and recognize the importance of that in candidates. They look for someone that they can trust to be involved in and aware of things that are not public and trust the person's judgment. . . . My constituents are more concerned about vulnerability and security. They know it's a serious subject—one that's produced important legislation, such as the Patriot Act. They are aware of the big impact, but in terms of the event, which led to more trust.

Yet some members view the change through glass less rose-colored. When asked to reflect on the potential impact of homeland security to legislative activity, a senior staff member for a Democratic senator suggested, "Homeland security has profoundly affected every decision we make here. It has affected appropriations and created a lack of budget and fiscal discipline. Our work is colored by 9/11 and the American psyche. Elections are now about protecting the American people."

Because of the salience of the "homeland security" issue, the committee restructuring seems permanent, at least for now. The new structure provides a high-profile vehicle for legislative action and oversight on an issue of public concern. As far as the prestige of the committee assignment to members of Congress, the committees will be somewhat attractive so long as the homeland security issue remains salient. As a chief of staff for a senior Republican member of Congress suggested: "The Homeland Security committees will be around for a while. The issue will continue for a long time. The committee will continue to be somewhat prestigious, I guess. Not like Ways and Means or Appropriations. They don't have the budget. It is high profile because the issue has come into the spotlight. But it has got a lot of work to do. It has to figure out what works and what doesn't work . . . with grant programs, etc. The committee has to fashion a formula that won't make New York mad." A historian affiliated with the U.S. Capitol Historical Society reflected on the new committees: "Prestige is clearly going to decline unless there are more attacks. The intel side is very glamorous, but this part of it is going to end up with the same people that end up on House Administration—either somebody nobody likes or somebody just interested in the nitty gritty."

Finally, it appears that one of the most important factors influencing the long-range success of the committees involves legislative jurisdiction. As one Republican member of the House Homeland Security Committee noted: "Even though we now have a Homeland Security Committee, you still have people arguing that we need a centralization of authority. There are still elements of responsibility before so many other committees." Whether party leadership is able to untangle this jurisdictional ball of yarn may be key in determining the long-term legislative productivity and administrative oversight provided by the new committees.

5

GATEWAY TO AMERICAN HISTORY OR FORT CAPITOL?

Construction of the Capitol Visitor Center

They are political cathedrals. Lavishly decorated with native woods, indigenous stone and precious metals, lovingly packed with artwork and historic artifacts, they were built to celebrate democracy's promise. Today the U.S. Capitol and the state capitols represent democracy's dilemma. The lawmakers who work in them say they are "the people's houses." Yet these days, the people are having a harder time finding an open door. . . . Welcome to Fortress USA.
—"Post-9/11 Security Hinders Access at Capitols," *USA Today*

Donald Ritchie, associate historian of the Senate, reflected, "The Capitol was begun in 1793, when George Washington was president and laid the cornerstone, and it has never been finished."[1] While the Capitol has changed a great deal over the course of its two-hundred-year history, the greatest expansion in the history of the complex is the Capitol Visitor Center—a new subterranean facility spanning nearly 580,000 square feet, approximately three-quarters the size of the Capitol Building itself. Due to its enormous size, the Capitol Visitor Center (CVC) is the first construction project ever contracted out by the Architect of the Capitol. While the project originally was envisioned by the Architect in 1976, it did not receive adequate funding for significant progress until the 1998 Capitol shootings and the 9/11 and anthrax attacks of 2001.

This chapter explores the project development and management of the Capitol Visitor Center while it was under construction. It further examines the evolution of the policy debate surrounding the Capitol Visitor Center and the subsequent debate over management of the massive project. The evolving security demands and the escalating costs associated with construction have been central to the conflict surrounding the

CVC. It has been difficult for Congress to provide the necessary oversight in part because of the amorphous parameters of the project and in part because of its contracted-out management. The process of constructing the Capitol Visitor Center highlighted the frustrations inherent in collective decision making for a body like Congress, in which power is fragmented and decentralized. The CVC is now a critical feature of the Congress of tomorrow, serving as the first taste of congressional life for generations of future visitors to the nation's Capitol. For this reason, it warrants our attention, both for what it tells us by way of legislative behavior and project management and for what it tells America about Congress.

Before turning to the history of the development of the Capitol Visitor Center, it is useful to review the theoretical literature on how governmental entities manage public projects, including the use of contracted-out management. It is also useful to think about the people behind the construction of the CVC as a network of special interests, a view highlighted by the advocacy coalition framework in political science and public policy studies. The fact that the CVC was built in response to and during a time of crisis impacted the form that such management took. Crisis impacts the amount of resources decision makers are willing to spend on projects and the discretion they are willing to provide to project managers. From here, the chapter turns to the history of the Capitol Visitor Center, noting the political and administrative context of the project's development. Particular attention is paid to the chain of command in oversight of the project. The final pages conclude with a look at the reaction of political elite in Washington, D.C., to the opening of the CVC and with a summary assessment of the impact of the facility on the Capitol landscape.

Developing a Framework for Understanding the Project Evolution of the CVC

Three separate bodies of scholarship offer a framework for examining the development of the Capitol Visitor Center. First, the perspectives offered by scholarship on government contracting and the tool of privatization (also called contracting out, contractualization, or "outsourcing") are relevant to this case. Second, the perspective of the advocacy coalition framework developed by P. A. Sabatier and H. C. Jenkins-Smith is useful in understanding the complex range of actors and the importance of time in the policy process.[2] Finally, given that the CVC has been impacted by a series of crisis events, the literature on crisis management provides some unique understanding of the evolution of the policy process in this particular case. In the next few pages, the findings of these areas of research are summarized to provide an intersecting theoretical framework for examining the development of the CVC.

Project Management and Contracting Out

A growing trend is the use of contractualization in both the private and public sectors. As Carsten Greve suggests, contracting out is termed "outsourcing" in the private sector, but involves the same elements in the public sector. Just as in the private sector, "A principal decides on a job that it wants to be done, arranges for the service to be provided, and submits the task to a competitive bidding process, where independent agents are allowed to bid. The tender is rewarded to one or more agents. Principals aim to balance cost and quality in an effort to secure 'the best bid.'"[3] Given the growing popularity of contracting out and the relevance of the subject to the construction of the CVC, it is useful here to consider the value of privatization of government services.

A central debate in the public administration literature concerns the effects of privatization in public service delivery. Privatization involves moving functions performed by the public sector to the private sector. There are generally two principal reasons for privatization, one grounded in ideological justifications and the other grounded in economical justifications. According to ideological advocates of privatization, it is desirable to privatize government services and projects because big government is inherently bad government. The impact of government growth is increased regulation of private business and limitations on personal freedom. According to economical advocates of privatization, it is desirable to privatize government services and projects because, given competition and adequate government capacity for oversight, it can improve performance, eliminate wasteful public spending, and depoliticize decision making.[4] Private firms aim to cut costs in service provision in order to secure contracts in the competitive marketplace. Once the contract has been secured, however, a private firm might cut corners to increase its profit margin. On the other hand, government agencies might increase the costs of service provision in order to maximize funding in future budgetary cycles.[5] "The key question becomes simply which sector performs the function more efficiently and economically?"[6]

But many charge that privatization does not necessarily decrease the costs associated with delivery of government services and projects. Once the costs associated with "developing competition and providing meaningful oversight" are considered, it is unclear that privatization is more cost-effective.[7] In addition, opponents of privatization suggest that values other than efficiency warrant consideration when evaluating the practice's merits. When considering issues such as "accountability, equity, service quality, and governmental capacity," privatization does not necessarily produce desirable outcomes.[8] In a review of the scholarship on provision of government services by nonprofits, David Van Slyke reports a consistent finding of lack of competition, administrative capacity, and accountability.[9] In addition, privatization may actually increase the potential for corruption.[10]

In democratic societies, there is a public expectation that government will be accountable for the way in which it appropriates and utilizes revenue. When government contracts out work to private entities, this leads to "an inevitable weakening in the lines of political accountability."[11] No longer are elected officials or public employees solely responsible for federal spending. Private entities charged with performing a governmental function also exercise discretion over federal funds.[12] Elected officials continually are placed in the "position of being responsible for the programs they do not really control."[13] To fully oversee the activities of privatized service provision, government must have a certain degree of public management capacity. Only with expertise in contract management, public policy, mediation, auditing, and communication can public managers weather the challenges posed by privatized projects in the complex environment of contemporary politics.[14] "If government is to contract for services that are available in a private market, it should have the resources to manage, oversee, and enforce accountability," according to Van Slyke.[15]

In the end, the evidence on the benefits of privatization is mixed. In certain situations, privatization may offer a cost-efficient option for policymakers. The success of privatization efforts, however, seems somewhat contingent on the context. In situations involving abundant information, low risk, high competition, very specific contracts, and the capacity to enforce accountability and evaluate outcomes, privatization perhaps should be pursued.[16] Absent these criteria, public institutions should seriously question the value of privatizing services and projects. When public agencies privatize the delivery of services, they may be delegating the easiest aspects of policy implementation. "The conceiving, planning, goal-setting, standard-setting, performance-monitoring, evaluating, and correcting all remain with the government."[17]

Advocacy Coalition Framework

One framework Greve suggests for examining contracting out in the public sector is the advocacy coalition framework (ACF) developed by Sabatier and Jenkins-Smith.[18] The goal of this framework is to "provide a coherent understanding of the major factors and processes affecting the overall policy process—including problem definition, policy formation, implementation, and revision in a specific policy domain—over periods of a decade or more."[19] The ACF is useful in that its core assumptions provide a role for technical information, the passage of time, the policy subsystem, a range of participants, and learning in the policy process.[20] According to Sabatier and Jenkins-Smith, an advocacy coalition includes "people from a variety of positions, elected and agency officials, interest group leaders, researchers who share a particular belief system . . . and who show a non-trivial degree of coordinated activity over time."[21]

When applied to contracting out, the ACF approach requires observing "(a) the alliances formed between different actors; (b) the beliefs they hold; (c) the political, administrative, and organizational context of contracting out; and (d) the learning process that might take place."[22] Figure 5.1 suggests that the structure of the ACF provides for the important grounding of policy within an institutional and environmental context. Sabatier and Jenkins-Smith first consider the role of societal values, the basic constitutional structure, and natural resources in the evolution of a given policy subsystem. Because these factors are relatively stable, they are rarely the focus of coalition strategies, but they nevertheless critically affect coalitional behavior. They secondly point to the role of socioeconomic change, political change, and major policy change. While perhaps not central to the policy subsystem under examination, other policy subsystems can have spillover effects on the policy area of concern. These two categories of factors, separate but central to policy evolution, serve to constrain and support the activities of policy subsystems.[23]

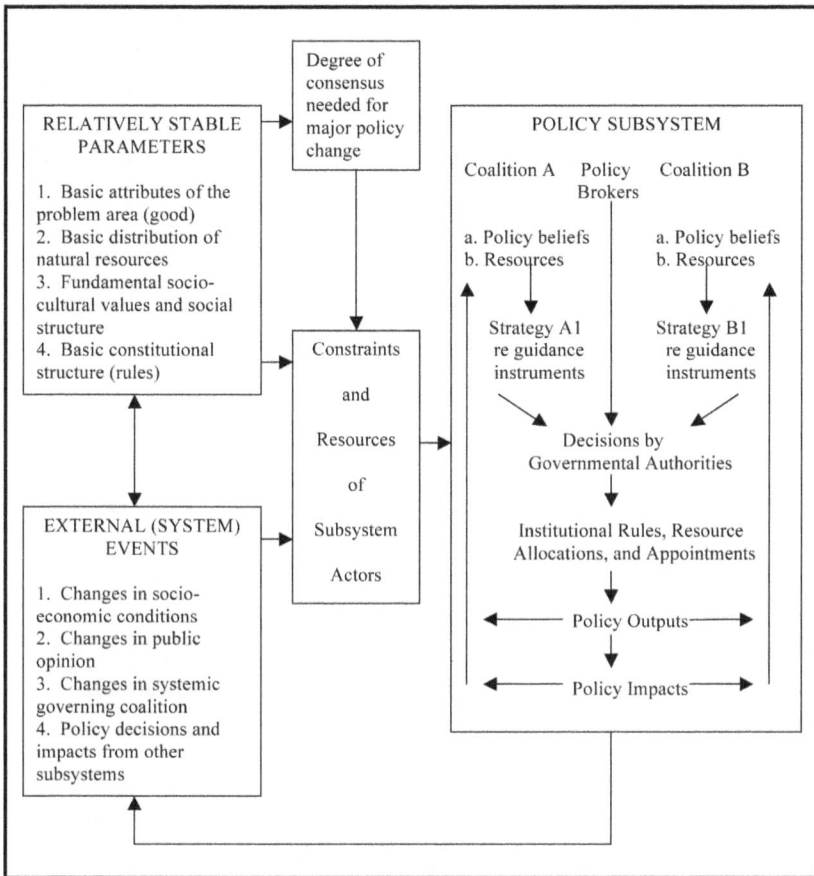

Figure 5.1: Diagram of the Advocacy Coalition Framework. *Source:* P. A. Sabatier and H. C. Jenkins-Smith, "The Advocacy Coalition Framework: An Assessment," in *Theories of the Policy Process,* ed. P. A. Sabatier, 149 (Boulder, Colo.: Westview Press, 1999).

Within a policy subsystem, a few advocacy coalitions will emerge that serve as conglomerates of actors who share the same beliefs concerning the policy area and engage in coordinated activity in support of these beliefs over an extended period of time. Uniquely, the ACF asserts that these actors come from a variety of both governmental and nongovernmental institutions. The framework thus recognizes the role of agencies, special interests, subnational government officials, researchers, and journalists in the policymaking process. The final element of the ACF of central concern here is the assumption that policy actors can learn from experience and/or new information and alter their policy strategy. Policy change can result from the combination of new knowledge of the problem, the policy's effectiveness, and the impact of policy alternatives with changes in the environment or turnover in personnel.[24] In terms of the present analysis, one particular aspect of the ACF should be noted. The ACF "encourages us to think of agency officials, researchers, and journalists as potential members of advocacy coalitions—as having policy beliefs very similar to those of interest group leaders and their legislative allies, and as engaging in some nontrivial degree of coordinated activity in pursuit of their common policy objectives."[25]

Crisis Management

A third valuable body of literature to the case of the CVC is the literature on crisis management. A crisis is "a serious threat to the basic structures or the fundamental values and norms of a social system, which—under time pressure and highly uncertain circumstances—necessitates making critical decisions."[26] In order to fully understand government crisis responses, Uriel Rosenthal and Alexander Kouzmin suggest an examination of:

- "the *administrative system* confronted with the threat"
- "the administrative *level* (local, regional, national, international) that eventually takes decisive action and controls the emergency response"
- "the dimension of the *speed* of government intervention"
- "the *scope* and strategy of government intervention—closed versus open response modes."[27]

The crisis management literature also emphasizes the subjective dimensions of crisis. Rosenthal and Kouzmin warn: "Crises are in the eyes of their beholders; if individuals (and the media) define a situation as a crisis, it is crisis in its consequences. Yet it should be noted that what certain groups within society deem a crisis well may be perceived by others as an opportunity to induce change. One's crisis is often another's opportunity."[28] It is to the advantage of some to create or capitalize on a crisis environment for personal, institutional, or political gain. Rosenthal and Kouzmin call this the creation of a "pseudo crises."[29] Even when there is widespread agreement on the nature and severity of the crisis, "differences may arise over appropriate implementation strategies for crisis resolution."[30]

One of the most important characteristics of crisis management is that in response to crisis there is a necessity for government decisions. The structure of modern democratic government favors specialization, departmentalization, and fragmentation of power. Nevertheless, crisis management often requires coordination and centralization of power. "Often, government authority is not of first importance in the face of disaster," according to Rosenthal and Kouzmin, "and in such a power vacuum situational leadership opportunities emerge."[31] They explain:

> On the one hand, prompt decision making is uncommon to public institutions. Democratic systems in particular have not been designed for this purpose. Rather, they are noted for their emphasis on formal consultation, deliberation, and sometimes-complex accountability procedures. The bureaucratic machinery derives both its strength and its weakness from a time-consuming modus operandi. It is designed to convert information into familiar and routine categories and is unable to respond at the very moment it is confronted with inputs that cannot be treated in that way. On the other hand, critical situations often require a quick response. . . . If government authorities and public agencies are not accustomed to the kind of setting created by crisis, they may have no alternative but to go for both prompt and risky decisions.[32]

Given great uncertainty and complexity, government entities may set aside normal operating procedures and engage in a strategy known as *concurrency*.[33] The hasty decisions made during these moments are likely to produce errors and inadequacies and require changes. "When applied to innovative or complex situations, concurrency may save time in the long term, but in the short term it invariably proves costly."[34]

Finally, the crisis management literature has evolved in a number of respects (see table 5.1). Rosenthal and Kouzmin challenge us to see the routine patterns of crisis management rather than treat each crisis as an irregularity. Second, crises are not necessarily brief episodes, but rather crisis management can evolve over extended periods of time. Third, political actors must not be assumed to fill a role of crisis prevention and relief. It is possible that political actors may exacerbate crisis for political or personal gain. Fourth, while it is easy to paint crises as unpleasant occurrences, it may be that crises bring about necessary change. Fifth, crisis must not be treated as an objective reality. Rather, crisis involves definition, perception, and interpretation, and thus management is confounded by the subjective dimensions of crisis. Sixth, while it is common to think of government response to crisis as centralized and consistent, much of crisis management and response is conducted by those with situation-based discretion over the problem. Finally, though conventional wisdom suggests tough and immediate response to crises, it may be that some situations call for restraint, deliberation, open communication, and a long-term policy strategy.[35]

The Capitol Visitor Center

The following section first traces the historical development of the CVC facility. From its initial conception to its opening day, the project received mixed reviews. Some praised the educational possibilities and spacious accommodations provided by the facility, and others criticized the cost overruns, public management, and architectural design. After tracing these reviews, this section ends with a detailed examination of the issues associated with administrative supervision of the CVC project.

History of the Facility

The plan was first proposed in the mid-1970s, with Capitol architects envisioning a facility "to make tourists—as many as 4 million a year—more comfortable and to add educational exhibits."[36] Not only were visitors required to wait outside regardless of the weather for entry into the Capitol, through security checkpoints and into the Rotunda; once inside the building, visitors had to look hard for public seating, restrooms, or restaurants. As Godfrey points out, "While it has become a living museum, almost every change to its design has been with Congress, not visitors, in mind."[37] The Capitol can only hold 2,200 people at a time above those who work in the building, yet during summer months the tourist site draws up to 20,000 a day.[38]

While the Capitol Visitor Center had been discussed for more than thirty years, specific material plans for the project were introduced in 1991 and then again in 1995 but not seriously considered by lawmakers until 1998.[39] During these years, the project was delayed by lack of adequate public funding or private donation of the estimated $71 to $125 million necessary to complete the facility. One of the leading opponents of the facility in 1991 was then–Minority Whip Newt Gingrich (R–GA).[40] While opponents of the project questioned "whether the benefits [were] worth the price tag," the congressional tune dramatically changed im-

Table 5.1: Competing Crisis Management Perspectives

Conventional Understanding	New Understanding
By their very nature, crises do not lend themselves to the usual examination of regularities of behavior and management.	Need to look past surprise and uncertainty in search of routine patterns of crisis behavior and management. May formulate empirical propositions and generalizations that can stand test of further empirical scrutiny.
Crises occur within a brief time period and are marked by a clear-cut beginning and a strictly demarcated end.	Processual notion of crisis and crisis management. Crises, contrary to being clear-cut episodes or events, may turn out to be protracted and exhaustive, with stress cumulating over time. They may also be considered in terms of circular processes involving mitigation and preparation, response as well as recovery and rehabilitation.
Particular actors assumed to adopt particular roles in crisis. Normative conceptions of roles of public officials and agencies explicate their formal contributions and exclusive responsibilities in preventing and controlling crisis.	Under some circumstances specific contributions by actors, including government officials and agencies, may only involve creating or heightening the fervor associated with a particular crisis.
Crises appear to be unpleasant situations. The focus in much analysis tends to be on the dysfunctionality of crisis situation.	Crises may be functional in many respects. They may generate social and political change. They may reactivate the core values and norms of a social and political order. They may put social and political elites to the test.
Respond to crises as concrete situations.	Multiple definitions of situation may exist. Divergent perceptions, interpretations, and interests may bear upon the processes of crisis management and may cause serious trouble in light of need for resolute and effective responses to severe threat.
Main pattern of government crisis management best depicted as consistent, monocentric, and centralized response.	Growing awareness of polycentric processes of crisis management and crisis response. Situation-based discretionary behavior of those who face critical predicaments does not reconcile with centralizing assumptions in government crisis decision making.
Immediate, tough measures to terminate challenges to social or political order are desirable.	Decisional restraint, prudence, media consciousness and media management, open communications, and a long-term policy perspective may be more effective in actual crisis management and in sensitizing decision makers to rich understanding that now exists in critically nonroutine administration.

Source: Adapted from Uriel Rosenthal and Alexander Kouzmin, "Crises and Crisis Management: Toward Comprehensive Government Decision Making," *Journal of Public Administration Research and Theory* 7, no. 2 (1997): 277–304.

mediately following the Capitol shootings in July 1998.[41] Senate Majority Leader Trent Lott (R-MS) stated one day after the shootings, "We are going to work in harmony with the House to get the necessary authorization this year."[42]

The idea "was given renewed impetus by the killings . . . of officers Jacob J. Chestnut and John Gibson" by a deranged man who entered the Capitol with a firearm.[43] While Capitol Police chief Gary Arbrecht could find no fault with the handling of the incident by Capitol security, he suggested that the problem was that security was confined by the structure of the building. The narrow doors only permitted a limited screening operation.[44] In the aftermath of the shootings, Congress proposed legislation for "an underground structure . . . provid[ing] security checkpoints outside the Capitol while offering tourists shelter and information."[45]

"'There's no question that the shooting of the officers acted as a catalyst,' said Senator Robert Bennett, R-Utah, who chair[ed] the Senate Appropriations subcommittee for the legislative branch."[46] Offering support for renewed interest in the project, Representative Eleanor Holmes Norton (D-DC) suggested that "Building a visitors center is 'the one major thing we can do' to protect the Capitol from a repeat of Friday's assault."[47] This structure would not be funded until 1999, but initial estimates suggested a target of three years for completion.[48] In addition, the leaders of the Senate Rules and Administration Committee and the House Oversight Committee immediately "announced plans to move forward with a 'perimeter security plan' that would upgrade safety features around the Capitol, House and Senate office buildings and the way vehicles [would be] allowed in to the main grounds."[49]

Nonetheless, congressional efforts reached a standstill for nearly a year after the shootings because of internal division within the Republican Party over who should have jurisdiction over the project.[50] A letter released in the fall of 1998 by Speaker Newt Gingrich (R-GA) giving jurisdiction of this "ambitious project of national importance" to the House Administration Committee caught the ire of Representative Bud Shuster, chair of the Transportation and Infrastructure Committee, which is responsible for public buildings.[51] Interestingly, Representative Bill Thomas (R-CA), chair of the House Administration Committee at the time, "was one of the few willing to buck the tide, saying he would not endorse the plan until someone could prove it was needed."[52] After a change in leadership at the beginning of the 106th Congress in 1999,

Speaker Dennis Hastert (R-IL) shifted jurisdiction of the project to the Capitol Preservation Commission (CPC), a bicameral group of congressional leaders that included the visitor center's sponsor, Representative John Mica (R-FL).[53] Authority over the project was officially transferred to the CPC through the 2000 spending bill for Congress. The commission included a bipartisan group of key committee leaders, but the eighteen-member group was ultimately controlled by party leadership.[54] See Appendix A for the roster of the Capitol Preservation Committee in the 109th and 110th Congresses. Shuster's ultimate appointment to the commission quieted his protest and paved the way for further dialogue concerning the project.

Alan Hantman, the Capitol Architect, received a $2.8 million appropriation in March 1999 to review and revise the initial 1995 proposal. From this review, the commission envisioned development of a blueprint for construction. Co-chairs Strom Thurmond (R-SC) and Dennis Hastert (R-IL) estimated this phase of the project to require twelve to eighteen months of design at a cost of $12 million.[55] At this point, the project was expected to cost a total of $200 to $250 million and hopefully be completed by January 2005.[56] Legislation in 1997 first introduced plans for the Capitol Visitor Center and appropriated $100 million in initial funds for the project, insisting that further funding come in the form of private donations. Some contributors did make charitable donations to support construction of the facility, including a gift of $10 million from Microsoft and the Bill and Melinda Gates Foundation.[57]

With these initial funds dedicated to the project, a congressional groundbreaking ceremony was held on June 20, 2000, to signify the greatest construction project at the Capitol since the 1850s. This event marked the beginning of pre-construction activities, "including testing the soil for hazardous materials and items of archaeological value."[58] Unable to raise more than $65 million in private funds, however, progress slowed until 9/11. In the aftermath of September 11 and the anthrax attacks of October 2001, the Republican Congress appropriated a $40 billion emergency package. This appropriation included additional funding for the "subterranean facility" that would provide enhanced security for Congress in case of a future attack.[59]

With President Bush and members of Congress committing to fully fund the CVC, the project totaled a budget of $373.5 million—more than five times the original $71 million projection.[60] Part of the increased cost was due to added office space and upgraded security requirements. "For example, plans were redrawn to ventilate the center through Capitol elevator shafts, protecting the rest of the building from a possible release of contaminants."[61]

By April 2004, the price tag had risen to $421 million. The CVC (officially the ninth addition to the Capitol) was to be "the largest, most expensive construction project in the 200-year history of the building."[62] Delays due to changes in the weather, the design, and the security for the facility had derailed the center from its target completion date of December 2005. Activities of crews involved in elements of the first phase, including the excavation and the foundation, were overlapping with activities of crews working on second-phase electrical and plumbing.[63]

In November 2004, the Government Accountability Office (GAO) released a performance review that found the April budget inadequate by more than $100 million. The report suggested the construction cost of the CVC could exceed $558 million and that the facility would take until the fall of 2006 to be completed. The GAO estimated that the $421.1 million for the center and the $33.3 million for a special ventilation system was unrealistic. The center would surely cost at least $60.7 million more, and potentially would require an additional $43.5 million above that to cover additional unforeseen construction costs.[64]

In a hearing in May 2005, Architect Hantman attempted to justify an additional request for $37 million to finish the project—at a total cost of $528 million. Hantman testified that he believed the CVC could be completed for the GAO estimate of $517 million, but members of the committee were not convinced. "The truth is, nobody around here really believes that. . . . I hope that you do, but I doubt if there are many people up on this dais that do," said Representative Ray LaHood (R-IL).[65]

In the 109th Congress (2005–2006), Republicans eliminated the Appropriations Subcommittee on the Legislative Branch, giving jurisdiction over appropriations to the full committee. Representative David Obey (D-WI), the ranking Democrat on Appropriations at the time, criticized the decision—particularly pointing out the ramifications for oversight of the CVC. In a press release, he stated: "The construction of the Capitol Visitor Center (CVC) has been a story of serious mismanagement and colossal government waste. There is a great need for increased oversight of this project. However, during the reorganization of the Appropriations Committee, the Legislative Branch subcommittee, the body with the institutional knowledge and day-to-day responsibility for overseeing the Architect, was eliminated. The cost of the CVC, first estimated at $95 million, has ballooned to over $500 million. I have raised my concerns about this project several times in the past, and I continue to have serious objections to the current plan."[66] Upon taking majority control of the newly organized 110th Congress, Democrats reinstated the Appropriations Subcommittee on the Legislative Branch, returning jurisdiction over appropriations for the CVC.

By September 2006, the GAO estimates for the facility ran close to $600 million and offered a possible completion date of 2007. According to the Architect, "problems with the fire protection system, gift shops and utility will cause more delays."[67] Senator Wayne Allard (R-CO), chair of the Appropriations Legislative Branch Subcommittee, upon review of an action plan submitted by the Architect in response to Allard's request in a September hearing, found it unclear whether the plan was "sufficient to complete the project by the end of 2007 and without breaching $600 million in total costs."[68] Following the release of these estimates, Representative Obey and Representative Dennis Cardoza (D-CA) held a press conference to present the "Golden Drain Award" to the Congress and the Architect of the Capitol "for their work pouring taxpayer dollars down the drain with the Capitol Visitor Center." Likening management of the center to the Republican management of the federal budget, Obey stated: "The absolute lack of oversight has led to financial disaster."[69]

In February 2007, Alan Hantman retired at the end of his ten-year term as Architect of the Capitol. In the fall of 2006, the Senate Rules and Administration Committee received a list of four potential candidates from the American Institute of Architects, which had been a central figure to the appointment process in decades past. Congress hired a search firm to review the candidates. In the meantime, Deputy Architect and Chief Operating Officer Stephen Ayers offered to serve as acting Architect of the Capitol.[70] As of December 2009, Ayers was still serving in this capacity.

On June 22, 2007, the House passed the FY2008 Legislative Branch Appropriations Bill, providing $34 million in additional funds for the Capitol Visitor Center. The bill passed by a vote of 216 to 176.[71] By August 2007, the completion date had been pushed back to the fall of 2008. Yet some members were heartened by the progress on the center and pushed for continued oversight. Senator Allard, as chair of the Senate Appropriations Legislative Branch Subcommittee during the 109th Congress, held fifteen monthly hearings to oversee management of the project.[72]

The appropriations package for the legislative branch for FY2008, signed into law on December 26, 2007, granted $28,753,000 for the CVC, of which up to $8,500,000 could be used for operating costs. The facility opened its doors to the public on December 2, 2008. The total cost of the center had risen to $621 million.

Mixed Reviews

Reviews of the original plan and early construction were mixed. Some touted the project as a long overdue renovation to complete the vision of Olmsted's original 1874 vision for the Capitol grounds. Reflecting on the plans, Ronald Sarasin, a former congressman from Connecticut and president of the U.S. Capitol Historical Society, stated: "I think it is going to be spectacular."[73] Others, however, were less enthusiastic. Senator Kent Conrad (D-ND) said, "It is a moonscape," while Brian Furness, an officer of the Capitol Hill Restoration Society, remarked, "It is just plug ugly."[74]

Part of the concern over construction stemmed from the project's necessary removal of dozens of historic trees from the east front of the Capitol. These trees included a spectacular variety of species—"Yoshino cherry, American linden, red-flowering dogwood, Japanese black pine, London planetree, and gingko."[75] Perhaps the greatest loss will be the hundred-year-old tulip trees lining East Capitol Street. Of 346 trees on this side of the Capitol, 85 were memorial trees. Some of the 68 trees removed for the project included memorial trees, and CVC planners faced great pressure to treat these special trees with care. While 6 of them were destroyed, 8 of them were transplanted, "including a 45-foot seedling of Maryland's Liberty Tree, which survived for 224 years until it was irreparably damaged by a storm in 1999; the transplanting of that seedling meant moving 92 tons of tree and root ball."[76] Those trees that did not survive the renovations include some dedicated to former members of Congress. Reflecting on the loss of the Staggers Tree (named for former Congressman Harley O. Staggers Jr. [D-WV]), his former aide, Marguerite Furfari, opined, "It's not necessary to dig up the whole Capitol grounds for a rest stop and a toilet."[77] To preserve the legacy of these trees, the Office of the Architect of the Capitol plans to replant cuttings from the memorial trees around the Capitol.

Central to the plans for the CVC were security upgrades. Spokesman Lieutenant Dan Nichols of the Capitol Police explained, "What we currently have is a 19th-century building that is having to support 21st-century technology."[78] The CVC creates distance between visitor screening and the actual Capitol Building.[79] In a *Washington Post* report on the early stages of construction, Alan Hantman, Architect of the Capitol, stated: "Let's face it. The Capitol has not been built as a Disney World. It's been built as the center of our government. But it has to function as a museum, a place where people meet and talk, and a conference center. This will be a tremendous change for tourists, and the driving force is concern for security."[80] Given the centrality of security in the design for the project, some questioned the suggested purpose of the new facility. "The Capitol Visitor Center moniker is a misnomer, in a sense. . . . [T]he Capitol will have a new virtual museum, office building and high-technology refuge for members of Congress in times of crisis."[81] The grounds ultimately will be ringed by metal bollards, "which will be used to control pedestrian and vehicle access and will replace the mishmash of barriers and planters now lining the perimeter."[82] While the original vision included many amenities and a price tag of $71 million, additions to the project over the past several years included hearing rooms, office space, and an auditorium to "serve as an emergency legislative chamber."[83] These additions drove up the cost of the facility and were partly responsible for the $621 million price tag.

Consequently, a second concern involved the extraordinary cost of the project. Way over budget and far past its projected deadline, the CVC failed to garner substantial funding through private fund-raising. While several commemorative coins were minted to raise money for the facility, the total dollars raised fell far short of expectations. Several years and several hundred million dollars ago, Godfrey observed, "Part of the problem is that, unlike a museum, where a benefactor's name might be featured prominently at an exhibit, Congress is unlikely to allow that in the visitors center. The other part of the problem is that while voters might support the project, $200 million seems a little steep."[84] In fact, a group of taxpayer advocates, Citizens against Government Waste, voiced deep concern over the project during its construction. CAGW president Tom Schatz warned that "the Capitol Visitor Center shows all the signs of becoming a quintessential government boondoggle: ambitious engineering, a long construction schedule, and lack of strong private interest."[85] Schatz feared that, with the price tag increasing by the year, we ultimately would replace "the halls of democracy with a 580,000-square-foot information desk."[86] Reporters following the project observed: "Complaints about the project's costs are not new, and the GAO briefing represents the latest evidence that, despite quarterly reports and congressional oversight, costs and delays are continuing to mount."[87]

Part of the reason for so much criticism of the costs associated with the project was lawmakers' confusion over the central purpose of the facility. The Office of the Architect of the Capitol repeatedly justified the expense of the CVC to members of Congress by pointing not only to the enhanced visitor experience offered by the center but also to the additional usable House and Senate workspace provided for members of Congress. Yet several members, most notably Chairman of Appropriations Representative Obey (D-WI), were quite skeptical of the second function. He stated in a press release in 2005:

> The CVC will provide the House with little, if any, usable new workspace. . . . Majority Leadership staff have made decisions about the CVC's design without any real recognition of the needs of the Congress and what it would take to make the House space within the CVC functional. The current design of the CVC House space includes 87,000 square feet of space, of which only 3,200 square feet is for hearing rooms where public business can be conducted, and even this is designed inefficiently. This is because the real work of the Congress was not a primary consideration in its construction. It was constructed in such a way as to make it ready for television. The media room takes up two floors, wasting significant space, with limited room for staff or the public. The chief value of this opulent hearing space, and the accompanying new Radio and Television Gallery, seems to be as a high tech propaganda tool. . . . In addition, CVC contains an enormous Congressional auditorium to seat 400 people. I asked the Architect of the Capitol why the theatre hall was needed in addition to the two orientation rooms. First, I was told that it could be used to host large constituent groups. I have never brought a group that large to the Capitol, and I doubt many other Members ever have either. Then I was told that the theatre could serve as an alternate chamber for the House if the current chamber was being renovated. However, it is my understanding that the Ways and Means hearing room in the Longworth Building was originally designed to serve this same purpose. . . . Given the apparent redundancy of an alternative chamber in the CVC, what is the true motivation for the space? It is found on page 25 of the Final Design Report done 10 years ago: "The Library [of Congress] has long needed facilities that meet the public

demand for greater access to its historical and education programs. The CVC provides a singular opportunity to do this well." We are building a movie theatre for the Library of Congress, even though the Center already includes two orientation theatres for visitors. . . . The Majority Leadership has not lived up to its obligation to responsibly manage taxpayer funds. It needed to create workspace. Instead, it has created Taj Mahal show space. This bill includes $40.3 million for the CVC. I do not support this funding and I will oppose any bill that contains additional funding for this project.[88]

In addition to concerns over the cost and the necessary renovations, several lawmakers expressed concern over the implications of the project for the environment of Capitol Hill. While Representative Norton (D-DC) long advocated for the Capitol Visitor Center to increase security on the Capitol grounds, she adamantly opposed blockading streets around the Capitol Building. Even before the 1998 Capitol shootings, Pennsylvania Avenue was closed to through traffic (after the Oklahoma City bombing) to protect the White House, and portions of Delaware Avenue NE and C Street NE were closed to protect Senate office buildings. "It's made a fortress, frankly, of the White House. I don't think anybody . . . is going to allow the Secret Service solution to come to the Capitol," stated Norton.[89] Though Senator Don Nickles (R-OK) thought the Senate should consider the project, he warned in 1998, "The Capitol is the people's house. We want [them] to have access to it."[90]

Also noting the extreme changes in security brought to the White House after the Oklahoma City bombing, an editorial in the *Washington Times* after the Capitol shootings suggested:

The distinction between a barricade and a long subterranean edifice that provides the only public access to the [Capitol] building is a distinction without a difference. The misguided plans for a visitors center are no more justified on security grounds in the wake of Friday's shooting than they were on security or other grounds before Friday's shooting. In the wake of the killings . . . everyone would do well to remember that the Capitol and its 535 elected members stand as powerful and living symbols of freedom and openness. To close the Capitol off, to begin limiting individuals' access to their representatives, could bring out the worst in our own government.[91]

From the perspective of landscaping, Jerry Baum, co-chair of the

National Association for Olmsted Parks, reflected in a letter to the *Washington Post* that, while Olmsted's landscape made the Capitol the central feature of the grounds for visitors to the nation's capital, the new Capitol Visitor Center "destroys the visual and spatial relationships of the East Lawn and severs the continuity of the historic circulation pattern with a descending approach ramp."[92] For neighborhood residents of Capitol Hill, the CVC was not necessarily a welcome change to the D.C. landscape. Though the designers went to great pains to preserve the Capitol view, residents worried that the subterranean facility would send the wrong message to the community and visitors to the site: "On a recent tour, for community representatives, of the underground Capitol Visitor Center, Nevitt [a retired foreign service officer and head of the Capitol Hill Restoration Society] said, a colleague looked up from the construction site toward the Capitol Dome through a large skylight—a view that millions of tourists will probably share in the future. Will it become a metaphor, Nevitt asked, where people see their Capitol through a peephole?"[93] Nevitt continued, "'Certainly, for people who have lived up here for a while, they miss it a lot. . . . For people who have come here lately and never had it in the first place, I guess they may not miss it that much.'"[94]

Regardless of the symbolic message that the CVC might send, other critics suggested that the facility might encourage increased tourism at the nation's Capitol, ultimately causing a bottleneck of visitors trying to gain access to the building itself. Clarence Brown, a former congressman and president of the U.S. Capitol Historical Society, opposed the solution offered by the visitor center. He argued that creating the facility would simply exacerbate the crowding problem. He stated, "They are going to attract more people to the Capitol with this Disney-like visitors center." While room might be ample in the center, it is scarce in the Capitol, leading to a potential problem of rationing entrance into the building. Brown further reflected that if visitors are provided with the visitor center as a surrogate for viewing the actual Capitol or observing actual representatives at work, then "we will have lost something."[95]

Administrative Supervision of the Project

In 1991 Congress gave the Architect of the Capitol funds to develop a design concept for a Capitol Visitor Center along the lines of the project outlined in 1976. In 1993, after Appropriations approved the design concept, the Capitol Preservation Commission granted the Architect $2.6

million to develop a formal design. To accomplish this task, the Architect contracted RTKL Associates, Inc., and presented the product to Congress in 1995.[96] The CVC was to educate visitors, enhance security, and integrate into the existing landscape while improving the East Plaza.

With appropriation of necessary funds to begin the project, the Architect divided construction of the Capitol Visitor Center into two major phases. Sequence I, the first phase, included all excavation and foundation work. The Office of the Architect awarded the Sequence I contract to manage the construction project to the Gilbane Building Company in 2002. For a more detailed description of the chronology of project supervision, see Appendix B. Through a competitive bidding process, the Architect awarded the first major construction contract, worth nearly $100 million, to Centex Construction Company–Mid Atlantic Division. Centex was hired to do "site demolition, slurry wall construction, excavation, construction of columns, installation of site utilities, construction of the concrete and steel structure, waterproofing, and construction of a new service tunnel."[97]

Given rising congressional concern over the growing budget for the Capitol Visitor Center, in March 2003 the Architect hired Tishman Construction Corporation, a financial consulting firm, to do a financial analysis of the costs to date of the CVC. The Architect presented these findings to the GAO as well as to the House and Senate Appropriations Subcommittees on the Legislative Branch in June 2003. With additional appropriations through the FY2003 and FY2004 budgets for the Legislative Branch, the Architect awarded the Sequence II contract for infrastructure of the CVC to Manhattan Construction Company. This contractor worked to install all interior components, including but not limited to finish materials, marble floors, balcony seating, audio systems, light fixtures, ceilings, exhibit cases, photo murals, and bronze doors.

The Architect awarded the contract for designing the Exhibition Hall, a 16,500-square-foot space to orient visitors to the history of the Congress through artifacts and displays, to Ralph Appelbaum and Associates. The design also called for several films and interactive programs to be shown within the Exhibition Hall. These multimedia exhibits were created by Donna Lawrence Productions and Cortina Productions. Donna Lawrence produced three films for the CVC. The longest is a thirteen-minute orientation film to the U.S. Congress to be shown in the orientation theater at the entrance of the facility. The firm also created two shorter films on the House and the Senate for the Exhibition Hall. Cortina produced additional videos and interactive programs, including virtual tours and congressional quizzes for the Exhibition Hall.[98]

After the bulk of construction was completed in 2005 and 2006, the Architect requested funding from Congress to support operations of the CVC facility. The House Appropriations Committee was hesitant to provide operations funding in the FY2006 and FY2007 budgets due to the ever-fluctuating completion schedule. Nevertheless, the Architect awarded the CVC food service contract to Restaurant Associates starting May 31, 2007, and $8.5 million was appropriated for operations on December 26, 2007, through the FY2008 legislative branch appropriations bill. To manage the transition from a facility under construction to an operating visitor center, the Architect assembled a CVC Operations Transition Team. He further appointed Terrie Rouse as the chief executive officer for visitor services to begin acting as an administrative director in mid-September 2007. An operations consultant, JM Zell Partners, worked with the Architect to recommend personnel and procedures for the CVC.[99] For a diagram of the organization of supervision over the CVC, see figure 5.2.

CVC Oversight or the Lack Thereof

From an initial estimate of $71 million to the final cost of $621 million, the Capitol Visitor Center frustrated lawmakers, special interest groups, and citizens alike. Protesting such excessive costs to the federal government and thus the American taxpayer, the Blue Dog Coalition staged a press conference on October 29, 2003, on the steps of the Capitol Visitor Center construction site. In front of a literal hole, the group focused news media on the growing deficit hole facing the nation.[100] While there was general negative opinion concerning the cost overruns and construction delays, there was little consensus concerning the source of the problem. Oversight for the project, as illustrated in figure 5.2, spanned two branches of government, both houses of Congress, special commissions, administrative offices, working groups, and private management firms. In general, the failures of implementation were ascribed to poor planning, the ineptness of the Architect, the weak oversight of Congress and its representative bodies, the historical nature of the project, and unforeseen events.

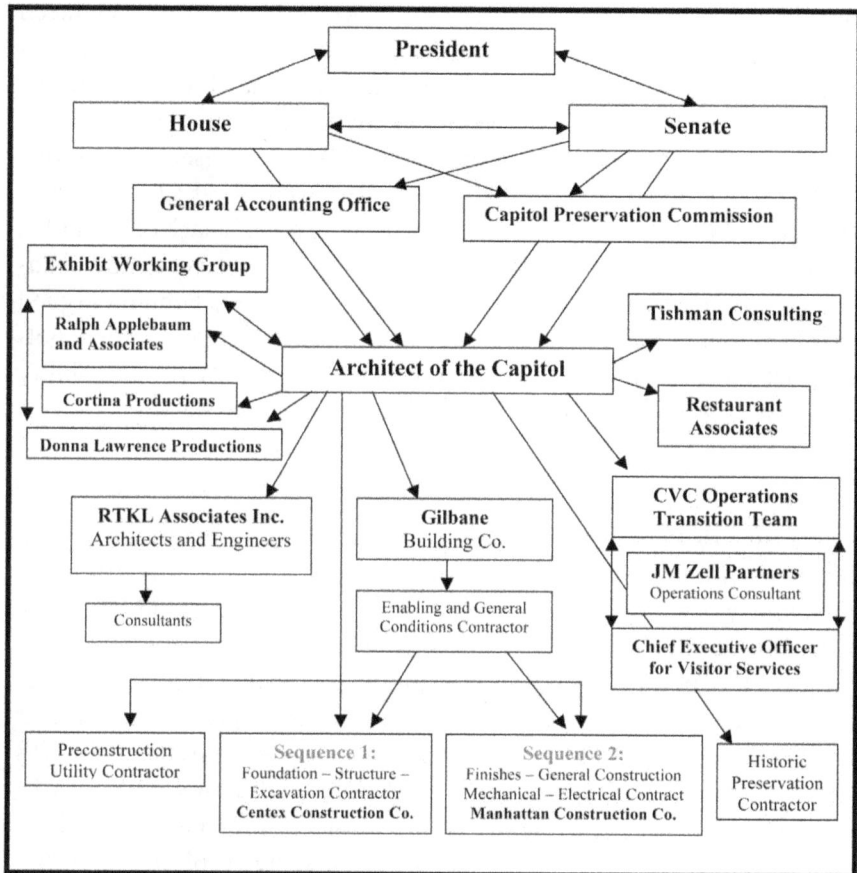

Figure 5.2: Organizational Chart Tracking Supervision of CVC. *Source:* Adapted from Debra K. Rubin and William J. Angelo, "Historic Expansion of U.S. Capitol," Engineering News–Record, June 17, 2002, http://www.construction .com/NewsCenter/Headlines/ENR/20020613a.asp (accessed on December 24, 2007); and Office of the Architect of the Capitol, "2005 Activities Summary," http://www.aoc.gov/cvc/project_info/milestones_2005.cfm (accessed on December 28, 2007).

Unforeseen Events

Oversight of the project was further frustrated by unforeseen events that led to additional costs and delays. For example, in preliminary excavation, workers discovered an unmapped well. Additionally, according to Tom Fontana, a spokesman for the Architect of the Capitol, not only did the weather and obstacles such as an Amtrak tunnel only eighteen inches below ground interfere with construction, certain developments required additional preconstruction activities that slowed down the project considerably. "Preconstruction activities such as the installation of noise reduction windows in the Capitol and tree preservation added to the cost of the project, as did the necessity to screen vehicles that enter the site."[101] While some of the delays were the result of a lack of a detailed design, other delays were attributable to unforeseen events and inadequate contingency funds.[102] Defending the Architect, Fontana argued that throughout the process all office expenditures were warranted, noting that the 2003 analysis provided by the Government Accountability Office did not cite "any instance of mismanagement or waste."[103]

Architect Hantman to Blame

According to Representative Jack Kingston (R-GA), Hantman was to blame for not predicting the engineering complications of the tunnel to the Library of Congress as well as for accepting unrealistic bid estimates. Kingston was not alone in his criticism of Hantman's management of the project. An omnibus spending measure in 2004 called for the "replacement of the architect's chief operating officer to improve management in the office, and . . . direct[ed] the GAO to study whether the architect's duties could be better performed by private contractors."[104] Similarly, H.R. 5521—Legislative Branch Appropriations Bill for Fiscal Year 2007 called for the Architect of the Capitol to be stripped of any authority over the CVC. "All functions of the office [were to be] transferred to the Government Accountability Office, effective October 1, until a new architect [could be] confirmed."[105] The Senate did not approve the measure in conference, but this gesture attests to the presence of those critical of the Architect's handling of the project.

Congress to Blame

Special interest groups critical of the center found Congress to be at least equally to blame for the delays. Steve Ellis, of Taxpayers for Common Sense, called the architect "a convenient whipping boy." Members of Congress, in his mind, were ultimately responsible for an "untenable plan" and the failure to adequately manage costs. "Congress has the fiduciary responsibility to oversee this boondoggle in their backyard, and they are conveniently putting their head in the ground and only popping up every time the GAO comes out with another criticism and a cost increase."[106] Some members of Congress similarly held congressional leadership accountable for the lack of effective oversight. Representative James Moran (D-VA), a member of the Appropriations Committee, refused to hold Hantman entirely responsible for the overruns because Congress consistently expanded the scope of the project over the course of a decade. Much like with the highway and tunnel project in Boston called the "Big Dig," the cost overruns seemed to be limitless. "Right now, it's an enormous excavation project, and I think the members are concerned," Moran said.[107]

The GAO also claimed that a major source of the problem was weak congressional oversight. According to Comptroller General David M. Walker, "There was an expectation gap. . . . Everybody has their idea of what they thought they were getting for their money. And some of those ideas were based on artist renderings—but those artist renderings may or may not have been funded for. It was pretty clear that there needed to be a more rigorous and disciplined process."[108]

As a representative body of the Congress, the Capitol Preservation Commission is a small group of nearly twenty members of leadership that was given decision-making authority over the project in 1999 and exercised this authority during the formative phases of the CVC. While the Capitol Preservation Commission was ultimately responsible for making important decisions regarding the CVC, the body met infrequently. A report by Lee suggested in 2003, "Instead, the work [was] handed off to senior congressional staffers who attend[ed] weekly meetings with the Office of the Architect of the Capitol and representatives of three contractors."[109] Rather than approving of changes in a group forum, key members serving on the commission offered individual approval.[110] In September 2002, finding the oversight provided by the CPC inadequate, Congress stipulated in a $48 million appropriations package for the CVC that all expenditures be authorized by leadership of the House and Senate Appropriations Committees. In addition, the Architect was required to comply with GAO reviews of project progress on a quarterly basis.

After a tour of the construction site, Representative Kingston explained the logic behind the change in the chain of command: "The architect ended up having 10 or 15 different Type A personalities telling him what to do at any given moment. . . . So we've changed it so that if somebody comes to him that he's got to run it back to the committee process. . . . The poor guy was trying to keep a lot of people happy, and we're protecting him from that type of thing."[111] Tom Fontana, the project communications officer through the Office of the Architect of the Capitol, reiterated, "The Capitol is unlike any other building. . . . The security concerns, the needs of Congress—here, you've got a lot of bosses."[112] With each member pushing for a particular CVC element, it was difficult for the full body of appropriators to cut costs for the project. In the end, Comptroller General David M. Walker argued that the escalating budget was due to "the continued growth in scope, the lack of a detailed design and the failure of Congress to rein in changes."[113]

Grandeur at Any Cost

Thomas Fontana, the Architect's project communications officer, suggested, "The Capitol is the front door to our nation. . . . [It's expensive, but] we didn't want to cut corners, we didn't want to sacrifice quality."[114] And this quality was costly. "The Tennessee Pink marble for flooring and decorative details costs up to $200 a cubic foot, depending on how it's cut and finished."[115] Valuable for its "density, color, and durability," the marble is the same as that used for the U.S. Capitol as well as that used for several other public buildings, including the Washington Monument, the Jefferson and Lincoln Memorials, the National Gallery of Art, the Smithsonian, the National Cathedral, the Metropolitan Museum of Art, and Philadelphia's city hall.[116] It is only mined from two active quarries, both owned by one company, the Tennessee Marble Company. According to John Barron of Manhattan Construction, one of the contractors for the CVC, the only other clients to take such a "spare-no-expense-approach" are Las Vegas hotels. "It's very substantial construction: the best marble that you can find in this country, tiles, bronze doors."[117] "'Is it off target? Yes, but I really can't blame one single individual,' said [Representative Bob Ney (R-OH)], citing the weather, outdated maps, new security concerns and other factors. 'It's the last great construction project for the Capitol. There's nowhere else to go.'"[118]

In conclusion, several distinct arguments were made to explain the cost and schedule overruns. Some suggested that the project suffered from poor planning on the part of both Congress and the Architect as well as unforeseen events, such as bad weather and unexpected preconstruction hurdles. Others suggested that the Architect was largely to blame for not providing a more realistic construction and cost schedule. Still others claimed that the ultimate responsibility for oversight of the center rested with Congress, and that members were unwilling to exercise restraint. Finally, there are those who argued that the CVC is historic in its design and purpose and consequently cutting corners was not possible.

The CVC building project was described on its opening day as "a perfect exemplar of bureaucratically conceived and executed architecture" by one article appearing in the *Washington Post*.[119] "It grew by fits and starts, reflecting the two prevailing political impulses of the past decade: fear of terrorism and growth of government. Eventually, the dog (the visitor center) was being wagged by the tail (everything else)."[120] The following section presents the advocacy coalition framework as a theoretical lens through which to understand the management and development of this massive addition to the U.S. Capitol.

Applying an Advocacy Coalition Framework to the CVC

One of the first requirements of the advocacy coalition framework (ACF) is to examine the overall policy process to more fully understand a given policy domain, from problem definition to evaluation and change. This type of perspective rests on a long-term analysis, typically spanning at least a decade or more. The previous examination of the Capitol Visitor Center attests to the value of this approach. Without looking at the evolution of this project over the course of the last full decade, it is impossible to appreciate the factors leading to the vision, design, appropriation, development, construction, and oversight of this major addition to the Capitol landscape. Originally envisioned in 1976, the Capitol Visitor Center did not open to the public until 2008. Utilizing the ACF perspective provides sensitivity to the "role for technical information, the passage of time, the policy subsystem, a range of participants, and learning in the policy process."[121]

The information and experience provided by the 1998 Capitol shootings and the events of 9/11 and anthrax both propelled the implementation of the CVC as well as led to its redesign to incorporate state-of-the-art security. The passage of time led to several unforeseen obstacles in construction and oversight, causing major schedule delays and extraordinary costs. The supervision of the CVC illustrates a policy subsystem that includes a complex advocacy coalition, including but not limited to members of the House and Senate Appropriations Subcommittees on the Legislative Branch; members serving as policy entrepreneurs (such as Representatives John Mica and Eleanor Holmes Norton); members of the budget-hawk Blue Dog Coalition as well as budget-hawk interest groups, such as Taxpayers for Common Sense and Citizens against Government Waste; the Office of the Architect; the Capitol Preservation Commission (including congressional leadership); the Exhibit Working Group (including Senate and House historians and other administrators); the Capitol Police; a laundry list of consultants, contractors, and financial analysts; the Government Accountability Office; and the president. Each of these actors played a nontrivial role in the development of this policy over the last decade. This analysis illuminates the core elements required by the ACF approach when applied to contracting out. As Greve suggests, it is critical to examine: "(a) the alliances formed between different actors; (b) the beliefs they hold; (c) the political, administrative, and organizational context of contracting out; and (d) the learning process that [has taken] place."[122]

Concerning the first element, the alliances formed between actors, the CVC policy subsystem was characterized by two distinct alliances. On the one hand, there were those supporting the Office of the Architect and the CVC for its facilitation of enhanced security, commitment to educational exhibits, and provision of amenable visitor facilities. This group included the Capitol Police, the Exhibit Working Group, the several contractors, the Capitol Preservation Commission, and a few interest groups, such as the U.S. Capitol Historical Society. On the other hand, there were those opposing the Office of the Architect for poor supervision of the construction schedule and costs associated with the CVC project. Actors in this alliance include members on the House and Senate Appropriations Subcommittees on the Legislative Branch, members of the Blue Dog Coalition, and special interest groups such as Taxpayers for Common Sense.

The beliefs held by these two groups also differed dramatically. Supporting coalitions were united in the belief that the CVC would enhance the educational experience as well as the comfort and safety of visitors to the nation's Capitol. Opposing coalitions were united in the belief that the CVC destroyed the historic landscape as well as the important symbolism of openness the U.S. Capitol has come to hold for visitors from around the world. While some of the enduring criticisms of the project seem to have come from minority protest of majority party leadership, opponents were to be found on both sides of the aisle. These opponents mourned the loss of days gone by when visitors could enter the Capitol from its grand steps rather than from its basement.

The second element examined in this analysis was the political, administrative, and organizational context of contracting out the design and construction of the CVC. The political context illustrated the importance of major events in influencing the allocation of resources and provision of oversight for contracted-out government services. Reflecting the literature on crisis management, certain critical events led to hasty decisions in the case of the CVC. On the one hand, these events led to action that had been delayed for multiple decades. On the other hand, the haste with which the design, construction, and implementation decisions were made was perhaps responsible for the inadequate construction schedule and hugely insufficient budget. It could also be argued that because the problem was defined in the context of crisis, lawmakers found it difficult to rein in costs associated with the ever-expanding project. Every expense could be justified in the name of security.

In terms of the administrative context of the contracting-out process, the CVC project marked the first time in the Capitol's history that the Congress had contracted out such a service. The sheer size of the project forced the Office of the Architect of the Capitol to bring in help from the private sector, but the sheer size of the project also made effective oversight nearly impossible. The organizational chart depicted above (figure 5.2) clearly illustrates the nightmare faced by those public officials tasked with overseeing the CVC project. Multiple chains of command, conflicting financial reports, construction delays, overlapping contract schedules, and appointed yet independent working groups joined to make this project a perfect storm. For all practical purposes, the Architect initially received a blank check issued in the name of "homeland security" and hastily began construction on a project that lasted nearly a decade.

But learning did happen within the policy subsystem. Blank checks became a thing of the past, and the Architect was required to appear before Congress on at least a monthly basis to give updated progress reports. To verify his claims, the Congress further requested frequent witness testimony by GAO representatives tasked with oversight of CVC activities. Members on the House side threatened to remove all authority over the CVC from the Office of the Architect and vest it in a CVC governing board, while members of the Senate threatened to appoint an executive director. In the end, it is clear that the Architect was eventually held more accountable for spending, but nevertheless the CVC took nine years to finish and cost nearly nine times the original estimate for the project. It seems from the CVC case that the existence of advocacy coalition frameworks, when government contracts out services, only frustrates the efficiency of service provision. This conclusion must be qualified by the fact that it is drawn from only one case. In addition, it is possible that the same problems could have surfaced even if the Architect had monopolized supervision of the project.

The CVC Opens

On December 2, 2008, the Capitol Visitor Center opened to the public. A grand opening ceremony was held in the morning and included an invocation and benediction; music by the U.S. Marine Band, the American Youth Chorus, and the Congressional Chorus; poetry by U.S. poet laureate Rita Dove; and addresses by members of Congress and Acting Architect of the Capitol Stephen Ayers.[123] This date marked the 145th anniversary of the raising of the Statue of Freedom to the top of the Capitol Dome. The year also celebrated the 200th anniversary of the birth of President Abraham Lincoln—the single person most responsible for the emancipation of slaves during the Civil War. This significant moment in U.S. history would be immortalized in the expansive Emancipation Hall of the Capitol Visitor Center. The largest space of the CVC was given this name to honor the slaves "who built the Capitol by clearing the ground, quarrying stone, sawing timber, and performing other tasks."[124]

At the ceremony, several dignitaries and lawmakers made speeches about the facility. Speaker Nancy Pelosi (D-CA) noted the significance of the name of the grand hall in the CVC and reflected on the role of slaves in the construction of the Capitol and the role of President Lincoln as the "Great Emancipator." She further stated: "This new addition to our majestic Capitol embodies our nation's ability to adapt while preserving our essential American character. . . . As both members and visitors enjoy the educational benefits of [the] Capitol Visitor Center, we will be inspired to explore new paths and to write new chapters in our nation's great history."[125] The Historian of the Library of Congress, Dr. James H. Billington, concluded that the CVC "provides a splendidly presented civics lesson within a glorious new structure that will make the Capitol—the icon of our republic—more accessible than ever before."[126] House Minority Leader John Boehner (R-OH) and other legislators recognized the sacrifice of Jacob Chestnut and John Gibson—the two U.S. Capitol Police officers shot in the line of duty in 1998—and attributed the construction of the facility largely to this event.[127] Senate Majority Leader Harry Reid (D-NV) reflected on the transformation of the East Front of the Capitol from a parking lot for members of Congress in the 1960s to a magnificent and safe Capitol Visitor Center.

The final structure covers 580,000 square feet and includes three levels. The space dedicated to visitors includes two levels of the facility. Emancipation Hall alone is 20,000 square feet.[128] Six huge skylights illuminate the room, which is lined with twenty-three statues moved from the Capitol's Statuary Hall. Through these skylights visitors see the Capitol Dome towering above. The crowing gem of the hall is the nineteen-foot plaster model of Thomas Crawford's Statue of Freedom, housed since 1993 in the basement rotunda of the Russell Senate Office Building. The bronze Statue of Freedom was raised to sit atop the Capitol Dome on December 2, 1863.[129] The plaster model stands in Emancipation Hall at the entrance to the interactive Exhibition Hall.

Entering the lower level of the CVC, visitors find an eleven-foot-tall model of the Capitol Dome. This hands-on model provides the keystone to *A More Perfect Union*—the exhibit space of the hall. Significant documents from the Library of Congress and the National Archives address various themes to illustrate the role and impact of Congress in American society. Artifacts include George Washington's letter to the Continental Congress announcing the victory over the British at Yorktown, President Jefferson's confidential letter to Congress requesting funding for the Lewis and Clark expedition, President Roosevelt's "Day of Infamy" speech to Congress, and many others.[130] Six alcoves use multimedia to trace the history of policy issues faced by Congress and adaptations to congressional life. Within these alcoves, architectural models capture the evolution of the Capitol itself over the last two hundred years. At each end of the hall, visitors find copies of the original Constitution highlighted to emphasize the role of the two branches of Congress in our system of separated powers.

Exhibition Hall includes two small theaters, one modeled after the

House and one after the Senate. These theaters provide live feeds of the House and Senate floors when Congress is in session. In these rooms, visitors can also utilize touch-screen displays to find out information about their members of Congress. While the Statue of Freedom stands guard at the entrance of the hall, the Lincoln catafalque is enshrined at the rear. This catafalque is the structure on which President Lincoln's casket rested as he lay in state in the Capitol Rotunda in 1865. This exhibit stands testament to the ceremonial functions of Congress, including lying-in-state ceremonies often held in the Capitol Rotunda to honor American presidents, among others.[131] Before leaving the facility, visitors watch a preliminary film in one of two large orientation theaters to prepare them for the final experience, a guided forty-five-minute Capitol tour.

Even given the high praise bestowed on the new facility at the grand opening, the event was not without controversy. Senate Majority Leader Harry Reid praised the center for providing a shelter for visitors who wait in long lines in the summer and winter to enter the Capitol. In an offhand comment, however, Reid further noted that "[in] the summertime, because of the humidity and how hot it gets here, you could literally smell the tourists coming into the Capitol."[132] While the comment was met with laughter, news coverage of the remark was not so kind to Senator Reid.

Also clouding over the ceremonies and press conferences surrounding the opening of the facility was widespread criticism concerning budget overruns and delay. The final cost of the CVC was $621 million. Given the original budget of $71 to $125 million and the revised budget of $265 million, many inside and outside of Washington, D.C., cringed at the expense of the new structure. House Appropriations Committee Chairman David Obey (D-WI) periodically suggested abandoning the project and "burying the giant hole dug on the east front of the Capitol." He charged that the CVC was "full of glitzy stuff, without addressing the real needs of this institution." With Representative Dennis Cardoza (D-CA), Representative Obey used news conferences to decry the facility. Similarly, Steve Ellis, vice president of the watchdog group Taxpayers for Common Sense, commented: "They could actually have an educational display on this project . . . called the Anatomy of a Congressional Boondoggle."[133] In light of the overruns, critics further questioned the timing of the opening of the facility. One reporter suggested that the delays and overruns had led the CVC to be regarded as a "bloated, behind-schedule

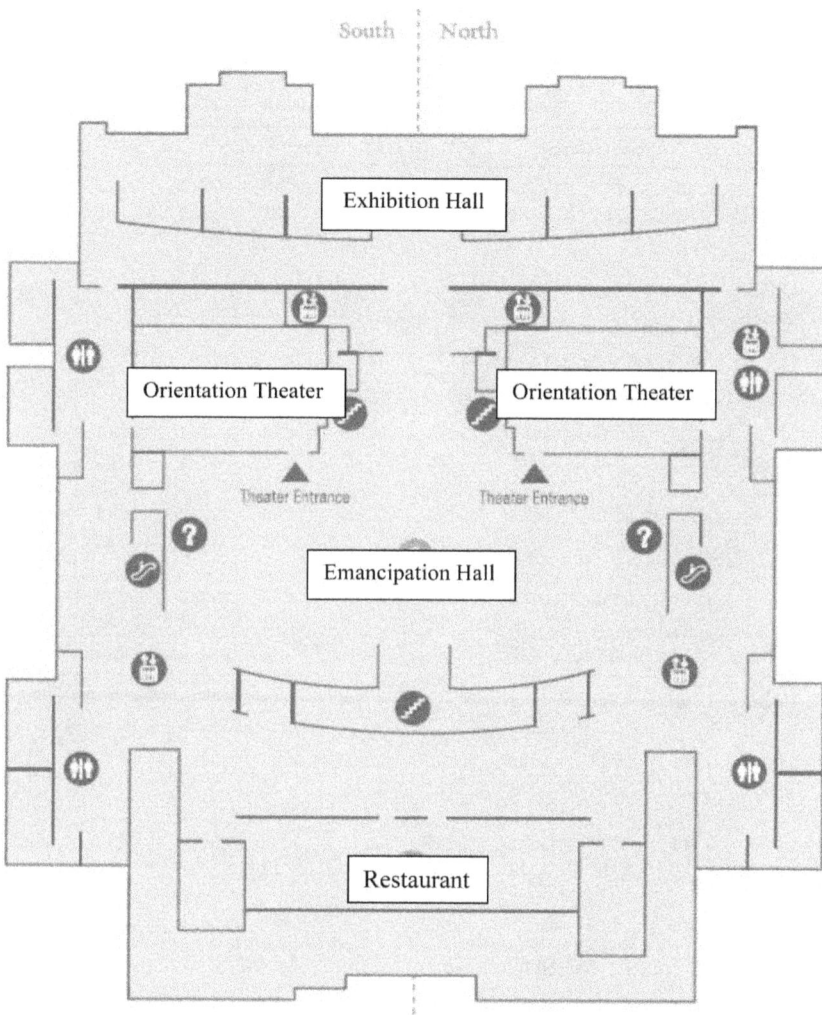

South : North

Exhibition Hall

Orientation Theater   Orientation Theater

Theater Entrance   Theater Entrance

Emancipation Hall

Restaurant

Lower level of the U.S. Capitol Visitor Center. (Adapted from "U.S. Capitol Visitor Guide: Lower Level," U.S. Capitol Visitor Center, available from http://www.visitthecapitol.gov/Visit/US_Capitol_Visitor_Guide.pdf.)

Taj Mahal—a public project symbolic of Washington waste and inefficiency. It's no coincidence that the media tour was put off until after the elections."[134]

    Facing criticism over the cost overruns for the new facility, Stephen Ayers, as the Acting Architect of the Capitol, defended the CVC at a news

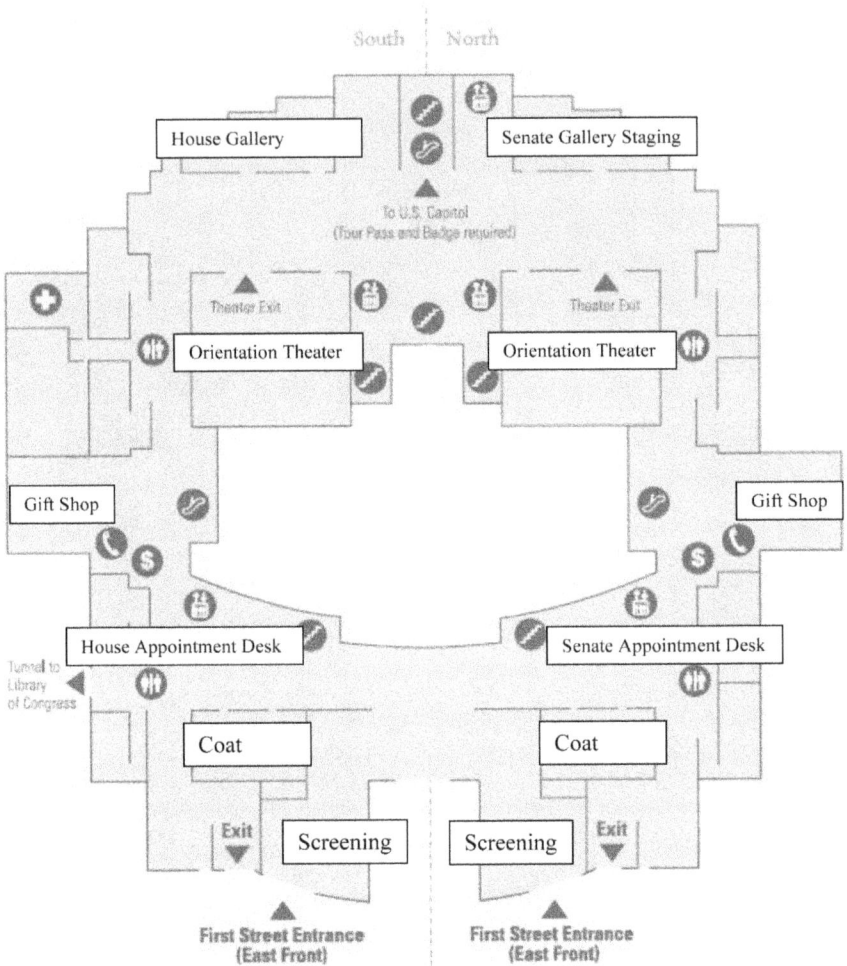

Upper level of the U.S. Capitol Visitor Center. (Adapted from "U.S. Capitol Visitor Guide: Upper Level," U.S. Capitol Visitor Center, available from http://www.visitthecapitol.gov/Visit/US_Capitol_Visitor_Guide.pdf.)

conference before the grand opening. He called it "a treasure in itself" and stated, "I don't think it's extravagant. We have built a building that's here to last another 215 years."[135] Only the finest materials were used in construction of the project, including mahogany, bronze, granite, and marble. Ayers suggested that the facility provides "a respectful and dignified way to enter the People's House."[136]

The CVC also came under fire by certain lawmakers arguing that the exhibits lacked reference to the nation's religious heritage. Senator Jim DeMint (R-SC) particularly protested the facility, demanding that changes be made to recognize this heritage through displays of our national motto ("In God We Trust") and the Pledge of Allegiance. In a press release, DeMint stated: "The Capitol Visitor Center is designed to tell the history and purpose of our nation's Capitol, but it fails to appropriately honor our religious heritage that has been critical to America's success."[137] He further asserted that political correctness should not lead to censorship of historical reference to God.[138] DeMint was joined by Congressman Randy Forbes (R-VA) and members of the Congressional Prayer Caucus in his protests. To avoid delay to the opening of the CVC, Senate leadership agreed to consider changes. One of these changes included the prominent placement of a stone engraved with "In God We Trust," which would cost an additional $150,000.[139] The engraving was added to the CVC in September 2009.

In light of this agreement, the Freedom From Religion Foundation filed suit against the Architect of the Capitol for establishment of religion. The organization claimed that congressional funding of these engraved additions to the CVC gave "actual and apparent government endorsement and advancement of religion" and discriminated against nonreligious Americans.[140]

The final set of criticism stemmed from the imagery created by the architectural features of the CVC. The facility was built entirely underground in an effort to enhance security while preserving the original Olmsted vision for the Capitol grounds. Visitors enter the CVC by descending from the street down a set of outdoor stairways. Upon entering the underground building, they proceed through screening with magnetometers at least three hundred feet from the Capitol itself.

Not only does this design choice symbolically express a view of and stance toward the public, it also physically limits public access to the Capitol. Besides concern over the cost of the project, Ellis further worried that lawmakers might use the CVC to excuse restricted Capitol access. "We spent $621 million of taxpayers' money in this project and I hope that it doesn't end up restricting or limiting access or become an impediment to access to the Capitol, the 'people's house,' where they can interact with their elected representatives."[141]

Two separate critical reviews of the CVC ran in major newspapers

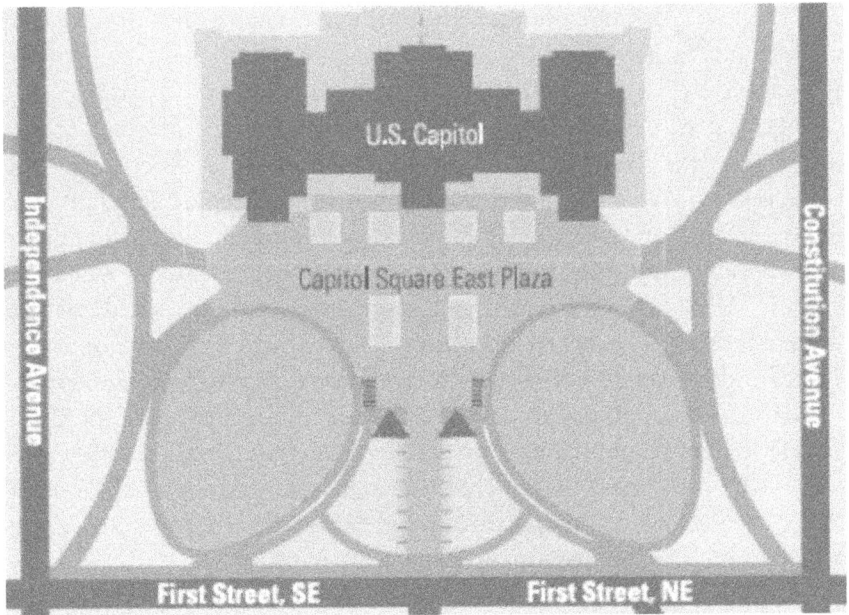

Location of the Capitol Visitor Center. (Adapted from "U.S. Capitol Visitor Guide: Capitol Location," U.S. Capitol Visitor Center, available from http:// www.visitthecapitol.gov/Visit/US_Capitol_Visitor_Guide.pdf.)

on its opening day. Catesby Leigh, who writes about public art and architecture for the *Wall Street Journal,* questioned the underground design, the location, the size, and the purpose of the facility. In terms of design, Leigh suggested that lawmakers had other options. They could have adopted the original design concept of "a monumental gateway, situated well in front of the building," as proposed by Benjamin Henry Latrobe in 1811 for the Capitol Building.[142] Latrobe's design called for a Greek Doric portico, "a temple-like entrance gate," on the Capitol's West Front (the side facing the Mall rather than the Supreme Court).[143] According to Leigh, this above-ground design would have "provided a dignified public entrance" and "an inspiring, secure new approach to—as well as screening at a safe distance from—the existing building."[144] Not only did he criticize the symbolism of the subterranean structure of the CVC, he further lamented the loss of the experience once shared by awe-struck visitors traversing the grand steps to the Capitol Rotunda. "The magic of the thrilling outdoor ascent is gone." When faced with an opportunity to build a Capitol Visitor Center in an environment of terrorism as a

Aerial view of the U.S. Capitol and Capitol Visitor Center. (Adapted from photograph provided courtesy of the Architect of the Capitol.)

"monumental expression of America's defense of civilization," Leigh concluded that "Washington chose to dig itself into a hole."[145]

Philip Kennicott of the *Washington Post* used the two fronts of the Capitol, West and East, as physical expressions of the dualistic nature of American government. The West Front, with its grand staircases and stately view of the National Mall, represents the grandeur, authority, tradition, and ceremony of a republic. The East Front, with its modest view and accessible entries, represents the equality, accessibility, and popular sovereignty of a democracy. According to Kennicott, "the East face has been demolished by the new Visitor Center, a tragically misconceived and overscale addition" to the Capitol.[146]

Visitors enter the facility by descending two long, gradual stairways from the street to the entrance of the CVC. These two walkways are divided by a raised promenade, creating what some have likened to a "bridge, which seems to cross a kind of moat."[147] At the end of the descent, visitors are greeted by cubic modernistic gates reminiscent of

Northeast entrance to the underground U.S. Capitol Visitor Center.
(Photograph taken on April 26, 2009, by Fletcher6. This file is licensed under
Creative Commons Attribution ShareAlike 3.0. Use of this photograph does not
suggest endorsement by its author.)

entrances to bunkers or "guard towers." While one of the major goals
of building the facility underground was to minimize the visual impact
of the CVC on the original landscaping design of Frederick Olmsted,
Kennicott charges that the end result of the design is a "tragically misconceived and overscale addition . . . a historical and aesthetic jumble,
a nonsensical place and a gross disfigurement of one of this country's
most important and iconic buildings."[148] The avenues are now very well
defined, with rows of tulip poplars bounded by ever-rising walls of stone.
This is a somewhat different setting than Olmsted's green curvilinear
landscape sprinkled with a variety of commemorative trees and dot-
ted with park benches, creating unanticipated picturesque views of the
Capitol Dome for visitors to the nation's capital. For some, this change is
welcome in that it provides much greater accessibility and better quality
accommodations to Capitol visitors. For others, "the loss of green space,

Visitors entering the U.S. Capitol Visitor Center on its opening day. (Courtesy of the Office of the Architect of the Capitol.)

the loss of old trees, the loss of the gentle, democratic approach to the Capitol is huge."[149]

In the midst of the pomp and circumstance surrounding the opening of the facility, lawmakers, historians, and journalists made reference to the symbolic importance of the U.S. Capitol to democratic nations around the world. Speaker Pelosi ended her remarks at the opening ceremony stating: "With that reverence for our history and dedication to progress, may this Temple of Democracy continue to be a place where people of diverse background and opinion can find common ground for the common good."[150] Some noted the inscription in the U.S. Capitol as well as on an engraving at the entrance to the CVC that invokes the words of Rufus Choate, a member of Congress from Massachusetts in the mid-nineteenth century. "We have built no temple but the Capitol. We consult no common oracle but the Constitution." Others referred to the Capitol as "America's great temple of democracy."[151] The Historian of the Library of Congress, Dr. Billington, drew parallels between Thomas Jefferson's vision for the Capitol and the vision realized by the CVC. "Thomas Jefferson described the Capitol as 'the first temple dedicated to

Emancipation Hall—View of the U.S. Capitol through skylight. (Adapted from photograph provided courtesy of the Architect of the Capitol.)

the sovereignty of the people,' and he worked with his architect Latrobe to make it more inviting to the public by adding a grand stairway to its entrance."[152] For Billington and several others in attendance at the event, the magnificent facility invited the public to experience Congress by figuratively (and somewhat physically) rolling out a red carpet on the East Front of the Capitol.

Upon closer review of Jefferson's vision, however, it seems that the Capitol as a "temple" was significant because it served as an edifice erected to acknowledge and venerate the power of the people. As Benjamin Franklin noted at the Constitutional Convention, "In free Governments the rulers are the servants, and the people their superiors & sovereigns."[153] Jefferson wanted the entrance to this secular temple to capture this relationship through a grand stairway that would welcome the people to their house. It is hard to believe that he would have expected citizens to descend into a subterranean facility to clear a security checkpoint before entering the Capitol through its basement. Lawmakers at the opening ceremony recognized and glorified the Capitol as a temple, but the setting surrounding their words and the view of the towering Capitol Dome through a literal glass ceiling begged observers to question the contemporary deity glorified by this iconic building.

Conclusion

Julian Zelizer suggests in his book *On Capitol Hill* that congressional reform "is the work of the tortoise, not the hare."[154] I can offer no better summary of the evolution of the Capitol Visitor Center than his. This chapter examines the evolution of the policy debate surrounding the Capitol Visitor Center and the subsequent debate over management of the massive project. The evolving security demands and the escalating costs associated with construction were central to the political debate surrounding the construction of the CVC. It was difficult for Congress to provide the necessary oversight in part because of the amorphous parameters of the project and in part because of the contracted-out management. The mission of the CVC seemed constantly in flux. At times, the mission focused on greeting, orienting, and educating visitors to the Capitol. At times, the mission focused on protecting the Capitol Building and its inhabitants from numerous security threats. At still other times, the mission focused on providing additional office space to members of Congress that would be in close proximity to the House and Senate floors. Without a central and consistent goal, those responsible for overseeing the management of the project lacked the means for holding the Office of the Architect accountable for cost overruns and construction delays. This problem was exacerbated by the numerous players involved in the design, execution, and oversight of the project as a whole. The old adage that "too many cooks in the kitchen spoils the soup" could not provide a truer picture of the management of the CVC construction project. In this way, the CVC speaks to the broader problem of inefficiency that is an inherent and enduring characteristic of congressional life.

The advocacy coalition framework developed by Sabatier and Jenkins-Smith has proven useful for understanding the evolution of the Capitol Visitor Center from its initial conception more than three decades ago to its completion in late 2008.[155] The complex range of actors within the policy subsystem, the long-term issue evolution, and the role of both institutional design and environmental forces shaping the development of the CVC lend support for the theoretical assumptions of the

ACF. In the relatively partisan-free policy environment of congressional administration, the advocacy coalitions take on unique shape and give us a glimpse at possibly new avenues for exploring the applications of the ACF.

While not much research has focused on the Capitol Visitor Center, it is now a central component of visitors' experience when exploring the U.S. Capitol. It is an important addition to the Capitol landscape, and its story sheds light on legislative behavior and project management. Those who study Congress should pay attention not only to the historical evolution of congressional facilities and Capitol culture, but also to the atypical but significant policy domains affecting legislative spending and operations such as the CVC. Future studies on Congress might benefit from the areas of research utilized in this chapter, including government contracting, the advocacy coalition framework, and crisis management.

The chapter concludes with a consideration of the architectural significance of this addition to the Capitol Complex. Through a detailed treatment of the history and evolution of the CVC, these pages document an important period of the Capitol's architectural history. While great effort was made to limit the physical impact of the facility on the original Olmsted design for the Capitol grounds, the resulting structure has faced great criticism for the imagery it creates. In the final chapter, the symbolic meaning of this structure is revisited within the context of the overall impact of terrorism on the U.S. Congress.

6

THE SOCIAL MEANING OF CONGRESSIONAL CHANGE

Expressive, Behavioral, and Symbolic Elements of Institutional Reform

> Every beginning is a consequence—every beginning ends something.
> —Paul Valéry

This book explores the impact of terror on Capitol Hill. During the fall of 2001, two separate events combined to raise awareness among decision makers concerning the need for threat assessment, heightened security, and emergency preparedness. The Capitol and its inhabitants became a target for those who would do harm to our nation. The tentacles of change introduced in the aftermath of this period reached every office, every meeting room, every corridor, and even every sidewalk in and around Capitol Hill. From the handling of constituent mail, to the structure of the committee system, to the processing of visitors through the Capitol, these changes impacted the way Congress conducts business on a daily basis.

It is the argument of this book that Congress is an evolving institution with a definite culture. As an institution, Congress responds to change in its political and social environment. These responses carry expressive, behavioral, and symbolic implications for the people, the processes, and the climate of the institution at large. The measures taken by the Congress to respond to the threat of terrorism in the fall of 2001 are laden with meaning. The unifying theme of all of these changes is an increased focus on security, which holds implications for the actual and perceived openness of our democratic legislative institution.

As Goodsell argues, there is social meaning in the construction and operations of buildings that house democratic politics.[1] First, the design

Table 6.1: Social Meanings of Structural and Procedural Changes

	Expressive	Behavioral	Societal
Types of social meaning sought	Ideals and values embedded in features of design	Design elements that shape user conduct	Symbolic impact of design on the public
Topics of analysis (by chapter)			
History of attacks on Capitol Complex (chapter 1)	Capitol grounds kept open, scenic, and accessible to demonstrate popular sovereignty; attacks lead to more focus on security while maintaining openness	Gradual structural and procedural changes increase security; introduction of security cameras, magnetometers, restricted areas, and barriers	Unobtrusive security suggests openness and accessibility, but increased measures cloud image with security reminders that distinguish people from their government
Member office administration (chapter 2)	Restructured to emphasize security, emergency preparedness, and enhanced communication	Offices equipped with limited gas masks and other resources, noisy PA systems, BlackBerrys, and emergency coordinators	Constant state of readiness; Congress understood as target; imminent danger to inhabitants; everything in environment suspect
Representation and the mail (chapter 3)	Restructured to ensure safe handling and provide easy accessibility and efficient processing	New security protocol requires irradiation of paper mail, which slows down delivery; dramatic shift to e-mail and fax correspondence	Communication is immediate, constant, and casual; Web-based system makes less personal or meaningful for sender and receiver

of legislative buildings expresses values regarding democratic politics. Second, the design of these buildings shapes legislative behavior. Finally, the public perceives certain symbolic values embedded in the design of legislative buildings. It is perhaps useful to recap the social meaning present in the changes introduced to Congress in response to the threat of 9/11 and anthrax. Table 6.1 outlines these changes in terms of the expressive, behavioral, and symbolic social meaning they hold for the culture of Capitol Hill.

As suggested in chapter 2, one of the first responses to the threat

Table 6.1: Social Meanings of Structural and Procedural Changes

	Expressive	Behavioral	Societal
	Topic of analysis (by chapter)		
Homeland Security committees (chapter 4)	Centrality of issue to current agenda requires permanent attention; doubts about long-term significance of issue requires limited status	Restructured committee system to accommodate issue and reflect chamber cultures; jurisdictional disputes affect ability to provide oversight or produce legislation	Security is now permanent fixture of congressional business; no end to the "War on Terror"
Visitor Center (chapter 5)	New era requires new facility; built underground to preserve historical design and landscape, provide better experience for visitors, shelter visitors from elements, screen visitors offsite	Shapes visitor experience of Capitol; enter underground; screened outside Capitol; view dome through skylights; manage traffic flow like amusement parks; educate through simulations and multimedia	Underground facility suggests hierarchical superiority of government; screening protocol suggests distrust of people; museum experience suggests inaccessibility of actual members and building

Source: This theoretical framework is adapted from Charles Goodsell's (2001) analysis in *The American Statehouse: Interpreting Democracy's Temples.* This table is adapted rather directly from pg. 183.

posed by terrorism in the fall of 2001 was a dramatic change in office management. Expressing a need for heightened security and emergency preparedness, House administration altered the protocol for responding to threats by requiring every office to identify an emergency coordinator who would be responsible for office personnel in a crisis. Every employee was issued a BlackBerry so as to maintain communication during emergencies. Offices were equipped with enunciators to ensure the communication of public announcements by Capitol Police. Gas masks and emergency kits were placed in every office and even on the House floor. Decision makers expressed through these measures a concern for security and emergency preparedness. Instituting these changes has led to behavioral adjustments for congressional personnel as well. Symbolically, these changes highlight the emphasis placed on security around the Capitol Complex. With threat notices and drill reminders constantly sounding throughout member offices, one is struck by a sense of imminent danger. Rather than serving as the open, accessible seat of popular government, the Capitol has taken on an aura of suspicion, guardedness, caution, and inaccessibility.

The changes introduced since 2001 also hold implications for member responsiveness to constituents and thus for representation in general. The discovery of anthrax in Capitol office buildings wreaked havoc on the Hill. To warrant against a similar attack in the future, Capitol Police instituted new protocols for handling incoming mail. All mail is delivered to an off-site location, where it is screened and irradiated before delivery to Capitol Hill. As presented in chapter 3, this process is time consuming and destructive, leading to members and office staff finding alternative means of communicating with constituents. The motivations behind these procedural changes express a heightened sense of vulnerability and need for security. The intended and unintended behavioral changes introduced by this new protocol have impacted the management of office communications, the preferred modes of constituent contact, and the quality of the correspondence between members and constituents.

Symbolically, these changes are troubling. The simple act of writing a letter to your member of Congress is fraught with delivery problems. Your letter may take months to reach your member. Once it arrives at the office, the condition of the letter is likely to be compromised. To avoid these problems, you are encouraged by the member's Web site to use an automated system to send an e-mail. While e-mail is often much less personal, it is much more efficient. The sheer volume of e-mails received by offices on a daily basis ensures that no one individual e-mail will receive much attention. The symbolic impact of adjustments to mail handling is the perception that Congress is threatened by constituent contact, that Congress is less personal and yet somehow more casual, and that Congress is more automated.

These events have not only impacted member office operations. They have also had a significant impact on the committee system, as is suggested by chapter 4. The creation of a Department of Homeland Security to wage a domestic "War on Terror" has demanded similar restructuring of congressional committees to provide legislative authorization and congressional oversight. The decision to make these committee changes permanent expresses the sense of Congress that security holds lasting importance, and is a legislative priority not only today but for the foreseeable future. That this restructured committee design has persisted through two different partisan majorities suggests that these changes supersede partisanship and thus express deep values held by the institution as a whole. The actual behavioral impact of this restructured committee system has been intense jurisdictional fights that have precluded legislative effectiveness or efficiency and hampered congressional oversight. Zelizer suggests that "[t]he way in which the nation's elected officials [structure] Congress to solve problems says a great deal about the character of the nation's democracy."[2] From a symbolic lens, the addition of a Committee on Homeland Security to the rather short list of congressional committees in the House (and a similar adjustment in the Senate) suggests the relatively equal importance of domestic security to agriculture or transportation or education.

While several changes in protocol and process are readily apparent, there is an additional change that, while literally beneath the surface, is perhaps one of the most lasting and significant imprints on the culture of Capitol Hill. The Capitol Visitor Center is a subterranean edifice (two-thirds the size of the Capitol itself) that physically represents the impact of terrorism. Several values are expressed by members of Congress in the design of the facility. Built completely underground, the center is intended to shield visitors from the elements and provide them with a more meaningful educational experience at the nation's Capitol. The center is also intended to screen visitors off-site and underground to lessen the threat of a terrorist attack. Finally, the center is intended to provide a secure meeting place in case of a physical attack on the Capitol Building. Decision makers have long considered an addition of this sort to the Capitol, but it was the Capitol shootings of 1998 and the terrorist attacks of 2001 that catapulted the project to actual construction.

Now open to the public, the CVC has permanently changed the visitor experience of the Capitol. No longer will visitors walk directly up to the Capitol and enter its doors to view government in action. This is symbolically important. Once inside the CVC, visitors' first vision of the Capitol is through skylights, looking up at the corridors of power spatially superior to them. Their access to the building is more significantly curtailed now than at any point since 9/11 and is drastically more limited than in decades past. These changes symbolize a Congress, as a building, an institution, and a process, that is less accessible to the people it is elected to serve. Beyond the sheer cost of the facility, there is perhaps an even greater cost to be felt by generations to come.

In the end, Congress evolves to address changes in its environment. These changes can be related to policy developments, technological advancements, or even national or international crises. Rarely has the institution faced such threats to its existence as those presented in the fall of 2001. In addition, the institution now has access to unprecedented technology to address such threats. These combined circumstances facilitated massive change to the internal workings and external structures of the U.S. Congress. While the legislative process is largely the same as it was before these attacks, the climate in which this process operates is significantly different. No roll call votes or interest group scores will convey these changes in the culture of the Hill. Only through the personal stories and attitudes of members and support staff can the full extent of change truly be appreciated. Observers of the U.S. Congress should pay close attention to the experiences and concerns of members and staff as real people operating in a unique community in order to better understand the dynamics of congressional life.

A poignant reflection on the impact of terrorism on Capitol Hill is an excerpted passage from Senate Majority Leader Tom Daschle's (D-SD) book *Like No Other Time*. His memory of the evening of September 11, 2001, succinctly captures the essence of this text.

> The sun was just setting beyond the still smoking Pentagon as we came together on the Capitol's east front steps—senators and representatives, Democrats and Republicans. I was struck by the vulnerability we all felt and showed at that moment, by our collective humanity and, yes, determination. In the face of the unspeakable horror of that morning's events, our entire nation had been drawn together that day in a way few of us have experienced in this lifetime.
>
> Our differences, made so petty by the tragic enormity of what we had witnessed, fell away as our bare humanity drew us together, just as the American people were drawn together that day, neighbor to neighbor, colleague to colleague, parent to child, husband to wife, in homes and workplaces across this entire vast nation. I can't think of a time in my life when I have witnessed such deeply felt unity and connection among our countrymen as I saw and experienced that day—as we *all* saw and experienced.
>
> That emotional nakedness was palpably evident on the steps of the

Capitol as the men and women of Congress, so often divided by their beliefs, stood shoulder to shoulder in the dusk's fading light, some embracing, many with tears in their eyes, all joined together by sorrow and courage.

Dennis Hastert spoke first, and then I said a few words. When I closed with the straightforward sentence, "Congress will convene tomorrow," my colleagues burst into a loud cheer.

And then someone began singing.

This had not been rehearsed. This had not been planned. Even the most jaded cynic had to have been overwhelmed as these members of Congress all lifted their heads and their voices, singing "God Bless America" to a shaken nation in need of some faith and some hope.

To this day I don't know who started that song, but when it was finished we turned to one another like long-lost members of a large family and embraced once again.

And then we went home to face a new day.

And a world that was no longer the same.[3]

This recent period of terrorism, both foreign and domestic, was a pivotal one in the history of the U.S. Congress. It changed the American people, and it changed their government. Though life on Capitol Hill never will return to what it was before 9/11, the Congress once again proved resilient, adapting to new threats and providing greater security for the many members of Congress, staff, administrators, employees, and visitors around the Capitol Complex. This change permeated the structure and function of Congress—impacting office administration and constituent correspondence, committee organization and jurisdiction, and visitor orientation and access to the Capitol. With such an indelible mark, it will be several decades before the changes of 2001 fade from congressional memory.

The final question raised by this book is whether these changes are for the better. Have the changes to the Capitol landscape and to congressional culture been in the direction of progress? The central tension at the heart of these changes has been between protecting the openness and accessibility of the legislative branch and securing the facilities, the personnel, and the political leaders of our country from those who wish to do them harm. In the face of danger, the Congress took direct action to fortify its security. As the beacon of democracy around the world, the Capitol lost some of its democratic virtue along the way. Recognizing

Photograph of the author and her mother in front of the Capitol in the early 1980s. (Photograph from the author's collection.)

its vulnerability to attack, the Congress reexamined the openness of its grounds, its offices, and its temple. With innocence lost, it responded out of real fear. While the changes Congress introduced were warranted and seemingly effective, they hold certain repercussions. Democracy's temple may now be more secure, but it is also less accessible.

In ancient Greece and Rome, temples were structured to facilitate widespread access. Open porticos invited all visitors to pay homage to the divine. America's great temple of democracy, built to celebrate the sovereignty of the people, has closed its porticos and buried its public entrance. I believe that this action runs counter to the fundamental virtues and architectural vision undergirding the U.S. Congress. Perhaps the visitor experience created by the educational materials and historical documents available in the new Capitol Visitor Center will better convey the significance of Capitol Hill to American democracy. As a teacher, this is my hope. As a student of Congress, however, I worry that, for all the interactive information and hands-on activities the museum provides, nothing can serve as an adequate substitute for the awe-inspiring ascent up the Capitol's grand staircase to the seat of American legislative government. This experience may be gone for all future visitors to the Capitol, and that is a shame.

Appendix A

Members of the Capitol Preservation Commission: 109th–110th Congresses

	109th Congress	110th Congress
Co-Chairs	Senate President Pro Tempore Ted Stevens (R-AK)	Senate President Pro Tempore Robert C. Byrd (D-WV)
	Speaker of the House Dennis Hastert (R-IL)	Speaker of the House Nancy Pelosi (D-CA)
Senate	Maj. Leader Bill Frist (R-TN)	Maj. Leader Harry Reid (D-NV)
	Min. Leader Harry Reid (D-NV)	Min. Leader Mitch McConnell (R-KY)
	Chair of Appropriations Subcommittee on Legislative Branch Wayne Allard (R-CO)	Mary Landrieu (D-LA)
	Chair of Rules Trent Lott (R-MS)	Chair of Rules Diane Feinstein (D-CA)
	Robert Bennett (R-UT)	Ranking Member on Rules Robert Bennett (R-UT)
	Christopher Dodd (D-CT)	Dick Durbin (D-IL)
	Thad Cochran (R-MS)	Wayne Allard (R-CO)
	Richard Durbin (D-IL)	
House	Maj. Leader John Boehner (R-OH)	Maj. Leader Steny Hoyer (D-MD)
	Min. Leader Nancy Pelosi (D-CA)	Min. Leader John Boehner (R-OH)
	Chair of Appropriations Jerry Lewis (R-CA)	David Obey (D-WI)
	Chair of House Administration Vernon Ehlers (R-MI)	Chair of House Administration Robert Brady (D-PA)
	Ranking Member of House Administration Juanita Millender-McDonald (D-CA)	Ranking Member of House Administration Vernon Ehlers (R-MI)
	Chair of Transportation Subcommittee on Economic Development, Public Buildings, and Emergency Management Bill Shuster (R-PA)	Zach Wamp (R-TN)
	Marcy Kaptur (D-OH)	Marcy Kaptur (D-OH)
	John Mica (R-FL)	Michael Capuano (D-MA)
Ex-Officio Member	Alan M. Hantman, Architect of the Capitol	Stephen T. Ayers, FAIA, Acting Architect of the Capitol

Source: Adapted from the Office of the Architect of the Capitol, http:www.aoc.gov/cvc/project_info/cpc_list.cfm, March 2008.

APPENDIX B

Timeline of CVC Project

•	Progress made on CVC
•	Oversight of CVC provided by Congress
•	Appropriations granted to CVC

1976	Architect issues a report entitled "Toward a Master Plan for the United States Capitol" proposing a Capitol Visitor Center.
1991	Congress authorizes funding for conceptual planning and design of a visitor center.
11/10/1995	Architect submits final design report.
5/22/1997	House Subcommittee on Public Buildings and Economic Development holds hearing on H.R. 20.
10/21/1998	FY1999 Omnibus Appropriations Act provides $100 million for CVC.
3/1999	Architect receives approval to use $2.8 million to re-validate the 1995 design study.
1999	1995 report is revisited and revalidated by team headed by Architect to address changes in security needs and other safety and accessibility issues. They are guided by four fundamental goals: security, visitor education, visitor comfort, and functional improvements. Their results are presented in the 1999 Revalidation Study.
2/3/1999	House Committee on Appropriations, Subcommittee on Legislative Branch hearings.
3/3/1999	Senate Committee on Appropriations, Subcommittee on Legislative Branch hearings.

9/29/1999	FY2000 Legislative Branch Appropriations Bill (H.R. 1905) transfers approval authority for the CVC to CPC.
10/15/1999	Updated plan is presented to the CPC members at a meeting.
11/3/1999	CPC approves design update and Architect proceeds with design development.
11/1999–1/2000	Design and engineering obligation plan approved by House and Senate legislative appropriations subcommittees.
1/31/2000	Design development work for the CVC begun.
2/1/2000	House Committee on Appropriations, Subcommittee on Legislative Branch holds hearing.
6/20/2000	Members of CPC ceremonially break ground to signal the beginning of a process that is scheduled to culminate in late 2006 or in early 2007 when the CVC is expected to open its doors to the public.
10/2000	CPC approves final design plan and authorizes Architect to prepare final construction documentation.
2001	Construction documents are created and finalized, and competitive bids are solicited for the first phase of the project.
6/26/2001	Senate Committee on Appropriations, Subcommittee on Legislative Branch holds hearing.
6/27/2001	House Committee on Appropriations, Subcommittee on Legislative Branch holds hearing.
11/12/2001	FY2002 Legislative Branch Appropriations Act appropriates additional $70 million for construction of CVC.
12/3/2001	Early preparation work for center starts when workers begin removing the first of the memorial trees.
12/3/2001	President Bush authorizes the transfer of $290.4 million to the legislative branch. Of this amount, $100 million was for the completion of the CVC and $38.5 million for security enhancements, including funds for a new tunnel to the LOC, vertical circulation improvements within the East Front Extension, and new connections to the center from the House and Senate. These funds were drawn from the $20 billion made available to the president following the terrorist attacks for "disaster assistance, for anti-terrorism initiatives, and for the assistance in the recovery from the tragedy" that occurred on September 11, 2001.

Fall 2001	Pre-construction activities begin.
Fall 2001–Spring 2002	9/11 necessitates some additional design changes and prompts Congress to provide all necessary funding—an additional $100 million—to move the project into construction.
2002	Architect awards contract for Sequence I, hiring the Gilbane Building Company to manage the construction project.
Spring 2002	First major construction contract is awarded.
	"Sequence I—Foundation/Structure," worth nearly $100 million, is awarded to the Centex Construction Company–Mid Atlantic Division.
	Contract involves site demolition, slurry wall construction, excavation, construction of columns, installation of site utilities, construction of the concrete and steel structure, waterproofing, and construction of the service tunnel.
3/2003	Architect hires Tishman Construction Corporation, a financial consulting firm, to evaluate the CVC costs.
5/2003	Tishman Construction Corporation submits its analysis.
6/9/2003	GAO presents findings to CPC.
6/24/2003	House Committee on Appropriations holds hearing on Legislative Branch appropriations for FY2004.
7/11/2003	Senate approves legislation appropriating an additional $47.8 million for CVC. The bill stipulates that Architect must gain approval by House and Senate Appropriations Committees before obligating any of the funds.
7/15/2003	House Committee on Appropriations, Subcommittee on Legislative Branch holds hearing. GAO Comptroller General David M. Walker reports that Tishman's estimated cost should be adjusted by $7 million, bringing the total from $344.3 million to $351.3 million. Walker also tells committee that $70 million might be needed to complete the House and Senate expansion space, and $35 million for enhanced security, adding $100 million to estimate.
9/30/2003	President Bush signs into law FY2004 Legislative Branch Appropriations bill, including nearly $50 million in additional funding for the CVC.

1/2004	CVC spokesman Tom Fontana announces that unforeseen conditions and design changes had pushed back the project completion date to spring of 2006.
4/8/2004	Senate Appropriations Committee, Subcommittee on Legislative Branch holds hearing. Architect Hantman requests $14.5 million in new funding for opening the CVC.
5/12/2004	House Appropriations Committee, Subcommittee on Legislative Branch holds hearing. Architect Hantman makes identical request of $14.5 million.
7/2004	Senate Appropriations Committee reports bill that includes $7.6 million for transitional start-up operations costs. No start-up funds are included in the House bill.
12/2004	A new 1,000-linear-foot truck tunnel is completed and is used by Sequence II contractor for material deliveries. The tunnel will be available for Capitol deliveries late in 2006 when connecting corridors are completed and new freight elevators in the CVC are installed.
12/8/2004	Bush signs the Consolidated Appropriations Act of 2005, authorizing Hantman to transfer $10.6 million from the Capitol Building to the CVC. Conferees for the FY2005 Legislative Branch Appropriations bill (as part of the consolidated act) include language in their report expressing frustration with Hantman.
1/2005	The western half of the roof slab is completed to the extent necessary to support inaugural activities, such as the troop review and presidential motorcade, maintaining a historic tradition.
1/2005	Work begins on the primary utility tunnel for the CVC.
Early 2005	Sequence II contractor completes fireproofing the entire steel structure, and begins installing mechanical, electrical, plumbing, fire, and life-safety systems throughout facility.
4/13/2005	Senate Appropriations Committee, Subcommittee on the Legislative Branch holds hearing. Hantman emphasizes GAO conclusion that 75 percent of cost increases are largely beyond his control. GAO estimates cost of CVC could reach $515 million.

5/3/2005	House Committee on Appropriations holds hearing on Legislative Branch Appropriations for FY2006. Discussion focuses on the specifics of the unfinished House office space in the CVC. AOC emphasizes that plans had received approval of House Office Building Commission, but Ranking Member Obey (D-WI) suggests his intent to oppose the project unless changes are made.
5/11/2005	President Bush signs the Emergency Supplemental Appropriations Act for Defense, the Global War on Terror, and Tsunami Relief, 2005. The act strikes the language requiring leadership approval for obligation of appropriations.
5/17/2005 6/24/1005 7/14/2005 9/15/2005 10/18/2005 11/16/2005	Senate Appropriations Committee, Subcommittee on the Legislative Branch holds series of hearings on progress of CVC. GAO emphasizes during May, June, and July hearings that costs could increase to between $522 million and $559 million, but no accurate cost estimate could be provided until completion date is known. In November hearing, GAO suggests minimum cost of $542.9 million, but additional uncertainties may alter figure.
6/16/2005	House Committee on Appropriations reports FY2006 Legislative Branch Appropriation bill providing $36.9 million for CVC project. This amount is half the amount request by the Architect ($72.2 million). It does not include any of the $35.285 million requested for CVC operations.
Summer 2005	Bulk of mechanical work is completed, including installation of twenty air-handling units. With most of the block walls installed and mechanical and ductwork nearly complete, the contractor begins installing finish wall stone in many areas. In all, the Sequence II contractor is installing $35 million worth of finish stone throughout the CVC. Approximately thirty stone mason teams are working both inside and outside the facility to complete stone installation.
7/2005	Centex completes all excavation and structural activities and the roof deck covers the entire CVC structure.

8/2/2005	President Bush signs FY2006 Legislative Branch Appropriations bill granting an additional $44.2 million for the CVC, including $41.9 million for the project and $2.3 million for operating budget as well as $3.4 million for costs associated with House expenses. The final bill drops the House language for a CVC governing board and the Senate language for an executive director.
8/2005	Excavation of the tunnel is completed, and the pre-cast tunnel sections are in place.
8/2005	Wall stone is completed along the north pedestrian ramp and masons begin work on the south wall.
8/2005	Filming and photography schedules for films and interactive computer stations are submitted by production contractors.
9/2005	Crews install forty-foot-long sections of chilled water and steam pipes and welding connections throughout the tunnel. Nearly all major utility re-routing is completed. Tunnel is scheduled to become operational in February 2006.
9/2005	Stone is completed in the food service area and nearly complete in the north and south orientation theaters. Three of four walls inside the Great Hall are also complete as well as the stone on eight of sixteen columns inside the Hall.
9/2005	Approximately 150,000 8-inch square pavers are installed across the plaza and installation continues.
10/2005	Filming and photography is scheduled to begin.
2005	Exhibit Gallery content working group continues efforts to refine script for orientation film, House and Senate Theater orientation films, and text for all exhibit reading rails and captions.
2005	Historic preservation contractor completes the installation of much of the stone for the historic Frederick Law Olmsted–designed lanterns and fountains that had been removed before site excavation began.

2/15/2006 4/27/2006 5/24/2006 6/28/2006	Senate Appropriations Subcommittee on the Legislative Branch holds a series of oversight hearings on the progress of the CVC. Hearings focus on factors affecting CVC construction schedule and cost. While Architect offers completion date of March 2007–July 2007, GAO estimates May 2007–July 2007 is reasonable. GAO further reports that total cost to date is $530 million. Total cost for CVC should be between $556 and $584 million. Other concerns at the hearings include: 1) delays in delivery and installation of stone for interior walls and floors; 2) "acceptance testing" of fire and life-safety systems; and 3) completion of utility tunnel due to asbestos.
3/14/2006	House Appropriations, Subcommittee on the Legislative Branch holds hearing. Architect responds to Ranking Member Obey's questioning concerning escalating cost and projected completion date. Hantman stands by completion date of March 2007 and formal opening in April 2007.
3/15/2006	Senate Appropriations, Subcommittee on the Legislative Branch holds hearing. GAO's Terrell G. Dorn suggests Architect's projected completion dates are too optimistic. Architect Hantman stands by March 2007 completion date. GAO estimates final cost between $556 and $584 million.
5/25/2006	House Appropriations Committee version of the FY2007 Legislative Branch funding bill includes an amendment by Obey to transfer authority over supervision of contracts and employees for the CVC project to the Comptroller General effective 10/1/2006 until the Architect can be replaced. Committee appropriates $46.2 million in additional CVC funding, reflecting the GAO estimate rather than the Architect's estimate.
6/22/2006	Senate Appropriations Committee version of the FY2007 Legislative Branch funding bill approves $40 million for CVC, but does not include Obey amendment.
2/16/2007	GAO's Dorn reports progress on CVC project's heating, ventilation, and air-conditioning system; interior floor stone and ceiling installation; and other interior and exterior construction work.

3/1/2007	House Appropriations, Subcommittee on the Legislative Branch holds hearing. Architect requests $20 million for CVC project and $13.9 million for operating costs.
3/2/2007	Senate Appropriations, Subcommittee on the Legislative Branch holds hearing.
3/2007	Most of the construction on the CVC is complete.
5/31/2007	The food service contract is awarded to Restaurant Associates.
6/8/2007	House Subcommittee on Economic Development, Public Buildings, and Emergency Management of the Committee on Transportation and Infrastructure holds a hearing on transportation access to the CVC and security-related issues. The director of the D.C. Department of Transportation testifies that the preferred transition option is the Circulator bus from Union Station to the CVC.
6/12/2007	House Appropriations Committee version of the FY2008 Legislative Branch funding bill includes renaming the hall of the CVC "Emancipation Hall" and contains an extra $20 million in construction funding and $7.545 million for CVC operational costs. The House passes the bill on June 22.
6/21/2007	The Senate Appropriations Committee version of the FY2008 Legislative Branch funding bill contains $28,753,000 for the CVC, including $8,000,000 for CVC operations, but does not contain a provision renaming the hall of the CVC "Emancipation Hall." Most of these funds are eventually provided through the FY2008 Consolidated Appropriations Act on December 26, 2007.
9/25/2007	House Subcommittee on Economic Development, Public Buildings, and Emergency Management holds a hearing on H.R. 3315, naming the great hall of the CVC "Emancipation Hall." The bill is sponsored by Representatives Jesse Jackson Jr. (D-IL) and Zach Wamp (R-TN).
10/17/2007	House Administration Committee holds oversight hearing focused on the visitor experience provided by the CVC. Witnesses included representatives from CVC Visitor Services, Capitol Police, and the U.S. Capitol Visitor Service.

11/13/2007	The House overwhelmingly approves renaming the hall of the CVC "Emancipation Hall"; the Senate agrees on 12/6/2007; and President Bush signs the bill into law on 12/18/2007.
12/26/2007	Congress appropriates $28,753,000 for CVC, of which up to $8,500,000 may be used for operating costs.
2/7/2008	House Subcommittee on the Legislative Branch holds oversight hearing. Acting Architect of the Capitol Stephen Ayers reports that completion cost should be $621 million and the estimated opening date is November 2008.
3/5/2008	The House passes a bill to create the Office of the Capitol Visitor Center within the Office of the Architect of the Capitol. This office is to be headed by the chief executive officer for visitor services.
3/12/2008	House Subcommittee on the Legislative Branch holds hearing on visitor access to CVC, Web site design for the CVC, and the facility's advance-reservation system.
4/1/2008	House Subcommittee on Economic Development, Public Buildings, and Emergency Management holds hearing on environmental impact of the CVC as well as transportation-related issues.
4/15/2008	House Subcommittee on the Legislative Branch holds hearing on visitor access to CVC and expresses frustration with the options available for transporting visitors to the center.
5/22/2008	House Subcommittee on the Legislative Branch holds hearing on visitor access to CVC, as well as other miscellaneous issues requiring attention before the CVC receives its Certificate of Occupancy.
6/24/2008	Congress passes and President Bush signs into law the legislative branch appropriations bill for FY2009, which provides $40.227 million for the CVC. This figure includes roughly $31 million for remaining construction costs and roughly $9 million for operating costs.
7/8/2008	House Subcommittee on the Legislative Branch holds hearing on private tour bus access to CVC and funding for CVC staff.

7/21/2008	CVC receives a Temporary Certificate of Occupancy after successful testing of the fire detection and life-safety systems.
7/2008	Visitor Services launches outreach initiative to orient congressional staff with the reservation system for CVC visits, new Visitor Assistants, gift shops, restaurants, and the Congressional Historical Interpretative Program (CHIP), a training program for congressional staff providing tours of the Capitol.
9/27/2008	The Senate substitutes much of the language of the House bill creating an Office of the Capitol Visitor Center to protect the supervisory role of the Senate Committee on Rules and Administration, the House Administration Committee, and/or the Architect of the Capitol. The House agrees to this version in October, and President Bush signs it into law on October 20.
12/2/2008	The CVC opens to the public.
2/23/2009	The Architect of the Capitol requests $24.56 million for FY2010 for operating costs of the CVC.

Source: Adapted from the Office of the Architect of the Capitol, "2005 Activities Summary," 2005; Terrell G. Dorn, "Capitol Visitor Center: Update on Status of Project's Schedule and Cost as of February 16, 2007," Testimony before the Subcommittee on the Legislative Branch, Committee on Appropriations, House of Representatives, United States Government Accountability Office, 2007; Stephen W. Stathis, "The Capitol Visitor Center: An Overview," Congressional Research Service, Order Code RL31121, updated July 5, 2006, and "The Capitol Visitor Center: An Overview," Congressional Research Service, Order Code RL31121, updated January 16, 2009; Tim Dillon, "U.S. Capitol Visitor Center Nears Completion," *USA Today,* January 7, 2007, and Public Law No: 110-161.

NOTES

Preface

1. Tom Daschle with Michael D'Orso, *Like No Other Time: The 107th Congress and the Two Years That Changed America Forever* (New York: Crown Publishers, 2003), 108.

2. Richard F. Fenno Jr., *Watching Politicians: Essays on Participant Observation* (Berkeley, Calif.: Institute of Governmental Studies, University of California at Berkeley, 1990).

Introduction

1. Charles T. Goodsell, *The American Statehouse: Interpreting Democracy's Temples* (Lawrence: Univ. Press of Kansas, 2001), 159.

2. Ibid., 160.

3. Ibid.

4. Ibid.

5. Elaine K. Swift and David W. Brady, "Out of the Past: Theoretical and Methodological Contributions of Congressional History," *PS: Political Science and Politics* 24, no. 1 (1991): 61.

6. Nelson W. Polsby, "The Institutionalization of the U.S. House of Representatives," *American Political Science Review* 62 (1968): 144–168.

7. Thomas E. Cavanaugh, "The Dispersion of Authority in the House of Representatives," *Political Science Quarterly* 97, no. 4 (1982): 623–637.

8. Hugo Gurdon, "New Member Guide," *The Hill,* 2009, http://thehill.com/new-member-guide.html.

9. David T. Canon, "The Institutionalization of Leadership in the U.S. Congress," *Legislative Studies Quarterly* 14, no. 3 (1989): 415–443.

10. James G. March and Johan P. Olsen, "The New Institutionalism:

Organizational Factors in Political Life," *American Political Science Review* 78, no. 3 (1984): 734–749.

11. Peter A. Hall and Rosemary C. R. Taylor, "Political Science and the Three New Institutionalisms," *Political Studies* 44 (1996): 939.

12. Ibid.

13. Ibid. See also: James G. March and Johan P. Olsen, *Rediscovering Institutions: The Organizational Basis of Politics* (New York: Free Press, 1989).

14. Hall and Taylor, "Political Science and the Three New Institutionalisms," 955.

15. See March and Olsen, "The New Institutionalism."

16. David Easton, *The Political System: An Inquiry into the State of Political Science* (New York: Knopf, 1953). See also: David Easton, *A Framework for Political Analysis* (Chicago: Univ. of Chicago Press, 1979).

17. Ibid.

18. John W. Kingdon, *Agendas, Alternatives, and Public Policies* (Boston: Little, Brown, 1984).

19. Andrew P. Cortell and Susan Peterson, "Altered States: Explaining Domestic Institutional Change," *British Journal of Political Science* 29, no. 1 (1999): 177–203. See also: Michael McFaul, "State Power, Institutional Change, and the Politics of Privatization in Russia," *World Politics* 47 (1995): 210–243.

20. Ronald D. Hedlund, "Organizational Attributes of Legislatures: Structure, Rules, Norms, Resources," *Legislative Studies Quarterly* 9, no. 1 (1984): 87.

21. Donald Matthews, *U.S. Senators and Their World* (Chapel Hill: Univ. of North Carolina Press, 1960).

22. John C. Wahlke et al., *The Legislative System: Explorations in Legislative Behavior* (New York: Wiley, 1962). It should be noted that the behavioral movement in the social sciences impacted the study of Congress in significant ways. The study of Congress as an institution with norms of behavior was replaced by the study of Congress as individuals with goal-oriented behavior. As Hedlund suggests, this shift in focus led research problems "to be phrased in terms of individual phenomenon" and variables to be measured at "the individual level rather than the organizational or structural" level. Consequently, concerns of a structural or organizational nature were "ignored" or "overlooked" (Hedlund, "Organizational Attributes of Legislatures," 51). This shift has had an enduring impact on the quality of scholarship produced on the institution of Congress. Cooper and Brady suggest that institutional analysis has lagged behind behavioral analysis since the early 1950s, and this lag has hurt our ability to handle questions that concern institutional collectives in complex environments (Joseph Cooper and

David W. Brady, "Toward a Diachronic Analysis of Congress," *American Political Science Review* 75, no. 4 [1981]: 994).

23. Charles M. Price and Charles G. Bell, "Socializing California Freshmen Assemblymen: The Role of Individuals and Legislative Sub-Groups," *Western Political Quarterly* 23, no. 1 (1970): 169.

24. Ross K. Baker, *House and Senate* (New York: Norton, 1989), 215.

25. Ibid., 14–15.

26. Ibid., 12.

27. Quoted in Matthews, *U.S. Senators and Their World* (Chapel Hill: Univ. of North Carolina Press, 1960), 92.

28. Marvin L. Overby and Lauren C. Bell, "Rational Behavior or the Norm of Cooperation? Filibustering among Retiring Senators," *Journal of Politics* 66, no. 3 (2004): 921.

29. Alan Rosenthal, *Legislative Life: People, Process, and Performance in the States* (New York: Harper and Row, 1981), 111.

30. Roger H. Davidson and Walter J. Oleszek, "Adaptation and Consolidation: Structural Innovation in the U.S. House of Representatives," *Legislative Studies Quarterly* 1 (1976): 37–65.

31. Hedlund, "Organizational Attributes of Legislatures," 73.

32. Julian Zelizer, ed., *The American Congress* (Boston: Houghton Mifflin, 2004).

33. Davidson and Oleszek, "Adaptation and Consolidation," 40.

34. Nelson Polsby, *How Congress Evolves: Social Bases of Institutional Change* (Oxford: Oxford Univ. Press, 2004), 3–4.

35. Ibid., 4.

36. See Stephen D. Krasner, "Approaches to the State: Alternative Conceptions and Historical Dynamics," *Comparative Politics* 16 (1984): 233–244. Also see John T. S. Keeler, "Opening the Window for Reform: Mandates, Crises, and Extraordinary Policy-Making," *Comparative Political Studies* 25 (1993): 433–486.

37. Julian Zelizer, *On Capitol Hill: The Struggle to Reform Congress and Its Consequences, 1948–2000* (Cambridge: Cambridge Univ. Press, 2006), 268.

38. Ibid.

39. Cortell and Peterson, "Altered States," 186.

40. Goodsell, *The American Statehouse,* 7.

41. Ibid., 8.

42. Ibid.

43. Ibid.

44. Ibid., 10–11.

45. Ibid., 11. See Robert Rhodes James, ed., *Winston S. Churchill: His Complete Speeches, 1897–1963* (New York: Chelsea House, 1974), 7:6869–6873.

46. Stewart Brand, *How Buildings Learn: What Happens After They're Built* (London: Phoenix Illustrated, 1994), 3.

47. Charles de Secondat Montesquieu, *Considerations on the Causes of the Greatness of the Romans and Their Decline,* trans. David Lowenthal (Ithaca, N.Y.: Cornell Univ. Press, 1968).

48. Goodsell, *The American Statehouse,* 12.

49. Ibid., 185.

50. Zelizer, *On Capitol Hill,* 3.

51. Polsby, *How Congress Evolves,* 158.

52. Richard F. Fenno Jr., *Home Style: House Members in Their Districts* (Glenview, Ill.: Scott, Foresman, 1978).

53. The interview data consist of transcripts of seventy-six elite interviews conducted in Washington, D.C., in the summers of 2005 and 2006. These data include interviews with twenty-eight members of Congress serving in the 109th Congress (twenty-five representatives and three senators). It further includes an interview with one former member of Congress who retired approximately thirty years ago. In addition to twenty-nine members of Congress, the data include interviews with thirty-eight congressional staff, four historians representing both the Office of the House Historian and the Office of the Senate Historian, one representative of the U.S. Capitol Historical Society, one representative of the Capitol Police, one lobbyist, one tourism representative, and one academic expert on homeland security. The staff interview set includes six committee staff, five chiefs of staff, three legislative directors, five legislative assistants, five press secretaries, one communications director, one legislative correspondent, one administrative employee, and eleven other staff with no job description provided.

Twelve of the interview subjects had affiliation with the House Committee on Homeland Security, including seven members and five staff in personal offices of members on the committee. Of the Senate interviews, one senator and one staff had affiliation with the Senate Committee on Homeland Security and Governmental Affairs. Four of the interview subjects had affiliation with the House Permanent Select Committee on Intelligence, including three members and one staff. Similarly, four of the subjects had affiliation with the Senate Select Committee on Intelligence, including one senator and three staff.

Not all of the interview subjects had an obvious partisan affiliation. Of those who did, twenty-four were Democrats and forty-one were Republicans. These figures include eleven Democratic members, thirteen Democratic staff, eighteen Republican members (including one former member), and twenty-three Republican staff. The interview set includes more respondents with Republican affiliation (approximately 60 percent R; 40 percent D) than it should, given the partisan composition of the 109th Congress (House: 53 percent R, 47 percent D; Senate: 55 percent R, 45 percent D). This could be a result of a number of factors. First, in contacting offices, I contacted members on the House and Senate Homeland Security committees and members on the House and Senate intelligence committees. Republicans constituted 56 percent of the House Homeland Security Committee and 57 percent of the House Permanent Select Committee on Intelligence in the 109th Congress. Second, I further used a snowball sampling technique. In this method, respondents are asked to recruit additional interview subjects. While this approach may have increased my sample size, it is possible that Republicans were more willing and ready to discuss terrorism and Capitol security as well as the project management of the Capitol Visitor Center. In the end, it is unlikely that the partisan orientation of respondents introduces much bias into the findings of this study, given the focus of the analysis on the specific security measures introduced on the Hill, changes to office administration, handling of office mail, changes to the committee structure, and construction of the CVC.

54. Goodsell, *The American Statehouse,* 12.

55. Zelizer, *On Capitol Hill,* 264.

56. Ibid.

57. Goodsell, *The American Statehouse.*

58. Susan Webb Hammond, "Recent Research on Legislative Staffs," *Legislative Studies Quarterly* 21, no. 4 (1996): 543–576.

59. For an overview of the scholarship on legislative staff, see: Christine DeGregorio, "Congressional Committee Staff as Policy Making Partners in the U.S. Congress," *Congress and the Presidency* 21 (1994): 49–66. And see Susan Webb Hammond, "Recent Research on Legislative Staffs," *Legislative Studies Quarterly* 21, no. 4 (1996): 543–576.

60. For an explanation of the advocacy coalition framework, see P. A. Sabatier and H. C. Jenkins-Smith, eds., *Policy Change and Learning: An Advocacy Coalition Approach* (Boulder, Colo.: Westview Press, 1993). See also P. A. Sabatier and H. C. Jenkins-Smith, "The Advocacy Coalition Framework: An Assessment," in *Theories of the Policy Process,* ed. P. A. Sabatier, 117–166 (Boulder, Colo.: Westview Press, 1999).

1. Reconciling Security and Liberty

1. Quoted in Linda Wheeler, "The Night 'the City was Light': Washington Marks 185th Anniversary of British Burning the Capitol, White House," *Washington Post,* August 24, 1999, B03.

2. "The British Burn Washington, DC, 1814," http://www.eyewitnessto history.com/pfwashingtonsack.htm.

3. Wheeler, "The Night 'the City was Light,'" B03.

4. Dolley Madison, "The Burning of Washington," http://www.national center.org/WashingtonBurning1814.html.

5. Anthony S. Pitch, *The Burning of Washington: The British Invasion of 1814* (Annapolis, Md.: Naval Institute Press, 1998), 103.

6. U.S. Congress, Senate, "September 19, 1814: The Senate Convenes in Emergency Quarters," http://www.senate.gov/artandhistory/history/min ute/Senate_Convenes_in_Emergency_Quarters.html.

7. U.S. Congress, Senate, "The Capitol Police," http://www.senate.gov /artandhistory/history/common/briefing/Capitol_Police.htm.

8. "Washington Reacts to the Capitol Hill Shooting," http://www.cnn .com/ALLPOLITICS/1998/07/24/quotes.shooting/.

9. Michael Grunwald and Juliet Eilperin, "Protection vs. 'The People's House,'" *Washington Post,* July 25, 1998, A1.

10. Elbert B. Smith, "Thomas Hart Benton: Southern Realist," *American Historical Review* 58, no. 4 (1953): 795–807.

11. Michael D. Pierson, "All Southern Society Is Assailed by the Foulest Charges: Charles Sumner's 'The Crime against Kansas' and the Escalation of Republican Anti-Slavery Rhetoric," *New England Quarterly* 68, no. 4 (1995): 548.

12. Nancy Gibbs, "Murder in the House: Shots, Screams and Heroism as a Gunman Invades the Capitol," *Time,* August 3, 1998, http://www.cnn.com /ALLPOLITICS/1998/07/27/time/capitol.killings.html.

13. U.S. Congress, Senate, "July 2, 1915: Bomb Rocks Capitol," http:// www.senate.gov/artandhistory/history/minute/Bomb_Rocks_Capitol.htm.

14. Ibid.

15. Samuel A. Tower, "Bullets of an Assassin Miss Bricker in Capitol Tunnel," *New York Times,* July 13, 1947, sec. 1, 34; U.S. Congress, Senate, "April 2, 1917: Senator Attacks Constituent," http://www.senate.gov/artand history/history/minute/Senator_Attacks_Constituent.htm.

16. Grunwald and Eilperin, "Protection vs. 'The People's House.'" See also Office of the Clerk of the U.S. House of Representatives, "A Gunman in the House Gallery in 1932," http://clerk.house.gov/art_history/highlights .html?action=view&intID=234.

17. Tower, "Bullets of an Assassin."

18. Ibid.

19. Manuel Roig-Franzia, "A Terrorist in the House," *Washington Post,* February 22, 2004, sec. 1, 34.

20. "A Bomb in the Senate," *Time Magazine,* March 15, 1971.

21. U.S. Congress, Senate, "November 7, 1983: Bomb Explodes in Capitol," http://www.senate.gov/artandhistory/history/minute/bomb_explodes _in_capitol.htm.

22. Ibid.

23. Philip Shenon, "U.S. Charges 7 in the Bombing at U.S. Capitol," *New York Times,* May 12, 1988, A20.

24. Ibid.

25. Ibid.

26. U.S. Congress, Senate, "November 7, 1983: Bomb Explodes in Capitol."

27. Grunwald and Eilperin, "Protection vs. 'The People's House."

28. "Washington Reacts to the Capitol Hill Shooting."

29. Ibid.

30. Roig-Franzia, "A Terrorist in the House."

31. "A Bomb in the Senate."

32. "Washington Reacts to the Capitol Hill Shooting."

33. "U.S. Capitol Changed Much in 5 Years Since Gunman Killed 2 Officers," *USA Today,* July 24, 2003, http://www.usatoday.com/news/washington/2003-07-24-capitolx.htm.

34. Grunwald and Eilperin, "Protection vs. 'The People's House," A1.

35. "A Bomb in the Senate."

36. Grunwald and Eilperin, "Protection vs. 'The People's House," A1.

37. "Washington Reacts to the Capitol Hill Shooting."

38. Baker references the following sources in this section. Roger H. Davidson and Walter J. Oleszek, *Congress and Its Members,* 2nd ed. (Washington, D.C.: CQ Press, 1985), 216; Lewis A. Froman Jr., *The Congressional Process* (Boston: Little, Brown, 1967), 7–15; and David C. Kozak, "House-Senate Differences: A Test among Interview Data," in *Congress and Public Policy,* ed. David C. Kozak and John D. Macartney, 79–94 (Chicago: Dorsey Press, 1987).

39. Baker, *House and Senate,* 38.

40. Baker, *House and Senate,* 9–10.

41. Timothy Burger, "Capitol Police Ask 21 Percent Funding Hike; Senate Leg. Apps. Chairman Reid Grills Chief Kerrigan on Certain Purchases, Pay Raises," *Roll Call,* March 25, 1991.

42. Karen Foerstel, "Why No Fire Drills on Hill? Mazzoli Raises Question in Wake of World Trade Center Bombing," *Roll Call,* March 4, 1993.

43. Ibid.

44. Juliet Eilperin, "House Entrances Closed to Traffic," *Roll Call,* April 24, 1995.

45. Ibid.

46. Jennifer Yachnin, "Security Unaffected by Attack in Madrid; Ney Cautions Not to Cut Cops' Budget," *Roll Call,* March 16, 2004.

47. Erin P. Billings, "Security Remains at Status Quo," *Roll Call,* July 12, 2005.

48. "U.S. Capitol Changed Much in 5 Years Since Gunman Killed 2 Officers."

49. Ibid.

50. Ibid.

51. "Washington Reacts to the Capitol Hill Shooting."

52. Ibid.

53. Ibid.

54. Ibid.

55. "Sources: Capitol 'Gunfire' Likely from Air Hammer," CNN.com, May 26, 2006, http://www.cnn.com/2006/POLITICS/05/26/house.shots/index.html.

56. Office of the Architect of the Capitol, "The Capitol Visitor Center," http://www.aoc.gov/cvc/index.cfm.

57. Office of the Architect of the Capitol, "Project Information: Planning Begins," http://www.aoc.gov/cvc/project_info/index.cfm.

58. Felicia Bell, "Commentary: Enslaved Labor and the Capitol," *The Capitol Dome: USCHS Quarterly Historical Newsletter*, Special Issues, 2003, http://www.uschs.org/04_history/subs_articles/04e_dome_b.html.

59. Turpin C. Bannister, "The Genealogy of the Dome of the United States Capitol," *Journal of the Society of Architectural Historians* 7, no. 1/2 (1948): 1.

60. "Washington Reacts to the Capitol Hill Shooting."

61. Roig-Franzia, "A Terrorist in the House."

62. Ibid.

63. Ibid.

2. Enunciators and BlackBerrys

1. Barbara Vobejda, "'Extensive Casualties' in Wake of Pentagon Attack," *Washington Post Online*, September 11, 2001, http://www.washingtonpost.com/wpsrv/metro/daily/sep01/attack.html.

2. National Commission on Terrorist Attacks, *The 9/11 Commission Report: Final Report of the National Commission on Terrorist Attacks upon the United States (Authorized Edition)* (New York: Norton, 2004), 14.

3. *Congressional Record*, April 10, 2002, S2504.

4. Hammond, "Recent Research on Legislative Staffs."

5. See Susan Webb Hammond, "Legislative Staffs," *Legislative Studies Quarterly* 9, no. 2 (1984): 271–317.

6. See Richard F. Fenno Jr., "The House Appropriations Committee as a Political System: The Problem of Integration," *American Political Science Review* 56, no. 2 (1962): 310–324. See Richard F. Fenno Jr., *The Power of the*

Purse (Boston: Little, Brown, 1966). And see John F. Manley, "Congressional Staff and Public Policy-Making," *Journal of Politics* 30 (1966): 1046–1067.

7. See John W. Kingdon, *Congressmen's Voting Decisions* (New York: Harper and Row, 1973). See also Harold L. Wolman and Dianna M. Wolman, "The Role of the U.S. Senate Staff in the Opinion Linkage Process: Population Policy," *Legislative Studies Quarterly* 2 (1977): 281–293. And see DeGregorio, "Congressional Committee Staff."

8. James D. Cochrane, "Partisan Aspects of Congressional Committee Staffing," *Western Political Quarterly* 27 (1964): 338–348.

9. Matthews, *U.S. Senators and Their World.*

10. John S. Saloma III, *Congress and the New Politics* (Boston: Little, Brown, 1969).

11. Harrison W. Fox Jr. and Susan Webb Hammond, *Congressional Staffs: The Invisible Force in American Lawmaking* (New York: Free Press, 1977).

12. Hammond, "Recent Research on Legislative Staffs."

13. Randall Strahan, *New Ways and Means: Reform and Change in a Congressional Committee* (Chapel Hill: Univ. of North Carolina Press, 1990).

14. See Fenno, *Home Style.* See Steven H. Schiff and Steven S. Smith, "Generational Change and the Allocation of Staff in the U.S. Congress," *Legislative Studies Quarterly* 8 (1983): 457–468. And see Morris P. Fiorina, *Congress: Keystone of the Washington Establishment,* 2nd ed. (New Haven, Conn.: Yale Univ. Press, 1989).

15. Burdett A. Loomis, "The Congressional Office as a Small (?) Business," *Publius* 9 (1979): 35–55.

16. Michael J. Malbin, *Unelected Representatives: Congressional Staff and the Future of Representative Government* (New York: Basic Books, 1980).

17. Congressional Management Foundation, "How Is Anthrax Changing Congress and How Are Offices Using Technology to Cope?" http://www.congressonlineproject.org/november.html.

18. Ibid.

19. Daschle with D'Orso, *Like No Other Time,* 165–166, 170.

20. Congressional Management Foundation, "Congress Online: Special Report," http://www.cmfweb.org/techreports.asp#COP02.

21. Lorraine H. Tong and Barbara L. Schwemle, "Telework in the Federal Government: Background, Policy, and Oversight," Congressional Research Service, April 3, 2002.

22. Congressional Management Foundation, "How Is Anthrax Changing Congress."

23. Ibid.

24. Ibid.

25. Ibid.

26. U.S. Congress, House, Committee on House Administration, "Member's Handbook," http://cha.house.gov/model_employee.aspx.

27. See *Congressional Record,* April 21, 2004, H2228.

28. Carl Hulse, "Threats and Responses: Security; Despite 9/11, Study Finds 'Significant Safety and Health Hazards' at Capitol," *New York Times,* November 26, 2002, sec. A.

29. Online NewsHour with Jim Lehr Transcript, "Capital Defense," Public Broadcasting Service, April 6, 2004, http://www.pbs.org/newshour /bb/terrorism/july-dec04/security_8-6.html.

30. Ibid.

31. Adapted from Congressional Management Foundation, "Crisis Management," Washington, D.C., 2005, http://www.cmfweb.org/OfficeMg mtCrisisMgmt.asp (accessed on March 2, 2006).

32. One possible explanation for the difference in staff tenure for D.C.-based Senate offices and state-based Senate offices is compensation. In 1991 the average salary for a Senate staffer was $35,000; in 2001, it was $49,000. While Senate staff salaries kept up with inflation over this ten-year period, it was not commensurate with the salary increases for executive branch employees. According to the Congressional Management Foundation, "The average Senate staff member earned 18% less than an executive branch employee in 1991—that gap increased to 32% in 2001." See Congressional Management Foundation, "Senate Staff Employment Study—Salary, Tenure, and Demographic Data: 1991–2001" (Washington, D.C.: Congressional Management Foundation, 2005).

33. *Congressional Record,* February 14, 2003, S2516.

34. *Congressional Record,* September 22, 2004, H7410.

35. Hammond, "Recent Research on Legislative Staffs."

3. Is Writing a Letter to Your Member of Congress a Thing of the Past?

1. Brandon Keim, "Years Later, Anthrax Attack Remains a Mystery," Columbia News Service (April 5, 2005), http://jscms.jrn.columbia.edu/cns /2005-04-05/keim-anthraxmystery.

2. Ibid.

3. Scott Shane and Eric Lichtblau, "Scientist's Suicide Is Linked to Anthrax Inquiry," *New York Times,* August 2, 2008, A1.

4. David Willman, "Anthrax Mixture Led FBI to Ivins; Its Origins Pointed to One Conclusion: That Only the Government Scientist Could Be Behind the '01 Attacks," *Los Angeles Times,* August 4, 2008, A1.

5. Gerry Andrews, "Open Questions on a Closed Case," *New York Times,* August 10, 2008, sec. WK (10).

6. Daschle with D'Orso, *Like No Other Time,* 147.

7. Paul Reynolds, "Living with Bioterror," *BBC News Online,* 2001, http://news.bbc.co.uk/1/low/programmes/from_our_own_correspondent/1611314.stm.

8. Janice C. Blanchard et al., "In Their Own Words: Lessons Learned from Those Exposed to Anthrax," *American Journal of Public Health* 95, no. 3 (2005): 489.

9. Ibid., 491.

10. Ibid.

11. Ibid., 492.

12. The General Accounting Office was renamed the Government Accountability Office in July 2004. See the GAO Web site for full details: http://www.gao.gov/about/namechange.html.

13. General Accounting Office, "Capitol Hill Anthrax Incident: EPA's Cleanup Was Successful; Opportunities Exist to Enhance Contract Oversight," GAO-03-686, June 2003, 11.

14. Ibid.

15. Ibid., 13.

16. Iver Peterson, "Anthrax Cleanup Day Finally Comes for Mail Sorting Center," *New York Times,* October 24, 2003, http://query.nytimes.com/gst/fullpage.html?res=9C03EFDC1531F937A15753C1A9659C8B63&sec=&spon=&pagewanted=all#.

17. Hanna Fenichel Pitkin, *The Concept of Representation* (Berkeley: Univ. of California Press, 1967), 154–155.

18. Bryan D. Jones, "Competitiveness, Role Orientations, and Legislative Responsiveness," *Journal of Politics* 35, no. 4 (1973): 925.

19. Heinz Eulau and Paul Karps, "The Puzzle of Representation: Specifying Components of Responsiveness," *Legislative Studies Quarterly* 2, no. 3 (1977): 235.

20. Ibid., 243.

21. Warren H. Butler, "Administering Congress: The Role of the Staff," *Public Administration Review* 26, no. 1 (1966): 5.

22. George Serra and David Moon, "Casework, Issue Positions, and Voting in Congressional Elections: A District Analysis," *Journal of Politics* 56, no. 1 (1994): 200–213.

23. Fiorina, *Congress: Keystone of the Washington Establishment.*

24. D. Rutter, *Commuting by Telephone* (New York: Pergamon Press, 1987).

25. Christopher B. Sullivan, "Preferences for Electronic Mail in Organizational Communication Tasks," *Journal of Business Communication* 32, no. 1 (1995): 49.

26. Ibid., 50. In this passage, Sullivan references Rutter as well as J. Short,

E. Williams, and B. Christie, *The Social Psychology of Telecommunication* (New York: Wiley, 1976).

27. Paul DiMaggio et al., "Digital Inequality: From Unequal Access to Differentiated Use," in *Social Inequality,* ed. Kathryn Neckermann, 355–400 (New York: Russell Sage Foundation, 2004). And Susannah Fox and Jessica Vitak, "Degrees of Access," *Pew Internet and American Life Project,* July 9, 2008, http://www.pewinternet.org/Presentations/2008/Degrees-of-Access-(May-2008-data).aspx.

28. Fox and Vitak, "Degrees of Access." And Sydney Jones and Susannah Fox, "Generations Online in 2009," *Pew Internet and American Life Project,* January 28, 2009, http://www.pewinternet.org/Reports/2009/Generations-Online-in-2009.aspx.

29. Paul S. Herrnson, Atiya Kai Stokes-Brown, and Matthew Hindman, "Campaign Politics and the Digital Divide: Constituency Characteristics, Strategic Considerations, and Candidate Internet Use in State Legislative Elections," *Political Research Quarterly* 60, no. 1 (2007): 31–42.

30. Eulau and Karps, "The Puzzle of Representation," 241.

31. John C. Wahlke, "Policy Demands and System Support: The Role of the Represented," *British Journal of Political Science* 1 (1971): 288.

32. David Mayhew, *Congress: The Electoral Connection* (New Haven, Conn.: Yale Univ. Press, 1974), 5.

33. Ibid. Also see Fenno, *Home Style.*

34. Fenno, *Home Style.*

35. E. Scott Adler, Chariti E. Gent, and Cary B. Overmeyer, "The Home Style Homepage: Legislator Use of the World Wide Web for Constituency Contact," *Legislative Studies Quarterly* 23, no. 4 (1998): 585–595.

36. Fenno, *Home Style.*

37. Bruce Cain, John Ferejohn, and Morris Fiorina, *The Personal Vote: Constituency Service and Electoral Independence* (Cambridge, Mass.: Harvard Univ. Press, 1987). See also Albert Cover, "Contacting Congressional Constituents: Some Patterns of Perquisite Use," *American Journal of Political Science* 24 (1980): 125–135. And see Laurily Epstein and Kathleen Frankovic, "Casework and Electoral Margins: Insurance Is Prudent," *Polity* 14 (1982): 691–700.

38. Lewis Anthony Dexter, "What Do Congressmen Hear: The Mail," *Public Opinion Quarterly* 20, no. 1 (1956): 16–27.

39. Butler, "Administering Congress," 5.

40. Mary J. Culnan, "Processing Unstructured Organizational Transactions: Mail Handling in the U.S. Senate," *Organizational Science* 3, no. 1 (1992): 119.

41. Ibid.

42. Graeme Browning, "Don't Call Me, Call Me E-mail," *National Journal* 20 (1994): 1146.

43. K. C. Swanson, "21st Century, Ready or Not," *National Journal* 22 (1996): 1215.

44. Kathy Goldschmidt et al., "E-mail Overload in Congress: Managing a Communications Crisis," *Congress Online Project*, 2001, http://www.cmfweb.org/storage/cmfweb/documents/CMF_Pubs/e-mailoverload.pdf.

45. Dexter, "What Do Congressmen Hear."

46. Ibid.

47. Adler, Gent, and Overmeyer, "The Home Style Homepage," 585.

48. Ibid., 587.

49. Butler, "Administering Congress," 4.

50. Goldschmidt et al., "E-mail Overload in Congress," 1.

51. Ibid.

52. Ibid., 5.

53. Ibid.

54. I used a logistic regression model to estimate members' preferred modes of contact. The independent variables, as mentioned above, included member party, sex, seniority, membership on the Homeland Security Committee, electoral security, entry in or after 2000, and distance from the district to D.C. Given the possibility of interaction effects between member electoral safety and year of entry, an interaction term was created to capture significant influences on member-preferred mode of constituent contact. The model is represented by the following equation:

$$Z = \beta_0 + \beta_1 X_1 + \beta_2 X_2 + \beta_3 X_3 + \beta_4 X_4 + \beta_5 X_5 + \beta_6 X_6 + \beta_7 X_7 + \beta_8 X_8$$

Where: Z = Preferred mode of constituent contact; X_1 = Membership on House Homeland Security Committee; X_2 = Republican; X_3 = Female; X_4 = Seniority; X_5 = Marginal at 55%; X_6 = Elected in or after 2000; X_7 = Marginal and elected in or after 2000; and X_8 = Distance from D.C. My hypothesis was that seniority would be associated with a preference for more traditional modes of contact, while relevant committee membership, electoral vulnerability, election since the 2001 attacks, and increased district distance would be associated with a greater preference for e-mail. I further hypothesized that members elected since 2000 who were also electorally vulnerable would be particularly inclined to favor e-mail over slower forms of communication. As the analysis suggests, the only two variables significantly associated with a member's preferred mode of contact were electoral vulnerability and year of congressional entry.

55. This relationship is significant at the $p < .05$ level.

56. This relationship is significant at the p<.05 level.

57. Pitkin, *The Concept of Representation*.

4. Terror Wars and Turf Wars

1. Walter Kravitz, "The Advent of the Modern Congress: The Legislative Reorganization Act of 1970," *Legislative Studies Quarterly* 15, no. 3 (1990): 375.

2. Michael L. Koempel, "Homeland Security: Compendium of Recommendations Relevant to House Committee Organization and Analysis of Considerations for the House, and 109th and 110th Congresses Epilogue," Congressional Research Service, March 2, 2007, 1.

3. Ibid.

4. U.S. Congress, House, Committee on Homeland Security, "Homeland Security Committee Overview," 2007, http://homeland.house.gov/about/index.asp.

5. U.S. Congress, Senate, *To Eliminate Certain Restrictions on Service of a Senator on the Senate Select Committee on Intelligence*, S. Res. 445, 108th Cong., 2nd sess. (Washington, D.C.: Government Printing Office, 2004).

6. Koempel, "Homeland Security," 2.

7. Ibid., 2–3.

8. Fenno, "The House Appropriations Committee."

9. Andrew Taylor, "Senators Fight over Turf in Revamp of Homeland Security Oversight," *CQ Weekly*, October 16, 2004, 2460.

10. Ibid.

11. Patrick Yoest, "Democrats' First 100 Hours: Security Initiatives Facing Short Funds, Turf Wars and Inertia," *CQ Weekly*, November 20, 2006, 3109.

12. Ibid.

13. Richard L. Hall, *Participation in Congress* (New Haven, Conn.: Yale Univ. Press, 1996).

14. Richard F. Fenno Jr., *Congressmen in Committees* (Boston: Little, Brown, 1973).

15. Tim Starks, "Committee OKs Cox Priority," *CQ Weekly—Weekly Report*, May 2, 2005, 1155.

16. Tim Starks, "Homeland Security under Attack by Lawmakers," *Congressional Quarterly Weekly*, June 26, 2006, 1772.

17. Jonathan Allen and Patrick Yoest, "110th Senate Committees: Homeland Security and Governmental Affairs," *CQ Weekly*, November 13, 2006, 3032.

18. Steven Maguire and Shawn Reese, "Department of Homeland Secu-

rity Grants to State and Local Governments: FY2003 to FY2006," Congressional Research Service, Order Code RL33770, December 22, 2006.

19. Ibid., 2.

20. Ibid., 3.

21. Ibid., 10.

22. Ibid., 10–11.

23. "Other Senate Committees in the 109th," *CQ Weekly*, November 6, 2004, 2614.

24. Sarah Laskow, "Is Congress Failing on Homeland Security Oversight?: Despite Calls for Consolidation, Over 80 Hill Panels Still Have a Say," Center for Public Integrity, July 15, 2009, http://www.publicintegrity.org /articles/entry/1549/.

25. Ibid.

26. Ibid.

27. Ibid.

5. Gateway to American History or Fort Capitol?

Epigraph: Kathy Kiely, "Post-9/11 Security Hinders Access at Capitols," *USA Today*, August 5, 2002.

1. Carl Hulse, "Workers Set to Transform East Front of the Capitol," *New York Times*, May 28, 2002.

2. Sabatier and Jenkins-Smith, *Policy Change and Learning.*

3. Carsten Greve, "New Avenues for Contracting Out and Implications for a Theoretical Framework," *Public Performance and Management Review* 24, no. 3 (2001): 270.

4. S. H. Hanke, ed., *Prospects for Privatization* (New York: Academy of Political Science, 1987).

5. E. S. Savas, *Privatization: The Key to Better Government* (Chatham, N.J.: Chatham House, 1987).

6. Ronald C. Moe, "Exploring the Limits of Privatization," *Public Administration Review* 47, no. 6 (1987): 453.

7. David M. Van Slyke, "The Mythology of Privatization in Contracting for Social Services," *Public Administration Review* 63, no. 3 (2003): 308.

8. Timothy K. Barnekov and Jeffrey A. Raffel, "Public Management of Privatization," *Public Productivity and Management Review* 14, no. 2 (1990): 138.

9. Van Slyke, "The Mythology of Privatization."

10. Moe, "Exploring the Limits of Privatization."

11. Ibid., 457.

12. Lester Salamon, "Rethinking Public Management: Third-Party Government and the Changing Forms of Government Action," *Public Policy* 29 (1981): 260.

13. Ibid., 260.

14. Van Slyke, "The Mythology of Privatization," 296–297. See also D. F. Kettl, *Sharing Power—Public Governance and Private Markets* (Washington, D.C.: Brookings, 1993).

15. Ibid., 308.

16. John R. Chamberlin and John E. Jackson, "Privatization as Institutional Choice," *Journal of Policy Analysis and Management* 6, no. 4 (1987): 602. See also Van Slyke, "The Mythology of Privatization," 297.

17. J. L. Sundquist, "Privatization: No Panacea for What Ails Government," in *Public-Private Partnership: New Opportunities for Meeting Social Needs,* ed. H. Brooks, L. Liebman, and C. S. Schelling, 307 (Cambridge, Mass.: Ballinger, 1984).

18. See Sabatier and Jenkins-Smith, *Policy Change and Learning.* See also Sabatier and Jenkins-Smith, "The Advocacy Coalition Framework."

19. P. A. Sabatier, "The Advocacy Coalition Framework: Revisions and Relevance for Europe," *Journal of European Public Policy* 5, no. 1 (1998): 98.

20. Ibid., 99.

21. Sabatier and Jenkins-Smith, *Policy Change and Learning,* 25.

22. Greve, "New Avenues," 273.

23. Sabatier and Jenkins-Smith, "The Advocacy Coalition Framework."

24. Ibid., 123.

25. Ibid., 127.

26. Uriel Rosenthal, Michael T. Charles, and Paul 't Hart, *Coping with Crises: The Management of Disasters, Riots and Terrorism* (Springfield, Ill.: Thomas, 1989), 10.

27. Uriel Rosenthal and Alexander Kouzmin, "Crises and Crisis Management: Toward Comprehensive Government Decision Making," *Journal of Public Administration Research and Theory* 7, no. 2 (1997): 296–297.

28. Ibid., 285; Ronald D. Crelinsten, "The Impact of Television on Terrorism and Crisis Situations: Implications for Public Policy," *Journal of Contingencies and Crisis Management* 2, no. 2 (1994): 61–72; Uriel Rosenthal, Paul 't Hart, and Alexander Kouzmin, "The Bureau-Politics of Crisis Management," *Public Administration* 69, no. 2 (1991): 221–233.

29. Rosenthal and Kouzmin, "Crises and Crisis Management," 290.

30. A. Kouzmin and A. M. G. Jarman, "Crisis Decision Making: Towards a Contingent Decision Path Perspective," in *Coping with Crises: The Management of Disasters, Riots and Terrorism,* ed. Uriel Rosenthal, Michael T. Charles, and Paul 't Hart, 408–410 (Springfield, Ill.: Thomas, 1989).

31. Rosenthal and Kouzmin, "Crises and Crisis Management," 292.

32. Ibid., 293–294; Uriel Rosenthal, "Politics in Administration: Max Weber and the Quest for Democratic Order," in *Dynamics in Australian Public Management: Selected Essays,* ed. Alexander Kouzmin and Nicholas Scott (Melbourne: Macmillan, 1990); Gregory M. Herek, Irving L. Janis, and Paul Huth, "Decision-Making during International Crises," *Journal of Conflict Resolution* 31, no. 2 (1987): 203–226.

33. See Kingdon, *Congressmen's Voting Decisions,* 60.

34. Rosenthal and Kouzmin, "Crises and Crisis Management," 294.

35. Ibid.

36. Spencer S. Hsu, "Congress Digs Deep for Visitors and Safety; Underground Center's Construction Begins," *Washington Post,* May 28, 2002.

37. John Godfrey, "Visitors Center Closer to Reality; Capitol Police Slayings Spur Security Measure," *Washington Times,* May 27, 2001.

38. Ibid.

39. See Appendix B for a more thorough timeline of events surrounding the design, construction, and oversight of the Capitol Visitor Center.

40. Jim Abrams, "Capitol Visitors Center Idea Mulled," Associated Press Online, July 27, 1998.

41. Wendy Koch, "Lawmakers Vow to Push for Capitol Visitors' Center," *USA Today,* July 30, 1998.

42. Ibid.

43. Samantha Critchell, "AP Top News at 5 A.M. EDT Wednesday, July 29, 1998," Associated Press Online, July 29, 1998.

44. John Godfrey, "Plans for Capitol Visitor Center Face Further Security Scrutiny," *Washington Times,* July 27, 1998.

45. Critchell, "AP Top News."

46. Eun-Kyung Kim, "Lawmakers Discuss Plans for Capitol Visitors Center," Associated Press, July 29, 1998.

47. David Goodman, "AP Top News at 3 P.M. EDT Sunday, July 26, 1998," Associated Press Online, July 26, 1998.

48. "Capitol Visitor-Center Plans Back on Track," *The Kiplinger Letter,* July 31, 1998.

49. Kim, "Lawmakers Discuss Plans."

50. Juliet Eilperin, "A Peace Plan for the Capitol Visitor Center," *Washington Post,* July 12, 1998.

51. Ibid.

52. Godfrey, "Visitors Center Closer to Reality."

53. Eilperin, "A Peace Plan."

54. John Godfrey, "Commission OKs Capitol Expansion; Visitors Center Needed for Extra Security," *Washington Times,* October 16, 1999.

55. Ibid.

56. Ibid.

57. Dan Carney, Amy Borrus, and Jay Greene, "Microsoft's All-Out Counterattack," *Business Week*, May 15, 2000.

58. David Ho, "Capitol Visitors' Center Planned," Associated Press Online, June 20, 2000.

59. Hsu, "Congress Digs Deep."

60. Christopher Lee, "Digging Deep for Capitol Visitors; Plan for New Center Turns from Modest to Monumental," *Washington Post*, November 11, 2003.

61. Hsu, "Congress Digs Deep."

62. Jim Abrams, "Work Accelerates on Biggest, Most Expensive Capitol Construction Project," Associated Press Online, April 30, 2004.

63. Ibid.

64. Christopher Lee and Spencer S. Hsu, "GAO Cites Capitol Facility's Costs, Delays," *Washington Post*, November 30, 2004.

65. Mary Dalrymple, "Capitol Visitor Center to Open Fall 2006, Architect Tells Lawmakers," Associated Press Online, May 3, 2005.

66. "Rep. Obey Comments on FY 2006 Legislative Branch Appropriations Bill," *US Fed News*, June 22, 2005.

67. "Update," *Washington Post*, July 5, 2006.

68. "Sen. Allard Chairs Final Legislative Branch Committee Hearing," *US FedNews*, November 15, 2006.

69. *States News Service*, "Obey-Cardoza Give 'Golden Drain Award for Waste, Fraud and Abuse' to Congress and Architect of the Capitol," September 21, 2006.

70. Bruce Buckley, "Search Begins for New Architect of Capitol," *Engineering News-Record*, March 5, 2007.

71. "Rep. Mitchell Votes against Legislative Branch Appropriations Bill," *US FedNews*, June 22, 2007.

72. Andrea Benda, "Capitol Center Aims for Fall of '08; Visitor Facility 3 Years Overdue," *Washington Times*, August 2, 2007.

73. Hulse, "Workers Set to Transform East Front."

74. Ibid.

75. Godfrey, "Visitors Center Closer to Reality."

76. Hulse, "Workers Set to Transform East Front."

77. Associated Press State and Local Wire, "Tree Planted in Memory of W.Va. Congressman to Be Removed," May 7, 2001.

78. Ibid.

79. Ibid.

80. Hsu, "Congress Digs Deep."

81. Ibid.

82. Hulse, "Workers Set to Transform East Front."

83. "U.S. Capitol Staircase to Be Repaired," Associated Press Online, January 27, 2006.

84. Godfrey, "Visitors Center Closer to Reality."

85. Bob Dart, "Big Changes on the Way for Prime Capitol Tourist Sites," Cox News Service, July 10, 2002.

86. Kiely, "Post-9/11 Security Hinders Access at Capitols."

87. Lee and Hsu, "GAO Cites Capitol Facility's Costs, Delays."

88. "Rep. Obey Comments on FY 2006 Legislative Branch Appropriations Bill."

89. Godfrey, "Plans for Capitol Visitor Center."

90. Ibid.

91. "America's Capitol," *Washington Times,* July 28, 1998.

92. Dart, "Big Changes on the Way."

93. Spencer S. Hsu, "Historic Capitol Hill Faces Uncharted Future; Security Needs, Business Boom Reshape Area," *Washington Post,* January 20, 2005.

94. Ibid.

95. Godfrey, "Visitors Center Closer to Reality."

96. Stephen W. Stathis, "The Capitol Visitor Center: An Overview," Congressional Research Service, Order Code RL31121, updated January 16, 2009, http://wikileaks.org/leak/crs/RL31121.pdf.

97. Office of the Architect of the Capitol, "2005 Activities Summary," 2005, http://www.aoc.gov/cvc/project_info/milestones_2005.cfm.

98. Ibid.

99. Ibid.

100. "The Blue Dog Coalition Holds a News Conference on the Deficit Hole," *Washington Daybook,* October 29, 2003.

101. Ibid.

102. Christopher Lee, "Visitor Center over Budget, Running Late; Costs up 16 Percent and Delay Is Months, GAO Report Says," *Washington Post,* July 9, 2003.

103. Ibid.

104. Lee and Hsu, "GAO Cites Capitol Facility's Costs, Delays."

105. "Weekly Report from Washington by Rep. Kilpatrick," *US FedNews,* June 14, 2006.

106. Lee and Hsu, "GAO Cites Capitol Facility's Costs, Delays."

107. Lee, "Visitor Center over Budget."

108. Lee, "Digging Deep for Capitol Visitors."

109. Ibid.

110. Ibid.

111. Ibid.

112. Isaac Wolf, "Funds Tight on Visitor Center; Capitol Project Delayed to '06," *Washington Times,* July 7, 2004.

113. Lee, "Digging Deep for Capitol Visitors."

114. Abrams, "Work Accelerates."

115. Dune Lawrence, "Scope, Cost of U.S. Capitol Welcome Center Continue to Grow," Knight Ridder Washington Bureau, July 6, 2003.

116. Ibid.

117. Ibid.

118. Abrams, "Work Accelerates."

119. Philip Kennicott, "The Capitol Addition That Takes Too Much Away," *Washington Post,* December 2, 2008.

120. Ibid.

121. Sabatier, "The Advocacy Coalition Framework," 99.

122. Greve, "New Avenues," 273.

123. C-SPAN, "CVC Opening Ceremony," December 2, 2008, http://www.aoc.gov/CVC-Opening-Ceremony.cfm.

124. Katherine Skiba, "Congress Unveils Stunning New Capitol Visitor Center—Late and Over Budget," USNews.com, November 11, 2008.

125. Nancy Pelosi, "Pelosi Remarks at Opening Ceremony of the Capitol Visitor Center," December 2, 2008, http://speaker.house.gov/newsroom/speeches?id=0151.

126. C-SPAN, "CVC Opening Ceremony."

127. Ibid.

128. "Years and Millions of Dollars Later, US Capitol Visitor Center Opens," Agence France-Presse, December 2, 2008.

129. Office of the Architect of the Capitol, "The Statue of Freedom," http://www.aoc.gov/cc/art/freedom.cfm.

130. U.S. Capitol Visitor Center, "Exhibition Hall General Description," January 2009, http://www.visitthecapitol.gov/For%20the%20Press/Press%20Materials/Fact%20Sheets/PDF%20-%20Exhibition%20Hall%20General%20Description%20%20.pdf.

131. U.S. Capitol Visitor Center, "Exhibitions at the U.S. Capitol Visitor Center," http://www.visitthecapitol.gov/Exhibitions/.

132. C-SPAN, "CVC Opening Ceremony."

133. Susan Ferrechio, "Costly Capitol Visitor Center Finally Ready," *Washington Examiner,* December 1, 2008.

134. Skiba, "Congress Unveils Stunning New Capitol Visitor Center."

135. Jim Abrams, "Capitol Visitor Center Opens after Delay, Overrun," Associated Press, November 12, 2008.

136. Ferrechio, "Costly Capitol Visitor Center Finally Ready."

137. Jim DeMint, "DeMint: New Capitol Visitor Center Omits History of Faith," press release from the office of U.S. Senator Jim DeMint, December 2, 2008.

138. Ibid.

139. Abrams, "Capitol Visitor Center Opens after Delay, Overrun."

140. Freedom From Religion Foundation, "FFRF Sues to Stop Religious Engravings at Capitol Visitor Center," July 14, 2009.

141. Jordy Yager, "CVC Opens, Can't Shake Controversy," *The Hill,* December 2, 2008.

142. Catesby Leigh, "In the Nation's Capital, an Uninviting Addition . . . ," *Wall Street Journal,* December 2, 2008.

143. Office of the Architect of the Capitol, "West Front," July 25, 2009, http://www.aoc.gov/cc/capitol/models/model_12.cfm.

144. Leigh, "In the Nation's Capital."

145. Ibid.

146. Kennicott, "The Capitol Addition."

147. Ibid.

148. Ibid.

149. Ibid.

150. Pelosi, "Pelosi Remarks."

151. Leigh, "In the Nation's Capital."

152. C-SPAN, "CVC Opening Ceremony."

153. James Madison, "Notes on the Debates in the Federal Convention," *The Avalon Project: Documents on Law, History, and Diplomacy,* 1787, http://avalon.law.yale.edu/18th_century/debates_726.asp.

154. Zelizer, *On Capitol Hill,* 3.

155. Sabatier and Jenkins-Smith, *Policy Change and Learning.*

6. The Social Meaning of Congressional Change

1. Goodsell, *The American Statehouse.*

2. Zelizer, ed., *The American Congress,* xvii.

3. Daschle with D'Orso, *Like No Other Time,* 117–118.

BIBLIOGRAPHY

Abrams, Jim. "Capitol Visitors Center Idea Mulled." Associated Press Online, July 27, 1998. http://www.lexisnexis.com (accessed August 12, 2009).
———. "Capitol Visitor Center Opens after Delay, Overrun." Associated Press Online, November 12, 2008. http://www.lexisnexis.com (accessed August 12, 2009).
———. "Work Accelerates on Biggest, Most Expensive Capitol Construction Project." Associated Press Online, April 30, 2004. http://www.lexisnexis.com (accessed August 12, 2009).
Adler, E. Scott, Chariti E. Gent, and Cary B. Overmeyer. "The Home Style Homepage: Legislator Use of the World Wide Web for Constituency Contact." *Legislative Studies Quarterly* 23, no. 4 (1998): 585–595.
Allen, Jonathan, and Patrick Yoest. "110th Senate Committees: Homeland Security and Governmental Affairs." *CQ Weekly,* November 13, 2006: 3032.
"America's Capitol." *Washington Times*, July 28, 1998, final edition.
Andrews, Gerry. "Open Questions on a Closed Case." *New York Times,* August 10, 2008. WK (10). http://www.nytimes.com/2008/08/10/opinion/10andrews.html (accessed August 12, 2009).
Associated Press State and Local Wire. "Tree Planted in Memory of W.Va. Congressman to Be Removed," May 7, 2001. http://www.lexisnexis.com (accessed August 12, 2009).
Baker, Richard A. *200 Notable Days: Senate Stories, 1787 to 2002.* Publication of the U.S. Senate Historical Office. Washington, D.C.: Government Printing Office, 2006.
———. Interview with Leonard Ballard, Inspector, United States Capitol Police (1947–1984): Interview #7. *United States Senate Historical Office—Oral History Project.* (October 20, 1983). www.senate.gov (accessed October 6, 2006).

———. Interview with Leonard Ballard, Inspector, United States Capitol Police (1947–1984): Interview #8. *United States Senate Historical Office —Oral History Project.* (October 27, 1983). www.senate.gov (accessed October 6, 2006).

Baker, Ross K. *House and Senate.* New York: Norton, 1989.

Bannister, Turpin C. "The Genealogy of the Dome of the United States Capitol." *Journal of the Society of Architectural Historians* 7, no. 1/2 (1948): 1–31.

Barnekov, Timothy K., and Jeffrey A. Raffel. "Public Management of Privatization." *Public Productivity and Management Review* 14, no. 2 (1990): 135–152.

Bell, Felicia. "Commentary: Enslaved Labor and the Capitol." *The Capitol Dome: USCHS Quarterly Historical Newsletter,* Special Issues, 2003. http://www.uschs.org/04_history/subs_articles/04e_dome_b.html (accessed March 4, 2007).

Benda, Andrea. "Capitol Center Aims for Fall of '08; Visitor Facility 3 Years Overdue." *Washington Times,* August 2, 2007, final edition.

Bernick, E. Lee, and Charles W. Wiggins. "Legislative Norms in Eleven States." *Legislative Studies Quarterly* 8, no. 2 (1983): 191–200.

Billings, Erin P. "Security Remains at Status Quo." *Roll Call,* July 12, 2005. http://www.rollcall.com/issues/51_3/news/9972-1.html (accessed August 12, 2009).

Blanchard, Janice C., Yolanda Haywood, Bradley Stein, Terri L. Tanielian, Michael Stoto, and Nicole Lurie. "In Their Own Words: Lessons Learned from Those Exposed to Anthrax." *American Journal of Public Health* 95, no. 3 (2005): 489–495.

"The Blue Dog Coalition Holds a News Conference on the Deficit Hole." *Washington Daybook,* October 29, 2003. http://www.lexisnexis.com (accessed August 12, 2009).

Bly, Laura. "The Capitol Says 'Welcome.'" *USA Today,* November 27, 2008. http://www.usatoday.com/travel/destinations/2008-11-27-capitol-visitor -center_N.htm (accessed November 27, 2008).

"A Bomb in the Senate." *Time Magazine,* March 15, 1971. http://www.time.com/time/magazine/article/0,9171,904830-1,00.html (accessed March 6, 2007).

Boyne, George A. "Bureaucratic Theory Meets Reality: Public Choice and Service Contracting in U.S. Local Government." *Public Administration Review* 58, no. 6 (1998): 474–484.

Brand, Stewart. *How Buildings Learn: What Happens After They're Built.* London: Phoenix Illustrated, 1994.

"The British Burn Washington, DC, 1814." *EyeWitness to History,* 2003. http://www.eyewitnesstohistory.com/pfwashingtonsack.htm (accessed July 16, 2006).

Browning, Graeme. "Don't Call Me, Call Me E-mail." *National Journal* 20 (1994): 1146.

Buckley, Bruce. "Search Begins for New Architect of Capitol." *Engineering News-Record,* March 5, 2007. http://enr.ecnext.com/coms2/article _newaar070305a (accessed August 12, 2009).

Burger, Timothy. "Capitol Police Ask 21 Percent Funding Hike; Senate Leg. Apps. Chairman Reid Grills Chief Kerrigan on Certain Purchases, Pay Raises." *Roll Call,* March 25, 1991. http://www.lexisnexis.com (accessed August 12, 2009).

Butler, Warren H. "Administering Congress: The Role of the Staff." *Public Administration Review* 26, no. 1 (1966): 3–13.

Cain, Bruce, John Ferejohn, and Morris Fiorina. *The Personal Vote: Constituency Service and Electoral Independence.* Cambridge, Mass.: Harvard Univ. Press, 1987.

Canon, David T. "The Institutionalization of Leadership in the U.S. Congress." *Legislative Studies Quarterly* 14, no. 3 (1989): 415–443.

"Capitol Visitor-Center Plans Back on Track," *The Kiplinger Letter,* July 31, 1998. http://www.lexisnexis.com (accessed August 12, 2009).

Carney, Dan, Amy Borrus, and Jay Greene. "Microsoft's All-Out Counterattack." *Business Week,* May 15, 2000. http://www.businessweek .com/2000/00_20/b3681219.htm (accessed August 12, 2009).

Casey, Chris. *The Hill on the Net: Congress Enters the Information Age.* Boston: AP Professional, 1996.

Cavanaugh, Thomas E. "The Dispersion of Authority in the House of Representatives." *Political Science Quarterly* 97, no. 4 (1982): 623–637.

Chamberlin, John R., and John E. Jackson. "Privatization as Institutional Choice." *Journal of Policy Analysis and Management* 6, no. 4 (1987): 586–604.

Cochrane, James D. "Partisan Aspects of Congressional Committee Staffing." *Western Political Quarterly* 27 (1964): 338–348.

Cooper, Joseph, and David W. Brady. "Toward a Diachronic Analysis of Congress." *American Political Science Review* 75, no. 4 (1981): 988–1006.

Cooper, Phillip J. "Government Contracts in Public Administration: The Role and Environment of the Contracting Officer." *Public Administration Review* 40, no. 5 (1980): 459–468.

Congressional Management Foundation. "How Is Anthrax Changing Congress and How Are Offices Using Technology to Cope?" November 2, 2001. http://www.congressonlineproject.org/november.html (accessed March 2, 2006).

———. "Congress Online: Special Report." 2003. http://www.cmfweb.org/ techreports.asp#COP02 (accessed April 12, 2006).

——. "2004 House Staff Employment Study." Washington, D.C.: Congressional Management Foundation, 2005.

——. "Crisis Management." 2005. http://www.cmfweb.org/OfficeMgmt-CrisisMgmt.asp (accessed March 2, 2006).

——. "Managing a Congressional Office in War Time," 2005. http://www.cmfweb.org/OfficeMgmtWarTime.asp (accessed March 2, 2006).

——. "Senate Staff Employment Study—Salary, Tenure, and Demographic Data: 1991–2001," 2005. http://www.cmfweb.org/storage/cmfweb/documents/CMF_Pubs/cmfsenatesalarystudy1991-2001.pdf (accessed January 13, 2010).

Cortell, Andrew P., and Susan Peterson. "Altered States: Explaining Domestic Institutional Change." *British Journal of Political Science* 29, no. 1 (1999): 177–203.

Cover, Albert. "Contacting Congressional Constituents: Some Patterns of Perquisite Use." *American Journal of Political Science* 24 (1980): 125–135.

Crewe, Ivor, and Anthony King. *The Birth, Life and Death of the Social Democratic Party.* Oxford: Oxford Univ. Press, 1995.

Critchell, Samantha. "AP Top News at 5 A.M. EDT Wednesday, July 29, 1998." Associated Press Online, July 29, 1998. http://www.lexisnexis.com (accessed August 12, 2009).

C-SPAN. "CVC Opening Ceremony." December 2, 2008. http://www.aoc.gov/CVC-Opening-Ceremony.cfm (accessed August 12, 2009).

Culnan, Mary J. "Processing Unstructured Organizational Transactions: Mail Handling in the U.S. Senate." *Organizational Science* 3, no. 1 (1992): 117–137.

Dalrymple, Mary. "Capitol Visitor Center to Open Fall 2006, Architect Tells Lawmakers." Associated Press Online, May 3, 2005, final edition.

Dart, Bob. "Big Changes on the Way for Prime Capitol Tourist Sites." Cox News Service, July 10, 2002. http://www.lexisnexis.com (accessed August 12, 2009).

Daschle, Tom, with Michael D'Orso. *Like No Other Time: The 107th Congress and the Two Years That Changed America Forever.* New York: Crown Publishers, 2003.

Davidson, Roger H., and Walter J. Oleszek. "Adaptation and Consolidation: Structural Innovation in the U.S. House of Representatives." *Legislative Studies Quarterly* 1 (1976): 37–65.

DeGregorio, Christine. "Congressional Committee Staff as Policy Making Partners in the U.S. Congress." *Congress and the Presidency* 21 (1994): 49–66.

DeHoog, R. H. *Contracting Out for Human Services: Economic, Political and Organizational Perspectives.* Albany: State Univ. of New York Press, 1984.

DeMint, Jim. "DeMint: New Capitol Visitor Center Omits History of Faith." Press release from the office of U.S. Senator Jim DeMint, December 2, 2008. http://demint.senate.gov/public/index.cfm?Fuseaction=PressReleases .Detail&PressRelease_id=f90c4393-bcea-c76e-6c61-5dc0050b818e (accessed August 12, 2009).

Dexter, Lewis Anthony. "What Do Congressmen Hear: The Mail." *Public Opinion Quarterly* 20, no. 1 (1956): 16–27.

Dillon, Tim. "U.S. Capitol Visitor Center Nears Completion." *USA Today,* January 7, 2007. http://www.usatoday.com/news/washington/2007-01 -07-capitol-visitors-center_x.htm (accessed February 5, 2007).

DiMaggio, Paul, Eszter Hargittai, Coral Ceste, and Steven Shafer. "Digital Inequality: From Unequal Access to Differentiated Use." In *Social Inequality,* edited by Kathryn Neckermann, 355–400. New York: Russell Sage Foundation, 2004.

Dorn, Terrell G. "Capitol Visitor Center: Update on Status of Project's Schedule and Cost as of February 16, 2007." Testimony before the Subcommittee on the Legislative Branch, Committee on Appropriations, House of Representatives. United States Government Accountability Office. 2007. http://www.gao.gov/new.items/d07507t.pdf (accessed February 16, 2007).

Dougherty, Jill. "New Center Offers Warmer Welcome to Capitol Tourists." CNN, December 2, 2008. http://www.cnn.com/2008/TRAVEL/12/02 /capitol.visitor.center/index.html (accessed August 12, 2009).

Easton, David. *A Framework for Political Analysis.* Chicago: Univ. of Chicago Press, 1979.

———. *The Political System: An Inquiry into the State of Political Science.* New York: Knopf, 1953.

Eilperin, Juliet. "House Entrances Closed to Traffic." *Roll Call,* April 24, 1995. http://www.lexisnexis.com (accessed August 12, 2009).

———. "A Peace Plan for the Capitol Visitor Center." *Washington Post,* July 12, 1998, final edition.

Epstein, Laurily, and Kathleen Frankovic. "Casework and Electoral Margins: Insurance Is Prudent." *Polity* 14 (1982): 691–700.

Eulau, Heinz, and Paul Karps. "The Puzzle of Representation: Specifying Components of Responsiveness." *Legislative Studies Quarterly* 2, no. 3 (1977): 233–254.

Fenno, Richard F., Jr. *Congressmen in Committees.* Boston: Little, Brown, 1973.

———. *Home Style: House Members in Their Districts.* Glenview, Ill.: Scott, Foresman, 1978.

———. "The House Appropriations Committee as a Political System: The Problem of Integration." *American Political Science Review* 56, no. 2 (1962): 310–324.

———. *The Power of the Purse.* Boston: Little, Brown, 1966.

———. *Watching Politicians: Essays on Participant Observation.* Berkeley, Calif.: Institute of Governmental Studies, University of California at Berkeley, 1990.

Ferrechio, Susan. "Costly Capitol Visitor Center Finally Ready." *Washington Examiner,* December 1, 2008. http://www.washingtonexaminer.com /local/120108_Costly_Capitol_Visitor_Center_finally_ready.html (accessed August 12, 2009).

Fiorina, Morris P. *Congress: Keystone of the Washington Establishment,* 2nd ed. New Haven, Conn.: Yale University Press, 1989.

———. "The Presidency and Congress: An Electoral Connection?" In *The Presidency and the Political System,* 3rd ed., edited by Michael Nelson. Washington, DC: Congressional Quarterly, 1990.

Foerstel, Karen. "Why No Fire Drills on Hill? Mazzoli Raises Question in Wake of World Trade Center Bombing." *Roll Call,* March 4, 1993. http:// www.lexisnexis.com (accessed August 12, 2009).

Fox, Harrison W., Jr., and Susan Webb Hammond. *Congressional Staffs: The Invisible Force in American Lawmaking.* New York: Free Press, 1977.

Fox, Susannah, and Jessica Vitak. "Degrees of Access." *Pew Internet and American Life Project,* July 9, 2008. http://www.pewinternet.org/ Presentations/2008/Degrees-of-Access-(May-2008-data).aspx (accessed August 12, 2009).

Fram, Alan. "Senate Votes to Give Troubled AmeriCorps Another $100 Million." Associated Press State and Local Wire, July 11, 2003. http://www .lexisnexis.com (accessed August 12, 2009).

Freedom From Religion Foundation. "FFRF Sues to Stop Religious Engravings at Capitol Visitor Center." July 14, 2009. http://ffrf.org/news/2009 /ayers.php (accessed August 12, 2009).

Galbraith, J. *Designing Complex Organizations.* Reading, Mass.: Addison Wesley, 1973.

General Accounting Office. "Capitol Hill Anthrax Incident: EPA's Cleanup Was Successful; Opportunities Exist to Enhance Contract Oversight." GAO-03-686, June 2003, 11. http://www.gao.gov/products/GAO-03-686 (accessed August 12, 2009).

Gibbs, Nancy. "Murder in the House: Shots, Screams and Heroism as a Gunman Invades the Capitol." *Time,* August 3, 1998. http://www.cnn.com /ALLPOLITICS/1998/07/27/time/capitol.killings.html (accessed August 12, 2009).

Godfrey, John. "Commission OKs Capitol Expansion; Visitors Center Needed for Extra Security." *Washington Times,* October 16, 1999, final edition.

———. "Plans for Capitol Visitor Center Face Further Security Scrutiny." *Washington Times,* July 27, 1998, final edition.

———. "Visitors Center Closer to Reality; Capitol Police Slayings Spur Security Measure." *Washington Times,* May 27, 2001, final edition.

Goldschmidt, Kathy, Nicole Folk, Mike Callahan, and Rick Shapiro. "E-mail Overload in Congress: Managing a Communications Crisis." *Congress Online Project,* 2001. http://www.cmfweb.org/storage/cmfweb/documents/CMF_Pubs/e-mailoverload.pdf (accessed August 12, 2009).

Goodman, David. "AP Top News at 3 P.M. EDT Sunday, July 26, 1998." Associated Press Online, July 26, 1998. http://www.lexisnexis.com (accessed August 12, 2009).

Goodsell, Charles T. *The American Statehouse: Interpreting Democracy's Temples.* Lawrence: Univ. Press of Kansas, 2001.

Greve, Carsten. "New Avenues for Contracting Out and Implications for a Theoretical Framework." *Public Performance and Management Review* 24, no. 3 (2001): 270–284.

Grunwald, Michael, and Juliet Eilperin. "Protection vs. 'The People's House." *Washington Post,* July 25, 1998, A1.

Gurdon, Hugo. "New Member Guide." *The Hill,* 2009. http://thehill.com/new-member-guide.html (accessed August 12, 2009).

Hall, Peter A., and Rosemary C. R. Taylor. "Political Science and the Three New Institutionalisms." *Political Studies* 44 (1996): 936–957.

Hall, Richard L. *Participation in Congress.* New Haven, Conn.: Yale Univ. Press, 1996.

Hammond, Susan Webb. "Legislative Staffs." *Legislative Studies Quarterly* 9, no. 2 (1984): 271–317.

———. "Recent Research on Legislative Staffs." *Legislative Studies Quarterly* 21, no. 4 (1996): 543–576.

Hanke, S. H., ed. *Prospects for Privatization.* New York: Academy of Political Science, 1987.

Hastert, Speaker Dennis. "Remarks in the House." *Congressional Record,* daily edition 149 (January 7, 2003): H5.

Hedlund, Ronald D. "Organizational Attributes of Legislatures: Structure, Rules, Norms, Resources." *Legislative Studies Quarterly* 9, no. 1 (1984): 51–121.

Herrnson, Paul S., Atiya Kai Stokes-Brown, and Matthew Hindman. "Campaign Politics and the Digital Divide: Constituency Characteristics, Strategic Considerations, and Candidate Internet Use in State Legislative Elections." *Political Research Quarterly* 60, no. 1 (2007): 31–42.

Ho, David. "Capitol Visitors' Center Planned." Associated Press Online, June 20, 2000. http://www.lexisnexis.com (accessed August 12, 2009).

Hodge, G. *Privatization. An International Review of Performance.* Boulder, Colo.: Westview Press, 2000.

Hulse, Carl. "Threats and Responses: Security; Despite 9/11, Study Finds 'Significant Safety and Health Hazards' at Capitol." *New York Times,* November 26, 2002, sec. A.

———. "Workers Set to Transform East Front of the Capitol." *New York Times,* May 28, 2002, final edition.

Hsu, Spencer S. "Congress Digs Deep for Visitors and Safety; Underground Center's Construction Begins." *Washington Post,* May 28, 2002, final edition.

———. "Historic Capitol Hill Faces Uncharted Future; Security Needs, Business Boom Reshape Area." *Washington Post,* January 20, 2005, final edition.

———. "New Needs Transform Capitol Security: Anti-terror Funds Bolster Police Force." *Washington Post,* November 29, 2001, final edition.

James, Robert Rhodes, ed. *Winston S. Churchill: His Complete Speeches, 1897–1963,* vol. 7. New York: Chelsea House, 1974, 6869–6873.

Jones, Bryan D. "Competitiveness, Role Orientations, and Legislative Responsiveness." *Journal of Politics* 35, no. 4 (1973): 924–947.

Jones, Sydney, and Susannah Fox. "Generations Online in 2009." *Pew Internet and American Life Project,* January 28, 2009. http://www.pewinternet.org/Reports/2009/Generations-Online-in-2009.aspx (accessed August 12, 2009).

Kammerer, Gladys M. "The Administration of Congress." *Public Administration Review* 9, no. 3 (1949): 175–181.

Keeler, John T. S. "Opening the Window for Reform: Mandates, Crises, and Extraordinary Policy-Making." *Comparative Political Studies* 25 (1993): 433–486.

Keim, Brandon. "Years Later, Anthrax Attack Remains a Mystery." Columbia News Service, April 5, 2005. http://jscms.jrn.columbia.edu/cns/2005-04-05/keim-anthrax%20mystery (accessed August 12, 2009).

Kennicott, Philip. "The Capitol Addition That Takes Too Much Away." *Washington Post,* December 2, 2008. http://www.washingtonpost.com/wp-dyn/content/article/2008/12/01/AR2008120103004.html (accessed December 2, 2008).

Kettl, D. F. *Sharing Power—Public Governance and Private Markets.* Washington, D.C.: Brookings, 1993.

Kiely, Kathy. "Post-9/11 Security Hinders Access at Capitols." *USA Today,* August 5, 2002, final edition.

Kim, Eun-Kyung. "Lawmakers Discuss Plans for Capitol Visitors Center." Associated Press, July 29, 1998, final edition.

Kingdon, John W. *Agendas, Alternatives, and Public Policies.* Boston: Little, Brown, 1984.

———. *Congressmen's Voting Decisions.* New York: Harper and Row, 1973.

Koch, Wendy. "Lawmakers Vow to Push for Capitol Visitors' Center." *USA Today,* July 30, 1998, final edition.

Koempel, Michael L. "Homeland Security: Compendium of Recommendations Relevant to House Committee Organization and Analysis of Considerations for the House, and 109th and 110th Congresses Epilogue." Congressional Research Service. Order Code RL32711. March 2, 2007. http://oai.dtic.mil/oai/oai?&verb=getRecord&metadataPrefix=html&identifier=ADA466550 (accessed August 12, 2009).

Kouzmin, A., and A. M. G. Jarman. "Crisis Decision Making: Towards a Contingent Decision Path Perspective." In *Coping with Crises: The Management of Disasters, Riots and Terrorism,* edited by Uriel Rosenthal, Michael T. Charles, and Paul 't Hart, 397–435. Springfield, Ill.: Thomas, 1989.

Krasner, Stephen D. "Approaches to the State: Alternative Conceptions and Historical Dynamics." *Comparative Politics* 16 (1984): 223–244.

Kravitz, Walter. "The Advent of the Modern Congress: The Legislative Reorganization Act of 1970." *Legislative Studies Quarterly* 15, no. 3 (1990): 375–399.

Lambright, W. Henry. *Governing Science and Technology.* New York: Oxford Univ. Press, 1976.

Laskow, Sarah. "Is Congress Failing on Homeland Security Oversight?: Despite Calls for Consolidation, Over 80 Hill Panels Still Have a Say." Center for Public Integrity, July 15, 2009. http://www.publicintegrity.org/articles/entry/1549/ (accessed August 12, 2009).

Lawrence, Dune. "Scope, Cost of U.S. Capitol Welcome Center Continue to Grow." Knight Ridder Washington Bureau, July 6, 2003.

Lee, Christopher. "Digging Deep for Capitol Visitors; Plan for New Center Turns from Modest to Monumental." *Washington Post,* November 11, 2003, final edition.

———. "Visitor Center over Budget, Running Late; Costs up 16 Percent and Delay Is Months, GAO Report Says." *Washington Post,* July 9, 2003, final edition.

Lee, Christopher, and Spencer S. Hsu. "GAO Cites Capitol Facility's Costs, Delays." *Washington Post,* November 30, 2004, final edition.

Leigh, Catesby. "In the Nation's Capital, an Uninviting Addition . . ." *Wall Street Journal,* December 2, 2008. http://online.wsj.com/article/SB122817512455970595.html (accessed August 12, 2009).

Loomis, Burdett A. "The Congressional Office as a Small (?) Business." *Publius* 9 (1979): 35–55.

Madison, Dolley. "The Burning of Washington," 1814. http://www.national-center.org/WashingtonBurning1814.html (accessed March 8, 2007).

Madison, James. "Notes on the Debates in the Federal Convention." *The Avalon Project: Documents on Law, History, and Diplomacy.* 1787. http://avalon.law.yale.edu/18th_century/debates_726.asp (accessed August 12, 2009).

Maguire, Steven, and Shawn Reese. "Department of Homeland Security Grants to State and Local Governments: FY2003 to FY2006." Congressional Research Service. Order Code RL33770. December 22, 2006. http://fas.org/sgp/crs/homesec/RL33770.pdf (accessed August 12, 2009).

Malbin, Michael J. *Unelected Representatives: Congressional Staff and the Future of Representative Government.* New York: Basic Books, 1980.

Manley, John F. "Congressional Staff and Public Policy-Making." *Journal of Politics* 30 (1966): 1046–1067.

March, James G., and Johan P. Olsen. "The New Institutionalism: Organizational Factors in Political Life." *American Political Science Review* 78, no. 3 (1984): 734–749.

———. *Rediscovering Institutions: The Organizational Basis of Politics.* New York: Free Press, 1989.

Marcum, Karissa. "House Approves Emancipation Hall Bill." *The Hill,* November 14, 2007. http://thehill.com (accessed January 8, 2008).

Matthews, Donald. *U.S. Senators and Their World.* Chapel Hill: Univ. of North Carolina Press, 1960.

Mayhew, David. *Congress: The Electoral Connection.* New Haven, Conn.: Yale Univ. Press, 1974.

McFaul, Michael. "State Power, Institutional Change, and the Politics of Privatization in Russia." *World Politics* 47 (1995): 210–243.

Miranda, Rowan. "Privatization and the Budget-Maximizing Bureaucrat." *Public Productivity and Management Review* 17, no. 4 (1994): 355–369.

Moe, Ronald C. "Exploring the Limits of Privatization." *Public Administration Review* 47, no. 6 (1987): 453–460.

Montesquieu, Charles de Secondat. *Considerations on the Causes of the Greatness of the Romans and Their Decline.* Translated by David Lowenthal. Ithaca, N.Y.: Cornell Univ. Press, 1968.

National Commission on Terrorist Attacks. *The 9/11 Commission Report: Final Report of the National Commission on Terrorist Attacks upon the United States (Authorized Edition).* New York: Norton, 2004.

Office of the Architect of the Capitol. "2005 Activities Summary." 2005.

http://www.aoc.gov/cvc/project_info/milestones_2005.cfm   (accessed December 28, 2007).

———. "The Capitol Visitor Center." http://www.aoc.gov/cvc/index.cfm (accessed March 10, 2007).

———. "The Current Capitol Preservation Commission List." 2007. http://www .aoc.gov/cvc/project_info/cpc_list.cfm (accessed December 28, 2007).

———. "Project Information: Planning Begins." http://www.aoc.gov/cvc /project_info/index.cfm (accessed March 6, 2007).

———. "The Statue of Freedom." http://www.aoc.gov/cc/art/freedom.cfm (accessed December 27, 2009).

———. "West Front." July 25, 2009. http://www.aoc.gov/cc/capitol/models/ model_12.cfm (accessed August 12, 2009).

Office of the Clerk of the U.S. House of Representatives. "A Gunman in the House Gallery in 1932." Historical Highlights (December 13, 1932). http:// clerk.house.gov/art_history/highlights.html?action=view&intID=234 (accessed August 12, 2009).

Online NewsHour with Jim Lehr Transcript. "Capital Defense." Public Broadcasting Service, April 6, 2004. http://www.pbs.org/newshour/bb /terrorism/july-dec04/security_8-6.html (accessed April 12, 2006).

"Other Senate Committees in the 109th." *CQ Weekly,* November 6, 2004, 2614.

Overby, Marvin L., and Lauren C. Bell. "Rational Behavior or the Norm of Cooperation? Filibustering among Retiring Senators." *Journal of Politics* 66, no. 3 (2004): 906–924.

Pelosi, Nancy. "Pelosi Remarks at Opening Ceremony of the Capitol Visitor Center." December 2, 2008. http://speaker.house.gov/newsroom /speeches?id=0151 (accessed August 12, 2009).

Perrow, C. *Complex Organizations: A Critical Essay.* New York: McGraw-Hill, 1986.

Peterson, Iver. "Anthrax Cleanup Day Finally Comes for Mail Sorting Center." *New York Times,* October 24, 2003. http://query.nytimes.com/gst /fullpage.html?res=9C03EFDC1531F937A15753C1A9659C8B63&sec=& spon=&pagewanted=all# (accessed August 12, 2009).

Pierson, Michael D. "All Southern Society Is Assailed by the Foulest Charges: Charles Sumner's 'The Crime against Kansas' and the Escalation of Republican Anti-Slavery Rhetoric." *New England Quarterly* 68, no 4 (1995): 531–557.

Pitch, Anthony S. *The Burning of Washington: The British Invasion of 1814.* Annapolis, Md.: Naval Institute Press, 1998.

Pitkin, Hanna Fenichel. *The Concept of Representation.* Berkeley: Univ. of California Press, 1967.

Polsby, Nelson W. *How Congress Evolves: Social Bases of Institutional Change.* Oxford: Oxford Univ. Press, 2004.

————. "The Institutionalization of the U.S. House of Representatives." *American Political Science Review* 62 (1968): 144–168.

Prager, J. "Contracting Out Government Services: Lessons from the Private Sector." *Public Administration Review* 54 (1994): 176–184.

Price, Charles M., and Charles G. Bell. "Socializing California Freshmen Assemblymen: The Role of Individuals and Legislative Sub-Groups." *Western Political Quarterly* 23, no. 1 (1970): 166–179.

"Rep. Kaptur Celebrates Women's History Month." *US Fed News,* March 30, 2006. http://www.lexisnexis.com (accessed August 12, 2009).

"Rep. Mitchell Votes against Legislative Branch Appropriations Bill." *US Fed News,* June 22, 2007. http://www.lexisnexis.com (accessed August 12, 2009).

"Rep. Obey Comments on FY 2006 Legislative Branch Appropriations Bill." *US Fed News,* June 22, 2005. http://www.lexisnexis.com (accessed August 12, 2009).

Reynolds, Paul. "Living with Bioterror." *BBC News Online,* October 21, 2001. http://news.bbc.co.uk/1/low/programmes/from_our_own_correspondent/1611314.stm (accessed August 25, 2008).

Robinson, Dan. "VOA [Voice of America News]: Capitol Security Breach Prompts New Review of Procedures." *U.S. Fed News,* September 19, 2006. http://www.voanews.com/english/archive/2006-09/2006-09-19-voa4.cfm?moddate=2006-09-19 (accessed August 12, 2009).

Roig-Franzia, Manuel. "A Terrorist in the House." *Washington Post,* February 22, 2004. http://www.washingtonpost.com/ac2/wp-dyn/A48918-2004Feb17 (accessed March 6, 2007).

Rosenthal, Alan. *Legislative Life: People, Process, and Performance in the States.* New York: Harper and Row, 1981.

Rosenthal, Uriel, Michael T. Charles, and Paul 't Hart. *Coping with Crises: The Management of Disasters, Riots and Terrorism.* Springfield, Ill.: Thomas, 1989.

Rosenthal, Uriel, and Alexander Kouzmin. "Crises and Crisis Management: Toward Comprehensive Government Decision Making." *Journal of Public Administration Research and Theory* 7, no. 2 (1997): 277–304.

Rubin, Debra K., and William J. Angelo. "Historic Expansion of U.S. Capitol Showcases Its Historic Use of CM." *Engineering News-Record,* June 17, 2002. http://www.construction.com/NewsCenter/Headlines/ENR/20020613a.asp (accessed December 24, 2007).

Rundquist, Paul S., and Christopher M. Davis. "S. Res. 445: Senate Committee Reorganization for Homeland Security and Intelligence Matters."

Congressional Research Service. Order Code RS21955. October 15, 2004. http://digital.library.unt.edu/govdocs/crs/permalink/meta-crs-5772:1 (accessed August 12, 2009).

Rutter, D. *Commuting by Telephone*. New York: Pergamon Press, 1987.

Sabatier, P. A. "The Advocacy Coalition Framework: Revisions and Relevance for Europe." *Journal of European Public Policy* 5, no. 1 (1998): 98–130.

Sabatier, P. A., and H. C. Jenkins-Smith, eds. "The Advocacy Coalition Framework: An Assessment." In *Theories of the Policy Process,* edited by P. A. Sabatier, 117–166. Boulder, Colo.: Westview Press, 1999.

———. *Policy Change and Learning: An Advocacy Coalition Approach*. Boulder, Colo.: Westview Press, 1993.

Sabatier, P. A., and Matthew Zafonte. "Policy Oriented Learning between Coalitions." Paper presented at the American Association for the Advancement of Science meeting, Seattle, Washington, February 1997.

Salamon, Lester. "Rethinking Public Management: Third-Party Government and the Changing Forms of Government Action." *Public Policy* 29 (1981): 260.

Saloma, John S., III. *Congress and the New Politics*. Boston: Little, Brown, 1969.

Sappington, D. E. M., and J. E. Stiglitz. "Privatization, Information, and Incentives." *Journal of Policy Analysis and Management* 6 (1987): 567–582.

Savas, E. S. *Privatization: The Key to Better Government*. Chatham, N.J.: Chatham House, 1987.

———. *Privatization and Public-Private Partnerships*. Chatham, N.J.: Chatham House, 2000.

Schiff, Steven H., and Steven S. Smith. "Generational Change and the Allocation of Staff in the U.S. Congress." *Legislative Studies Quarterly* 8 (1983): 457–468.

Schneider, Judy. "Committee System Rules in the House, 109th Congress." Congressional Research Service. Order Code RS22018. January 5, 2005. http://digital.library.unt.edu/govdocs/crs/permalink/meta-crs-7463:1 (accessed August 12, 2009).

"Sen. Allard Chairs Final Legislative Branch Committee Hearing." *US Fed News,* November 15, 2006. http://www.lexisnexis.com (accessed August 12, 2009).

Serra, George, and David Moon. "Casework, Issue Positions, and Voting in Congressional Elections: A District Analysis." *Journal of Politics* 56, no. 1 (1994): 200–213.

Shane, Scott, and Eric Lichtblau. "Scientist's Suicide Is Linked to Anthrax Inquiry." *New York Times,* August 2, 2008, A1.

Shenon, Philip. "U.S. Charges 7 in the Bombing at U.S. Capitol." *New York Times,* May 12, 1988, A20.

Shetterly, David R. "The Influence of Contract Design on Contractor Performance: The Case of Residential Refuse Collection." *Public Performance and Management Review* 24, no. 1 (2000): 53–68.

Short, J., E. Williams, and B. Christie. *The Social Psychology of Telecommunication.* New York: Wiley, 1976.

Skiba, Katherine. "Congress Unveils Stunning New Capitol Visitor Center—Late and Over Budget." USNews.com, November 11, 2008. http:// www.usnews.com/articles/news/politics/2008/11/11/congress-unveils -stunning-new-capitol-visitor-center--late-and-over-budget.html   (accessed on August 12, 2009).

Smith, Elbert B. "Thomas Hart Benton: Southern Realist." *American Historical Review* 58, no. 4 (1953): 795–807.

"Sources: Capitol 'Gunfire' Likely from Air Hammer." CNN.com, May 26, 2006.   http://www.cnn.com/2006/POLITICS/05/26/house.shots/index .html (accessed August 12, 2009).

Starks, Tim. "Committee OKs Cox Priority." *CQ Weekly—Weekly Report,* May 2, 2005, 1155.

———. "Homeland Security under Attack by Lawmakers." *Congressional Quarterly Weekly,* June 26, 2006, 1772.

States News Service. "Obey-Cardoza Give 'Golden Drain Award for Waste, Fraud and Abuse' to Congress and Architect of the Capitol," September 21, 2006. http://www.lexisnexis.com (accessed August 12, 2009).

Stathis, Stephen W. "The Capitol Visitor Center: An Overview." Congressional Research Service. Order Code RL31121. Updated July 5, 2006. http://digital.library.unt.edu/govdocs/crs/permalink/meta-crs-9754:1 (accessed August 12, 2009).

———. "The Capitol Visitor Center: An Overview." Congressional Research Service. Order Code RL31121. Updated January 16, 2009. http://wikile aks.org/leak/crs/RL31121.pdf (accessed August 12, 2009).

Strahan, Randall. *New Ways and Means: Reform and Change in a Congressional Committee.* Chapel Hill: Univ. of North Carolina Press, 1990.

Sullivan, Christopher B. "Preferences for Electronic Mail in Organizational Communication Tasks." *Journal of Business Communication* 32, no. 1 (1995): 49–64.

Sundquist, J. L. "Privatization: No Panacea for What Ails Government." In *Public-Private Partnership: New Opportunities for Meeting Social Needs,* edited by H. Brooks, L. Liebman, and C. S. Schelling, 303–318. Cambridge, Mass.: Ballinger, 1984.

Swanson, K. C. "21st Century, Ready or Not." *National Journal* 22 (1996): 1215.

Swift, Elaine K., and David W. Brady. "Out of the Past: Theoretical and Methodological Contributions of Congressional History." *PS: Political Science and Politics* 24, no. 1 (1991): 61–64.

Taylor, Andrew. "Senators Fight over Turf in Revamp of Homeland Security Oversight." *CQ Weekly,* October 16, 2004, 2460.

Tong, Lorraine H., and Barbara L. Schwemle. "Telework in the Federal Government: Background, Policy, and Oversight." Congressional Research Service. April 3, 2002. http://wikileaks.org/leak/crs/RL30863.pdf (accessed August 12, 2009).

Tower, Samuel A. "Bullets of an Assassin Miss Bricker in Capitol Tunnel." *New York Times,* July 13, 1947, sec. 1, 34.

"Update." *Washington Post,* July 5, 2006, final edition.

"U.S. Capitol Changed Much in 5 Years Since Gunman Killed 2 Officers." *USA Today,* July 24, 2003. http://www.usatoday.com/news/washington/2003-07-24-capitolx.htm (accessed October 6, 2006).

"U.S. Capitol Police." http://www.uscapitolpolice.gov/home.php (accessed on March 10, 2007).

"U.S. Capitol Staircase to Be Repaired." Associated Press Online, January 27, 2006. http://www.lexisnexis.com (accessed August 12, 2009).

U.S. Capitol Visitor Center. "Exhibition Hall General Description." http://visitthecapitol.gov/For%20the%20Press/Press%20Materials/Fact%20Sheets/PDF%20-%20Exhibition%20Hall%20General%20Description%20%20.pdf (accessed December 27, 2009).

———. "Exhibitions at the U.S. Capitol Visitor Center." http://www.visitthecapitol.gov/Exhibitions/ (accessed August 12, 2009).

U.S. Congress, House. "Are We Safer Now?" *Congressional Record,* 108th Cong., 2nd sess. Washington, D.C.: Government Printing Office, April 21, 2004.

———. "Honoring Congressional Staff and Government Employees." *Congressional Record,* 107th Cong., 2nd sess. Washington, D.C.: Government Printing Office, September 12, 2002.

———. "Defending Freedom and Democracy." *Congressional Record,* 108th Cong., 2nd sess. Washington, D.C.: Government Printing Office, September 22, 2004.

———. Committee on Homeland Security. "Homeland Security Committee Overview." 2007. http://homeland.house.gov/about/index.asp (accessed June 21, 2007).

———. Committee on House Administration. "Member's Handbook." September 2009. http://cha.house.gov/model_employee.aspx (accessed August 12, 2009).

U.S. Congress, Senate. "The Capitol Police." *U.S. Senate Art and His-*

tory. http://www.senate.gov/artandhistory/history/common/briefing/ Capitol_Police.htm (accessed March 9, 2007).

———. "Commending Courage and Professionalism Following the Release of Anthrax." *Congressional Record,* 107th Cong., 2nd sess. Washington, D.C.: Government Printing Office, April 10, 2002.

———. "April 2, 1917: Senator Attacks Constituent." *Senate Art and History Historical Minutes 1878–1920.* http://www.senate.gov/artandhis tory/his tory/minute/Senator_Attacks_Constituent.htm (accessed December 24, 2009).

———. "July 2, 1915: Bomb Rocks Capitol." *Senate Art and History Historical Minutes 1878–1920.* http://www.senate.gov/artandhistory/history /minute/Bomb_Rocks_Capitol.htm (accessed July 16, 2006).

———. "November 7, 1983: Bomb Explodes in Capitol." *Senate Art and History Historical Minutes 1964—Present.* http://www.senate.gov /artandhistory/history/minute/bomb_explodes_in_capitol.htm (accessed July 16, 2006).

———. "September 19, 1814: The Senate Convenes in Emergency Quarters." *Senate Art and History Historical Minutes 1801–1850.* http://www.senate .gov/artandhistory/history/minute/Senate_Convenes_in_Emergency_ Quarters.html (accessed July 16, 2006).

———. "A Trying Time for Our Nation." *Congressional Record,* 108th Cong., 1st sess. Washington, D.C.: Government Printing Office, February 14, 2003.

———. *To Eliminate Certain Restrictions on Service of a Senator on the Senate Select Committee on Intelligence,* S. Res. 445, 108th Cong., 2nd sess. Washington, D.C.: Government Printing Office, 2004.

———. Committee on Homeland Security and Governmental Affairs. "Committee on Homeland Security and Governmental Affairs: Full Committee and Subcommittee Jurisdictions for the 111th Congress." http:// hsgac.senate.gov/public/index.cfm?FuseAction=AboutCommittee .Jurisdiction (accessed August 12, 2009).

U.S. Department of Homeland Security. "Department Subcomponents and Agencies." July 30, 2009. http://www.dhs.gov/xabout/structure/#1 (accessed August 12, 2009).

Valéry, Paul. "Fragment from 'On Poe's Eureka.'" *Selected Writings of Paul Valéry.* New York: New Directions Publishing Corporation, 1964.

Van Slyke, David M. "The Mythology of Privatization in Contracting for Social Services." *Public Administration Review* 63, no. 3 (2003): 296–315.

Vobejda, Barbara. "'Extensive Casualties' in Wake of Pentagon Attack." *Washington Post Online,* September 11, 2001. http://www.washington post.com/wpsrv/metro/daily/sep01/attack.html (accessed April 11, 2006).

Wahlke, John C. "Policy Demands and System Support: The Role of the Represented." *British Journal of Political Science* 1 (1971): 271–290.

Wahlke, John C., Heinz Eulau, William Buchanan, and LeRoy C. Ferguson. *The Legislative System: Explorations in Legislative Behavior.* New York: Wiley, 1962.

"Washington Reacts to the Capitol Hill Shooting." *AllPolitics,* CNN, July 24, 1998. http://www.cnn.com/ALLPOLITICS/1998/07/24/quotes.shooting/ (accessed March 4, 2007).

"Weekly Report from Washington by Rep. Kilpatrick." *US Fed News,* June 14, 2006. http://www.lexisnexis.com (accessed August 12, 2009).

Wheeler, Linda. "The Night 'the City was Light': Washington Marks 185th Anniversary of British Burning the Capitol, White House." *Washington Post,* August 24, 1999, B03.

Willman, David. "Anthrax Mixture Led FBI to Ivins; Its Origins Pointed to One Conclusion: That Only the Government Scientist Could Be Behind the '01 Attacks." *Los Angeles Times,* August 4, 2008, A1.

Wolf, Isaac. "Funds Tight on Visitor Center; Capitol Project Delayed to '06." *Washington Times,* July 7, 2004, final edition.

Wolman, Harold L., and Dianna M. Wolman. "The Role of the U.S. Senate Staff in the Opinion Linkage Process: Population Policy." *Legislative Studies Quarterly* 2 (1977): 281–293.

Yachnin, Jennifer. "Security Unaffected by Attack in Madrid; Ney Cautions Not to Cut Cops' Budget." *Roll Call,* March 16, 2004. http://www.lexisnexis.com (accessed August 12, 2009).

Yager, Jordy. "CVC Opens, Can't Shake Controversy." *The Hill,* December 2, 2008. http://thehill.com/leading-the-news/cvc-opens-cant-shake-controversy-2008-12-02.html (accessed August 12, 2009).

"Years and Millions of Dollars Later, US Capitol Visitor Center Opens." Agence France-Presse, December 2, 2008. http://www.google.com/hostednews/afp/article/ALeqM5ixYp808Lhm0pc0XlEmCRUPQHyF9Q (accessed August 12, 2009).

Yoest, Patrick. "Democrats' First 100 Hours: Security Initiatives Facing Short Funds, Turf Wars and Inertia." *CQ Weekly,* November 20, 2006, 3109.

Zelizer, Julian. *On Capitol Hill: The Struggle to Reform Congress and Its Consequences, 1948–2000.* Cambridge: Cambridge Univ. Press, 2006.

———, ed. *The American Congress.* Boston: Houghton Mifflin, 2004.

INDEX

www.ingramcontent.com/pod-product-compliance
Lightning Source LLC
Chambersburg PA
CBHW030410100426
42812CB00028B/2902/J